"If you're in the information business (and we all are in the information business), Tercek's urgent manifesto will help you see the future, so you can prepare for it."

Seth Godin, author of *Unleashing the Ideavirus*

"Ignore this book at your peril. *Vaporized* tracks the move from atoms to bits in a funny and thought-provoking manner that will be a wake-up call to many industries."

Nolan Bushnell, founder of Atari, Inc.

"Robert Tercek is a technological provocateur. His book provides deep thinking about our digital world and its monumental possibilities in ways that you probably haven't ever considered."

Jarl Mohn, CEO of National Public Radio

"Tercek's vision is singular, unique, and unmatched in its insight. *Vaporized* is the next must-have strategy guide for every executive in media, manufacturing, retail, and marketing."

Gabe Zichermann, CEO of Gamification Co.
and author of *Gamification Revolution*

"*Vaporized* will certainly make you think. If you don't like change it will terrify you, but if you embrace the future, Tercek's book will justify your mission and spur you on to new heights."

Brett King, author of *Augmented* and founder of Moven

"A thoughtful and sharp look at the invisible forces transforming society today and in the near future. Never before in history have we experienced the scope of change being wrought by the networks, software, and real-time marketplaces explored in *Vaporized*."

Rio Caraeff, founder and former CEO of Vevo

"A worthy successor to *Blown to Bits* and *Being Digital*, *Vaporized* illustrates a new world order brought about by enabling software and a connected world."

Rishad Tobaccowala, chief strategist of the Publicis Groupe

"Robert Tercek is one of the keenest observers of the zeitgeists in media, culture, and technology, and *Vaporized* is where it all comes together. For anyone trying to understand the digital transformation of business, commerce, and society, this book is simply indispensable."

Gerd Leonhard, CEO of The Futures Agency and author of *The Future of Music*

"We've seen the headlines: software is eating the world. Physical things are dematerializing, disappearing before our very eyes. And yet amidst this disruption is exponential opportunity: for reinvention, for transformation, for new possibilities. Robert Tercek's *Vaporized* maps for us this new territory."

Jason Silva, host of National Geographic's *Brain Games*

"In this era of endless innovation, our world of things is being digitally blown to bits. In *Vaporized*, Robert Tercek puts the pieces back together so that anyone looking to succeed in the 21st century can better understand the economic forces at work and their impact on everyone's careers."

Jay Samit, author of *Disrupt You!*

"Robert Tercek's vision of the future of digital media provides indispensable strategic insight about the future of media, manufacturing, marketing and retail. *Vaporized* will be a must-read for the next generation of business and political leaders."

Katrina Cukaj, executive vice president of CNN Advertising Sales

"Super-fast access to data on mobile devices is vaporizing entire industries. Yours may be next. This book provides essential survival skills for the biggest business transformation of our lifetime."

Phil Braden, senior vice president of Technology
and Applications for PCCW

"*Vaporized* is a magnificent guide to the way software defines modern commerce: self-organizing, real-time, mobile markets that are devouring the material world. Tercek masterfully weaves his wide knowledge of both traditional and new businesses, showing us how it is less profitable to actually own things—and insanely profitable to control information about things."

Mark Jeffrey, author of *Bitcoin Explained Simply*

"Robert Tercek is one of the people who gets the transition happening in every corner of the economy from old, slow, solid, offline models to high-speed, digital, ephemeral ones. His insights matter to every industry and every business. Read the book. Listen to what he says."

Ramez Naam, author of *Nexus* and *The Infinite Resource*

"Robert Tercek is the Buckaroo Banzai of digital media. He literally travels to the future, and reports back foresights through a blend of provocative humor and actionable insights. He connects the dots like none other, and always energizes people with a creative call to arms for what is possible. Quite simply, Robert brings the thunder."

Michael Margolis, founder and CEO of Get Storied and StoryU

"This is the only book you need to understand how the mobile economy really works. An essential read for 21st century leaders, *Vaporized* provides an insightful look at how mobile data will transform our whole economy and, quite likely, our society."

Ned Sherman, co-founder and CEO of Digital Media Wire

"Robert Tercek's *Vaporized* theories provide a jolt of what's possible. Tercek convincingly poses breakthrough concepts that are both disturbing and promising about what will come."

Rod Perth, president and CEO of National Association
of Television Program Executives (NATPE)

"Too many 'aha moments' to list! In the spirit of *Megatrends*, *Vaporized* reveals what's right around the corner. This remarkable peek into the future is much more than a fascinating read. Follow Tercek's lead to be ahead of the change and the competition."

Marshall Goldsmith, author of the *New York Times* and
global bestseller *What Got You Here Won't Get You There*

"Robert Tercek takes us on a riveting ride through past tech-enabled disruptions to a profoundly reimagined future that is inspiring yet unnerving. Every corner of humankind will be impacted, and every business leader, thinker, doer, or spectator should be deeply concerned by the fresh questions, insights, and possibilities raised in this book."

Paul Zilk, CEO of Reed MIDEM

ROBERT TERCEK

VAPORIZED

SOLID STRATEGIES FOR SUCCESS IN A DEMATERIALIZED WORLD

Cataloguing data available from Library and Archives Canada
ISBN 978-1-928055-04-4 (cloth)
ISBN 978-1-928055-05-1 (epub)
ISBN 978-1-928055-06-8 (PDF)

Published by LifeTree Media Ltd
lifetreemedia.com

Distributed by Greystone Books Ltd.
greystonebooks.com

Editor: Maggie Langrick
Designer: Ingrid Paulson
Printed in Canada by Friesens

All monetary figures cited in the text are in US dollars.

CONTENTS

FOREWORD

Now You See It, Now You Don't

R ecords, film, newspapers, and, soon, books. What is so astonishing is not so much that they have been vaporized, but that so many people have clung to denial about this inevitability. Of course their physical forms would be made obsolete by digital media, as surely as the sun sets in the west. What's wrong with people that they could not see this coming?

Among the everyday items that featured heavily in my youth and young adulthood were little yellow boxes containing black plastic canisters. To use their contents properly, I had to learn all sorts of things: ASA numbers, the difference between color and chroma, and how to be cautious at airport security so as not to end up with clouded images. Consumers of this product exercised great parsimony and did considerable editing in front of the camera lens—it was so damn expensive to work behind the lens. Today, nobody under twenty-five knows what I am referring to.

Kodak, the source of these now obsolete iconic yellow boxes, was itself vaporized. Twenty years before it disappeared, Kodak was a founding member, in 1982, of the MIT Media Lab. I worked closely with their most senior management. I cannot tell you how many times I argued that film had no future, that imaging intelligence would move from the medium to the device. But no, they said, film has more resolution, more warmth, and more character than digital images. Huh, more character? Graininess was even touted as a feature, rather than a bug. Give me a break. Film was destined to be vaporized and fall out of use as assuredly as the Zeppelin.

Records, CDs, and videotapes came next. The same story happened with Tower Records and Blockbuster. Now newspapers and books. Personally, I won't even touch a newspaper these days, because it has low contrast ratio and poor images, it smells, and is filthy. Books will take longer to vaporize, unless you are one of the next billion readers, most of whom will be in the developing world. There are just too many new readers, too widely dispersed at low density, for us to continue to cut down trees, build inventory, and ship an atom-bound product. Notice that none of these arguments even touches upon interactivity, searching, sharing, or machine understanding, the key differentiators that make digital products better under any conditions.

The part of Robert Tercek's book that fascinates me most is beyond the traditional "move bits not atoms" story. Anything that can be bits will be. Any process that can be disintermediated will be. That is old news. What is new about vaporization is its unexpected consequences that reach far beyond media. Who would have imagined that taxis might be vaporized?

Ever since my own student years at MIT, people have been designing on-demand, multi-point to multi-point, personalized car services. In 1967 (yes, 1967) it was called Computer Aided Routing and Scheduling, or CARS. I remember it well, along with a dozen successor systems over the next fifty years. Question: why did Uber suddenly catch on? It was hardly a new idea.

Answer: Uber launched in a historic sweet spot at the confluence of smartphones, GPS, texting, email, and Google maps. Uber did not make any of these. CARS had none of them. My point is that vaporization takes more than just a kettle and a stove; it takes an entire kitchen. It arises when the context is right, with both a wide technical base and an overarching social acceptance. Therefore, I offer four pretty wild predictions of vaporization in the future, progressively more extreme and perhaps unbelievable. You do not need to agree with me, but think about them as you read this book.

1. Suburbs will disappear. By suburb I do not mean urban sprawl or slum, but the high-end, low-density residential districts to which people have traditionally decamped in search of clean air, backyards, safety, and good schools. The cities were left to rot. Now it is the suburbs' turn. No self-respecting young person is going to favor a picket fence and beagle over the excitement of the city. Whether it is parties, restaurants, no commute times, creative job opportunities, walkability, or arts and entertainment, cities win big time. All of these are tightly interwoven. The city zoning maps of the '60s looked like an Ellsworth Kelly. Today they look like a Georges Seurat.

2. A visit to the doctor's office will be vaporized. Why would you ever go to a doctor if it weren't strictly necessary? As our bodies are increasingly connected, we will become quantified people with every single function monitored 24/7. Whether it is a remote human doctor or an online artificial intelligence examining us, we can be assured their diagnosis will not be subject to the vagaries and approximations of human memory and discussion. I was recently within ten minutes of the knife for what was assumed to be appendicitis, but which turned out to be kidney stones. I was just explaining it wrong. Any little robot inside me would have known that.

3. Nations will be vaporized. Imagine redesigning the structure of the world today. We would never have come up with a taxonomy in which the smallest element is 1,000 people and the largest is 1.2 billion. The arbitrary nature of most national borders will give way to globalization of thought, especially once everybody in the world speaks two languages: English plus their own.

4. Large corporations will be vaporized. Many of the reasons for their existence have already disappeared. Today there are far fewer cases in which you have to lose $5 billion in order to make $50 billion. Also consider the social and scientific responsibilities of big corporations. I am thinking of Bell Labs and IBM Research, which has give way to petty corporate social responsibility programs that get divided into tiny chunks along marketing lines, across many countries and subsidiaries.

Large corporate research labs have lost their long-term focus. Civil leadership also has to wake up to the nonsense of public-private partnerships, which outsource civic responsibilities to private monopolies. The world has to return to a more equitable and civil society, in which government actually does run some things, as it does with roads and sidewalks. If you ask whether this is possible, I urge you take a train ride in Switzerland.

What I am trying to say is that vaporization is not a strategic cusp or tactical deviation. It is not simply the move from cellulose to silicon. It is an entire change of lifestyle, driven by equity and access for all. This book is a primer for that eventuality.

Nicholas Negroponte
June 2015

INTRODUCTION

Welcome to the software-defined society

B efore we embark on our excursion into the not-so-distant future, let's begin with a look back at the past. There's a patch of conceptual terrain I'd like to reclaim.

The phrase "Let's do more with less" has a bad rap. In recent decades, business managers had a tendency to use that phrase during downsizing and budget cuts. The boss was likely to say, "Now we have to do more with less," a few minutes after half the staff had been laid off. That's a lousy application of a great idea.

The person who popularized the phrase was the American philosopher, architect, author, and inventor R. Buckminster ("Bucky") Fuller, who happened to be a prodigious coiner of new terminology. In 1938 Fuller introduced the ungainly word "ephemeralization" in his history of technology called *Nine Chains to the Moon*. And he defined it as humanity's ability, through technological advancement, to do "more and more with less and less until eventually you can do everything with nothing."

In his final book, *Critical Path*, Fuller used this example to illustrate the process of doing more with less: "A one-quarter-ton communication satellite is now outperforming the previously used 175,000 tons of transatlantic copper cables, with this 700,000-fold reduction in system-equipment weight providing greater message-carrying capacity and transmission fidelity, as well as using vastly fewer kilowatts of operational energy." That's the right way to do more with less.

Fuller was an early proponent of environmental awareness and sustainability, and he saw ephemeralization as the path to ever-increasing living standards for humanity without depleting the planet's resources. In Fuller's view, there is no upper limit on the potential to increase productivity. Wasted resources, inefficiency, and garbage are the consequences of a lack of knowledge. Or, as he wrote, "Pollution is nothing more than the resources we are not harvesting. We allow them to disperse because we've been ignorant of their value."

Over the years, Fuller's concept has gone by many names: ephemeralization, digitization, dematerialization, and virtualization. A series of visionary authors have subsequently offered further refinements of his idea. For example, in the 1960s Canadian professor and media philosopher Marshall McLuhan speculated that information technology might dematerialize people. McLuhan was the first to observe that, as we rely increasingly on electronic media as a substitute and an extension of our physical senses, we too are being transformed. In 1971 he wrote, "What is very little understood about the electronic age is that it angelizes man, disembodies him. Turns him into software."

Author and futurist Alvin Toffler, in his 1970 manifesto *Future Shock*, forecasted dematerialized goods and services as an economic imperative. "As the general rate of change in society accelerates," he wrote, "the economics of permanence are—and must be—replaced by the economics of transience."

In 1985, Nicholas Negroponte and Jerome Wiesner, both of the Massachusetts Institute of Technology (MIT), founded the MIT Media Lab to conduct interdisciplinary research into media, technology, science, and design. There, Buckminster Fuller's coinage got an upgrade from "ephemeralization" to "digitization," a feat of linguistic finesse that locates the phenomenon squarely in the realm of the computer. Negroponte, the director of the Media Lab, urged us to "move bits, not atoms," and his book *Being*

Digital conveyed the implications of a dematerialized society to a general readership.

Since the publication of Negroponte's book in 1993, we've seen many of his predictions come true: broadband Internet, smart objects, artificial intelligence, and ultracheap, pocketable supercomputers sporting novel interfaces. Today these breakthroughs are taken for granted by a generation that grew up with YouTube, smartphones, selfies, Siri, and Wikipedia, but there was a time not too long ago when they were bold—even audacious—ideas.

In his 1998 book *New Rules for the New Economy,* author and technology journalist Kevin Kelly recast Fuller's idea in terms of digital information: "The three great currents of the network economy: vast globalization, steady dematerialization into knowledge, and deep, ubiquitous networking—these three tides are washing over all shores." The dematerialization theme has been echoed recently by many other commenters, ranging from Peter Diamandis, founder of the non-profit X Prize Foundation, to Al Gore, the former vice president of the United States.

What exactly are these bits that replace atoms? Software. In 2011 venture capital investor Marc Andreessen wrote a widely cited opinion piece in the *Wall Street Journal* claiming that "Software is Eating the World." It's a crude metaphor, perhaps, but a compelling way to inject Fuller's forecast into the context of the Internet. One year later Andreessen's venture capital partners published a widely circulated PowerPoint deck that refined the concept, contending that "Mobile is Eating the World."

Silicon Valley marketers, always keen to find a new term to push their products, have jumped on the bandwagon. VMware and other firms, for example, have used the term "virtualization" to describe how they can replace physical equipment with powerful software that can accomplish the same task. In other words, doing more with less material stuff.

Most recently, the computer networking industry has adopted a term called "software-defined" to describe what is coming next. The term is trendy in the information technology field: software-defined networking, software-defined storage, software-defined data centers, software-defined clouds, software-defined everything. This is a major tech trend that will replace stubbornly inflexible purpose-built systems embodied in physical hardware with highly flexible systems written in software. Software-defined architectures are adaptable. The entire system operates in real-time, responding to incoming data, as needs change and as demand ebbs and flows.

In this term, "software-defined," we capture some of the essence of the twenty-first-century society—not just because a growing part of our economy rides on top of digital information networks, but also because the rules that shape software are beginning to redefine the rules of everything that touches it, up to and including the rules that govern society.

THE SOFTWARE-DEFINED SOCIETY

What the bright minds in Silicon Valley have begun to realize is that they can replicate almost any business function in software. It's quite a feat to take a big physical thing like a data center or telecommunications network and replace it with code. If they can do that, they can probably write a software model for anything.

Of course, software still needs to run on physical equipment, but the end result will be more energy efficient, more flexible, faster, and much cheaper because—you guessed it—we're doing more with less.

A fundamental principle of the digital economy is this: as goods become information intensive they begin to lose the characteristics of physical *products* and take on the properties of a *service*. When a physical thing is replaced by a software replica, the very nature of ownership changes. The same piece of software can be used by hundreds or thousands or millions of people at once. That's because information has different economic properties than physical stuff: information is a non-rival good, which means that it can be used by more than one person at a time, and everyone is better off.

The concept of offering "anything as a service" opens up entirely new business models. Instead of outright purchase, a software-defined product can be shared freely or rented or used just once for a single micropayment. Innovative pricing puts the product-as-a-service within reach of millions of people who couldn't otherwise afford it.

This idea, "doing more with less by replacing physical stuff with digital information-as-a-service," began with networking technology but now touches just about every industry imaginable. What is being transformed? Manufacturing, distribution, retail sales, marketing and media, and the very concept of buying and owning physical products. That's what we're going to examine in this book. I believe that the phrase "Do more with less" is not just a hollow slogan; it is a global strategic imperative. Doing more with less is the right thing to do. Not only is this a valid choice in a world constrained by finite resources; it also happens to be the best business strategy in an economy that is, and will continue to be, defined by software.

From this point forward, by leveraging ubiquitous telecommunications networks and computer technology to make efficient use of abundant information resources, all of human society—not just companies, but also our civic institutions, educational establishments, and governing bodies—really will be able to do far more with less. Our economy will become more productive, and we will all be collectively much richer while consuming physical resources more wisely, making better use of both raw materials and finished goods. These are big claims, so what makes me so confident about them? What's the secret? Information.

I'm not talking about insider-trading information. Not the kind of "information as a proprietary edge" that gives a broker a momentary advantage over a less-informed rival. I don't claim to have that kind of insider scoop. I am arguing for "outside information." You see, we are getting better at extracting information from the world around us. Embedded inside every physical thing is a lot of information, and as more of the world is wired and more devices are connected to the network, more and ever more data about our world will be harvested in useful form from physical things. The collecting, organizing, and analyzing of this information will yield insights that will improve performance. And that's how we are going to be able to "do more with less."

We are in the process of liberating information that has been frozen inside of things. All those retail shelves stuffed with consumer products contain massive amounts of information, but it's all bound up inside the physical molecules and, therefore, it's not very useable. That's about to change. We're on the brink of extracting the data content from everything: from mute products and lifeless raw materials, from biology and natural processes, and from business practices and organizational structure. We'll even find ways to extract the raw data trapped inside human muscle and mind.

I believe that *everyone on Earth* can benefit from knowledge that is systematically harvested, organized, refined, and exploited for the purpose of making the economy and the rest of society more efficient. In the process, we have a chance to overhaul outdated government bureaucracies, crusty rules and regulations, old-fashioned education systems, and other relics from the industrial past. That's what this book is about.

These benefits are not evenly shared today, and they don't come without a cost. Information resources are not uniformly available. Some information is stolen, some is hoarded jealously, and a vast amount of information is frozen in proprietary formats and closed systems. This book will also highlight the problematic areas, and, where feasible, will suggest a solution and strategy to contend with these obstacles.

Today we have a chance to migrate away from institutions with inflexible laws and a mass market economy with one-size-fits-all products and rigid rules that govern transactions, to something radically different: a more flexible, evolving, editable, participatory, responsive, and inclusive digital economy. These are attributes of software, and they are also the characteristics of a society *defined* by software.

In the software-defined society, we will have the opportunity to make informed choices among known alternatives. We can choose a paradise or a dystopia. We can opt between closed and open systems. We can accept surveillance, tracking, recording of every nuance of behavior via sensors, beacons, and analytics, or we can resist it, taking steps to protect our data. Choice begins with an awareness of the options.

A software-defined society can be open or closed. It can favor mass participation or it can enable control by an elite. It can be inscrutable and resistant to reverse engineering, or it can be open for examination, critique, rewriting, and improvement. Such systems will record and track a billion data points that scale from the individual to the billions, and it will all be testable, iterative, and optimized.

The future society need not be governed by the legacy of the past nor burdened by an accumulation of superannuated laws and outdated regulations; it may instead be governed by real-time data flows that measure inputs and outputs and expose inefficiency.

This book provides a preview of the changes ahead, snapshots of a process in motion, and dispatches from the front line where the changes and conflicts are already discernable. If you are interested in the near future, if your desire is success and mastery of your destiny in an evolving landscape, then this book is for you. It is my hope to alert and inform those who care to participate in shaping this future. May this book equip you with signposts and guides to the radically new environment defined by software.

1

WHAT IS VAPORIZED?

EVERYTHING THAT CAN BE
INFORMATION WILL BE

"What happened to Tower Records?" This is the question that set me off on a six-year quest to understand a broad but intangible force that is rapidly transforming every part of the economy and our society. The question was put to me by a group of businessmen in Los Angeles in 2008. And though they were asking me about the demise of record shops in general, their question referred specifically to that iconic temple to pop music. I thought I knew the answer. However, what I learned changed my perspective on everything from television to health care, automobiles, startups, and education.

The old Tower Records shop on Sunset Boulevard was a Los Angeles institution, if there can be such a thing in LA's shaggy, laid-back cultural landscape. For thirty-six years the shop dominated one end of the Sunset Strip, walking distance from the Whisky a Go Go and Roxy nightclubs. Angelenos considered it the most famous record store in the world. In fact, celebrity sightings were so common that few shoppers made a fuss when they bumped into a movie star or performer in the aisles. The list of bands that played at the Tower Records shop ranged wildly, from Engelbert Humperdinck to Duran Duran to Mariah Carey. Legend has it that Guns N'

Roses frontman Axl Rose started out as a sales clerk there—and that he once challenged Mötley Crüe's Vince Neil to a fight in the parking lot. It was more than a record store; it was a fixture in LA's pop music scene. If the music industry had a hub, it was the Sunset Strip—and Tower Records was the anchor tenant.

But in 2006 it disappeared. After a long struggle on the brink of bankruptcy, the Tower Records chain closed up shops one by one until none were left. The famous marquee on the Sunset Boulevard location displayed a forlorn message borrowed from an REM lyric: "It's the end of the world as we know it. Thanks for your loyalty."

It wasn't just Tower Records. Rival music shops The Wherehouse and Sam Goody vanished one by one too, until there were only a handful of indie record shops left in all of Los Angeles. In the city where making hit entertainment for mass consumption is not just a cool career but the defining cultural lifestyle, these stores were contemporary landmarks. Their disappearance left a gaping void in the commercial landscape. Where did they go?

My answer was simple: "They got vaporized." Disintegrated. Zap. Gone in a puff of smoke, like a scene from a science fiction movie in which laser guns are used in battle.

It may sound like exaggeration but, figuratively speaking, that's exactly what happened. Not only did the Tower Records store vanish, so did the products it sold. Vinyl records, cassette tapes, and compact disks (CDs) were replaced by MP3s. And the music playback devices also disappeared. No more turntables, cassette decks, or boom boxes. An entire industry, its primary and secondary products, and most of its retail outlets were mostly gone within the span of five years.

Physical media, the CDs and tapes that lined shelves at homes across the country, were suddenly out of style. They became slightly embarrassing artifacts of a bygone era, like bell-bottom jeans stuffed in the back of the closet or a photo of your parents in their disco days. Today the CDs and digital video disks (DVDs) we find at flea markets remind us awkwardly that we no longer have devices to play them.

THE DIGITAL WAVE

The process that killed music retailers is now rippling across society like a seismic wave, reshaping one industry after another. We've entered a period in which more and more devices, products, companies, jobs, and stores will simply disappear forever to be replaced by invisible software. As consumers, we won't miss them much. We no longer want superfluous physical products cluttering up our lives. We don't miss standing in line at a shop. If we can get the job done with a digital version on our computers or smartphones, or by borrowing instead of buying, we're satisfied. We've lost the urge to collect tangible goods.

Substitution is just the beginning. As physical products are replaced by their digital counterparts, a new generation of innovators and entrepreneurs have begun to reimagine them entirely, turning them into apps and services with far greater flexibility and functionality, available at any time, in any context, on any device, for free or for a radically reduced price. After two or three rounds of this reinvention merry-go-round, the next-generation products are nearly unrecognizable when compared to their forerunners from the 1990s.

In music, to continue with our example, we've switched from the shiny compact disk to "rip, burn, mix" to rampant file sharing to legal downloads to Internet radio and subscription streaming-audio services—all in a fifteen-year span. We consume music in 2015 in ways that were unthinkable in 1999.

DIGITAL FIRST

I've spent most of my twenty-five-year career launching new businesses in digital media, from multiplayer games to mobile video to online courses, and in the process I have learned a great deal about the dynamics of these new systems. Business operates differently on digital networks. As more and more of our business is done in the digital domain, and more and more of the stuff we own lives in those networks, the process is beginning to change society, culture, who we are, what we talk about, and how we connect.

We're becoming a digital-first society. A lot of what we do, say, hear, watch, and own exists purely in the digital domain. That's very different from traditional society where possessions and products and cultural objects were tangible hallmarks of civilization. Some people call it a dematerialized society.

I call it a society defined by software. This digital aspect of our lives is expanding incredibly fast, but weirdly we cannot see it or touch it. It's vast but intangible, which makes it difficult to conceptualize, hard to describe, and even harder to predict its trajectory. It's scarcely noticeable until we start using it.

During the past twenty years I've worked with companies all over the world, big and small, helping them to craft a strategy so they can transition gracefully from the old world of tangible physical stuff to this strange new world of digital bits. I've had the good fortune to work with great companies such as Turner Broadcasting System, Viacom, NBCUniversal, Discovery Communications, Public Broadcasting System, Reed Exhibitions, Sony Computer Entertainment, Nokia, AT&T, as well as educational and government institutions.

I've found that many people, including some executive leaders, find abstract technology concepts confusing, especially when that technology seems to be far removed from their own business activities. The confusion is quite reasonable: information technology (IT) operates by completely different business rules and by radically different economics. Even more jarring, it threatens to dismantle, undercut, or subvert every step in their processes, from product development to manufacturing, marketing, and distribution. So it's no surprise that some executives tend to resist studying digital transformation until it is too late to catch up to the first movers. That's the wrong time to start paying attention.

When I work with these clients, I find it useful to illustrate this changing landscape with a conceptual metaphor. I tell them that their business is getting vaporized.

My motto is "Whatever can be vaporized will be." That means any part of your business or product that can be replaced by pure digital information almost certainly will be. No matter how badly you may wish to preserve your legacy business, you can't stop this transformation process because dozens or even hundreds of other companies are already working on it. And it's not just your stereo or your CD collection or your local record shop at stake. Your job, your company, even your identity are up for grabs as we make the transition from the real, tangible physical world to the digital domain.

That's why we are seeing so many companies crater and collapse completely, undone by nimbler rivals who use digital media to undermine their old-school counterparts. Just like Tower Records on the Sunset Strip, we're now seeing entire product categories and sometimes entire businesses vanish overnight, replaced by pure software. The strangest part is that this process is almost entirely imperceptible until it's complete. One day a store is selling familiar products, and the next day there's a vacant shop with a For Lease sign in the window. The vaporized phenomenon now extends to every part of the globe as digital media reaches into every industry. Those who feel immune to it may be the most vulnerable to being blindsided.

I want you to understand that it can happen to your business too. In fact, it's probably already happening.

VAPORIZED: THE METAPHOR EXPLAINED

We all learned in a grade-school science class that matter exists in three states:

> **Solid:** Matter can be a solid shape, like wood or plastic or metal. In solid form, molecules are packed tightly together and they don't move fast—or at all. Solid matter is dense, heavy, slow, and stable.
> **Liquid:** Matter can also exist in a liquid state, in which the molecules are packed loosely. In the liquid state, matter can move. It can flow in a certain direction. Matter in this state is fluid: looser, lighter, faster, and less stable.
> **Vapor:** Finally, matter can also exist in the state of vapor or gas. In this form, the molecules are very loose and free floating. They move very quickly and are quite far apart. Vaporized matter is diffuse, very lightweight, fast, and unstable.

Your grade-school science teacher probably used water to illustrate this principle. Water can exist in all three states, as a solid block of ice, a free-flowing stream of liquid, or as airborne vapor. Just like water, information exists in the same three states.

Solid

Information in solid form is embedded in a physical object. For example, consider a book: there's a huge amount of information contained in the book but it's all bound to the physical page. Until very recently, it was impossible to separate the information printed on the page from the physical book. The container and its content were a single unit.

The printing industry, and by extension the entire media industry, is based on this idea. We buy the container as a proxy for the contents—the books, not the ideas contained within them. Likewise, we used to buy CDs and DVDs, not the songs and movies encoded on them. Until fairly recently, the way we monetized content was to sell the container. There was no business model for selling just the content because we didn't have an easy way to deliver it without the container.

This physicality had some strong advantages. Physical books are remarkably stable. They can survive almost any catastrophe except fire or flood. They last a very long time, especially if they are printed on archival paper with non-acidic ink. Today it's still possible to read a bible printed in 1455 by Gutenberg, if you happen to know Latin.

But physical books have some serious defects too. They are heavy and they occupy a lot of space. Blame it on all those molecules packed together in the paper. Information in solid form therefore requires enormous amounts of energy to produce, transport, and store.

Even worse, books are scarce. They can be shared sequentially but not simultaneously, which means I can lend the book to another person but then I can't use it while she's got it. There is no practical way for one book to be used by two people at once. That's one reason the printing press mattered: it was the first time that multiple identical copies of the same text were available, a core requirement for the modern classroom and also for research in different locations.

Books are also instantly out of date. The delay between writing and publishing books made sense when society moved at the pace of a horse and carriage, but it's totally out of sync with our world today when science textbooks, for instance, are sometimes obsolete before they reach the schoolroom.

All of these factors taken together—the weight, the size, the scarcity, the obsolescence—mean that physical books are quite an expensive way to share information.

There was, of course, no way to know this in the past, because we didn't have alternatives. For a very long time, books were the best way to record and transmit information from one place to another or from one generation to the next. Books were less delicate than clay tablets and more portable than stones carved with runes. They were not as cumbersome as scrolls. And, thanks to Gutenberg, mechanically reproduced books were a heck of a lot cheaper to produce than hand-drawn codices.

For five hundred years, this was the best that human society could do. Sure, we tweaked the book format constantly and came up with paperbacks, posters, pamphlets, billboards, and magazines, but the basic template for information in solid form had been established in 1455 and is still pretty much the same.

Liquid

With the advent of the World Wide Web in the 1990s, something remarkable began to happen. We moved into our post-Gutenberg era. Written information was digitized and transformed into software displayed on a computer monitor. Books, brochures, and newspapers gave way to websites that freed information from its physical container. As people began to install Internet services in their homes and offices, information took on a life of its own, flowing through the telephone wires like water.

By the early 2000s, most households across North America and Northern Europe began to migrate from slower dial-up Internet services that rode over copper telephone wires to ever-faster, always-on broadband services delivered via optical fiber cables that transmit data at the speed of light. High-speed Internet turned information into a utility that was available at a keystroke, just like turning on the tap for water or flicking a switch for electricity. We came to expect immediately available, constantly updated information without delay. Even the language we casually use to describe the Web reflects this liquid quality: we talk about "fat pipes" of data, "web surfing," and "streaming media."

For the first time in history, information was freed from the constraints imposed by fixed physical media. It moved instantly from one site to another and then to users, who copied and pasted it into emails, downloaded it as text files, edited, excerpted, remixed, and shared it. Consumers began to think of the computer as an information appliance like a TV or radio, and this liquid information delivered over the wireline network to a terminal or desktop computer proved very handy for people at desks: office workers, academics, and researchers. But the transition to digital networks created problems for companies that were used to selling a physical container, such as a book or disk, as a proxy for content. The shift from solid to liquid form caused music labels and book publishers to lose control of their product. We'll take a closer look at those issues in the next two chapters.

For all of the advantages, there are plenty of circumstances where depending on a fixed wireline connection doesn't quite suit the needs of people who have come to rely on instant access to information. For instance, imagine a mechanic fixing a car in the garage. Covered in greasy overalls, she's unlikely to use a desktop computer to watch a video about the repair she is making. Ditto for chefs working with recipes in the kitchen, golfers tweaking their strokes, tennis players intent on improving their serve, or suburban kids learning a skateboard trick—or even cheating on a test in class. In these and similar cases, the computer just won't cut it. The desktop computer trailing a cable connected to a modem was not nearly as portable as a book.

Vapor

That's where the smartphone comes in. The next big step in the progression is to vaporize the information by making it available over the air to mobile devices. In this phase, information moves like atmosphere: fast, free, and rapidly evolving. Subject to constant change, it behaves in exactly the opposite way to fixed physical media. It's not bound to one place, it can be shared by millions of people at once, and it's instantly available any time.

During the past ten years we've seen the speed of downloading data to mobile phones increase by two orders of magnitude, and today mobile networks are 1,000 times faster than they were a decade ago. This means we now have access to data any time, no matter where we are or what we are doing. For those who grew up with home computers, "www" no longer stands for the World Wide Web: instead it means Whatever, Whenever, and Wherever. The computer has trained us to expect to receive information and content on our terms on the screen of our choice. Now mobile is literally reshaping the way we organize information, making it available anytime with just the touch of a virtual button on a screen.

During the broadband era, web content was organized in vast repositories known as portals. By necessity, huge sets of web pages were sorted into categories, similar to catalogs. It was a librarian's dream project to organize all of the world's information—or to make the attempt. This approach worked adequately on a desktop computer where users could browse massive information sets easily from big monitors where there is plenty of space to display many pages.

This approach did not work well on mobile phones, however. Phones have tiny screens, so ever-expanding web pages must be presented differently, divided up into lightweight formats optimized for a particular purpose. Today, instead of sprawling, one-size-fits-all information portals delivered to desktop computers, we now have concise mobile apps—more than 1.5 million of them—designed to solve specific problems. The curatorial power has shifted from the portal publisher to the end user who gets to classify, sort, and delete the apps on his or her phone.

Mobile data means that we can close the loop between the real world and the Internet. Now that car mechanic can pull an app-enabled device out of her pocket and access the information she needs at the time and place in which she needs it. The tennis player or the skateboard kid can watch an instructive YouTube video clip right when he or she needs it. Better still, millions of people can access the same information at once, and comment on it and share it with others. This is information as vapor, floating freely in the atmosphere around us, surrounding us, shared by all of us, pervading all places and circumstances.

THE VAPORIZATION OF DEVICES

If it feels like this evolution from solid-state information to vapor has occurred rapidly, that's because it has gained tremendous momentum in recent years. Things started slowly in the 1960s when scientists, government workers, academic researchers, and supergeeks began to define the protocols, or rules of data exchange, to link computer systems together.

In October 1968 the first two computers were linked via a network called ARPANET. In the 1970s many more computers were linked via a variety of rules governing the exchange of data, known as protocols. In 1983 ARPANET was upgraded to a new set of protocols called the Transmission Control Protocol/Internet Protocol (TCP/IP). This is the moment that many consider the beginning of the modern Internet. That year, in a poll conducted by Louis Harris & Associates, only 1.4 percent of Americans reported that they used the Internet.

Internet use began to gather great momentum a decade later when the American public first began to learn about the World Wide Web and dial-up bulletin board services, which were a digital version of the familiar cork boards used to post notices and information on college campuses. The United States Census Bureau did not even begin asking about home Internet use until 1994. By 1995, 14 percent of American homes were connected to the Internet via modems plugged into standard telephone lines. According to the Pew Research Center, 42 percent of Americans had not even heard of the Internet that year. By 2001, half of US households were online. After 2002, Americans began to migrate en masse to high-speed wireline broadband services. By 2013, more than 74 percent of US households were online, according to the US Census Bureau.

Mobile Internet grew much faster than fixed-line Internet. Various concepts for radio telephones date back to the early 1900s, but most historians agree that the first handheld mobile phone was introduced by Motorola in 1973. The establishment of the Global System for Mobile Communications (GSM) standard in 1991 marked the beginning of the modern era of digital mobile phones. CTIA—The Wireless Association, the trade group of US wireless service providers, reports that by 2000 about 109 million Americans owned mobile phones but very few of them were capable of more than voice calls. By 2005 that number doubled, and by 2010 more than 300 million Americans, 91 percent of the US population, owned a mobile phone. Sixty percent of them were using smartphones, effectively miniature supercomputers capable of handling video games, music, ebooks, and Web browsing in addition to voice calls, which were connected to fourth-generation (4G) wireless broadband Internet access. The modern smartphone era had arrived less than two decades after the first digital mobile phone. That's half the time it took for wireline Internet to attain broad diffusion.

In 2013, mobile phones also surpassed desktop computers as the preferred way to connect: Americans spend 33 percent more time accessing the Internet via their phones than via personal computers (PCs), reported eMarketer, a market research firm. Surprisingly, 25 percent of Americans connect to the Internet solely by smartphone.

There are 7.3 billion people on the planet: according to the Groupe Speciale Mobile Association (GSMA), 3.4 billion of them own a mobile phone of some kind, more than twice the number of PCs, and most of these phones are being upgraded to smartphones. In 2014 Google announced that more than a billion people use Android phones, and Apple's chief executive officer, Tim Cook, announced 800 million use iOS devices. Growth rates for mobile Internet continue to soar. Since 2007 mobile adoption rates in China and Russia have grown faster than in the US, and in many countries citizens are skipping the desktop computer phase altogether as they go straight for the mobile phone. Every kid growing up now in any country will reach the Internet first via a phone.

The modern smartphone era actually began long before Apple launched its first iPhone in 2007. Companies like Palm, Research In Motion (RIM), and Nokia had been experimenting with concepts for personal digital assistants (PDAs), personal communicators, and smartphones for nearly a decade—all of them preceded by the IBM Simon in 1993, which was the first mobile phone to include a calendar, address book, and email. The smartphones of the twenty-first century introduced ways to modify the device after it was purchased by adding new features and applications downloaded over the air or "side-loaded" via a tethered PC. Suddenly one device could handle three jobs: phone, written-word communicator, and media player.

In 2002, the state-of-the-art smartphone was a RIM BlackBerry pager. It was considered smart because it combined four separate things into a single device: a phone, an address book, a pager, and an email reader. Thanks to the relentless competition from other device manufacturers, new features were continuously added. Leveraging the ever-increasing processing power in new-generation devices, every new smartphone included special apps that rendered a previously separate device unnecessary. Games, MP3 players, FM radios, calculators, still photo cameras, voice message recorders, photo albums, web browsers, Global Positioning System (GPS) navigators, were all threatened as standalone products.

At first, the smartphone versions were poor substitutes. The resolution of the camera was low, the GPS navigation was slow, the games were grainy and low quality. But, as we've seen so many times with desktop and laptop computers, the processing power improved and gradually so did the rest of the device, including the apps. Today hardly anyone feels compelled to carry a separate camera or portable game player. They just don't add enough extra value to be worth the effort of hauling around a battery pack, display, keyboard, and charger.

While the features and processing power of smartphones were evolving, the iPhone paved the way to a major transition in 2008 when Apple added the ability to download apps with the single touch of a button. Previously, mobile subscribers needed to go through as many as thirty-five clicks on various menus to download a new app for their phone. Apple eliminated all of the complex steps, making the process irresistibly simple and massively improving the user experience.

Multiplied across the hundreds of millions of people who have adopted smartphones since that time, this trend toward vaporization has had a devastating effect on other industries. The sales of point-and-shoot cameras, 35mm film, and disposable cameras were crushed by the rise of mobile phones with embedded cameras. Next, consumer video cameras were wiped out. Case in point: in 2009, networking equipment giant Cisco Systems spent $590 million to acquire Flip, a promising new miniature high-definition (HD) camera that stole 30 percent of the HD video camera market from its competitors Sony and Sharp. But then, just two years later, Cisco simply shut Flip down. The company didn't sell it or spin it out as a standalone operation. It just turned the product off. Cisco could see the road ahead. Mobile phones would continue to improve in quality and processing power until there was no room left for a standalone miniature video camera, no matter how small and easy to use.

In short, the Flip camera was killed by an app. Vaporized. All of the precision functionality of a brilliantly designed and popular device was replicated by invisible software. And then the Flip disappeared.

The story of Flip is the story of many other consumer electronics products writ small. As the capabilities of the smartphone expand and improve, the distinct appeal of other standalone digital devices tends to disappear. Throughout the past eight years, as smartphone sales surged, the sales of video cameras, voice recorders, still cameras, portable music players, and DVD players and handheld game consoles have plummeted. In a word, they've been vaporized.

Vaporized is what happens when tangible physical products are replaced with invisible software that can be downloaded instantly over the air to a digital device.

Vaporized occurs when the neighborhood store is replaced with a digital storefront that exists in no particular place at all but is available anywhere, at any time, from any mobile phone connected to a data network.

Vaporized is what happens when the global supply chain for manufacturing, shipping, warehousing, and retailing consumer goods is decomposed and reorganized by software systems and digital networks.

Vaporized is the process of replacing real things with digital metaphors that can be replicated, updated, distributed, and deleted in seconds with the press of a button.

THE VAPORIZATION OF RETAIL

Vaporization is happening constantly, but it is very hard to monitor in the real world because there's very little to see except the aftermath: only some big signs that announce for a few weeks Everything Must Go, followed by a vacant storefront and an empty factory. So many things are changing at once now that it's hard to keep track of what's disappearing. Just like when a magician makes an elephant disappear from the stage in front of a live audience, vaporization involves a kind of vanishing act. Today it's those white elephants of the industrial economy—the big-box retailers—that are disappearing, and the magicians are the entrepreneurs who are reimaging the world in an entirely new form.

Economists use the term "demand destruction" to refer to a permanent shift downward in the demand for a commodity. The balance between supply and demand governs pricing in every market: fluctuations in supply and demand are routine. But demand destruction is rare. It has no connection to supply. Demand is destroyed when consumers find a substitute so perfect that a product is rendered irrelevant. The term is typically used in the context of the energy industry to describe, for example, what happens to demand for gasoline when a consumer trades in his gas guzzler for an electric car.

We're entering a new economic era in which demand destruction is becoming common, even normal. The smartphone has triggered a wave of demand destruction like nothing ever experienced in history. As more and more people migrate to smartphones and as the process of vaporization spreads through more sectors of the economy, consumers are finding perfect information substitutes for physical products and services in epic numbers.

On the day I was asked about what had happened to Tower Records, I explained to my interlocutors that American shoppers had developed a new preference for making their music purchases. They no longer wanted music in physical form. Their favorite new store looked nothing like Tower Records. It had no walls, no windows, no shelves, and indeed no physical inventory of any kind. It had no physical presence. There were no sales clerks or checkout counters. This new store existed solely in digital form.

I was referring to the Apple iTunes Store. It is unlike any store that ever previously existed. The iTunes Store is a virtual shop that exists entirely on the Internet in the form of electronic bits sent over the network and displayed on a device screen. It can't be seen without launching a software program made by Apple; the content plays only on Apple's music player, and all of the apps sold in the store work only on Apple devices.

By the time the iTunes Store was introduced in 2003, e-commerce was fairly mature. Online retailers had recovered from the dot-com crash of 2000–2002 that followed the bubble of speculation in Internet stocks. Survivors of the crash were already claiming victims in the real-world brick-and-mortar shopping center. During the ensuing years, the combination of big-box stores like Best Buy and Costco and online retailers like Amazon would doom national retail chains like the two big electronics retailers, The Good Guys and Circuit City.

But the Tower Records story was different. This wasn't just a matter of one store being beaten by another. It wasn't even about e-commerce beating traditional brick-and-mortar retail: Tower.com was already a major online seller of music on compact disks. The new competition from big-box stores definitely hurt Tower Records, as did the widespread sharing of MP3 files. Its demise was a novel twist on the classic tale of a nimbler competitor offering a more compelling way to sell the same merchandise.

This time the coup de grace was delivered by a completely different kind of store, with an entirely different product, sold in a completely different way, in a different environment altogether. Tower Records did not sell a single item that the Apple iTunes Store sold, but it was killed by Apple nevertheless. Apple's offering rendered Tower's utterly irrelevant: instead of selling a shiny hard disk packaged in a brittle jewel case sealed with sticky security seals, Apple offered a perfect substitute that consisted of pure information. The virtual emporium selling virtual products put a physical store selling physical merchandise completely out of business.

What makes the Apple iTunes Store even more radical as a departure from previous forms is that it's actually much more than a store. It comprises the total consumer experience, including packaging and promotion and displays as well as the inventory, warehousing, and provisioning systems that consumers never see. The entire retail supply chain that moves products from the manufacturer to the consumer had been compressed, compacted, and converted into a purely digital metaphor.

To guide consumers through this radically new experience, the iTunes Store makes liberal use of the old language of the traditional store: shopping cart, checkout, store sections, and best-seller charts. This mimetic echo of the past serves a dual function: it orients newcomers and helps them navigate the virtual store, and it also provides a sentimental connection to a familiar shopping experience that is core to our identity as consumers in a consumer society.

I know what you're thinking as you read this. You are probably saying: "Ah, Apple iTunes. Is this news? It's ten years old. Tell me something I don't know."

Here's what you need to know about Apple iTunes and the App Store. It's not just a music store. That name is a distraction. It's more than an app store. The iTunes software and services store is the centerpiece of a new kind of ecosystem for reinventing the economy in vaporized form. It is Apple's fastest-growing business segment with extremely high profit margins. It has transformed Apple from a maker of computers into a branded lifestyle company that provides high-margin devices bundled with software, digital media, and services. As it makes this transformation, Apple is literally sucking the profit out of the old industries that it vaporizes, and no industry is off-limits. The company has already conquered music, books, and video, and it is now expanding into retail, health and fitness, payments and transactions, automobiles, home automation, and more.

We hear the term "game changer" so often today that we sometimes forget what the phrase really means. Apple literally changed the rules of the music game so profoundly that Tower and its ilk had to exit the arena. This was demand destruction on an epic scale, rendering an entire retail category irrelevant, with all of the dominant players along with it.

Apple wasn't the first to sell digital downloads; it was just the best, and it blazed the trail for thousands of competitors. Tower Records wasn't the first company to be challenged by a virtual rival from cyberspace, nor was it the last. Today every company is facing some form of competition from a nimble, low-cost, purely digital rival. Or several.

THE NEW VALUE BUNDLE: DEVICE + SOFTWARE + CONTENT + COMMERCE

Apple's entire commerce offering is tightly bound to its proprietary operating system and its iconic devices. The store is now embedded in every Apple device. And together the device, the operating system, the store, the apps, and the content constitute a bundle of value that no other device maker can quite replicate.

Apple raised the stakes in the e-commerce game by re-envisioning the store as a purely digital experience that is inseparable from its device and impossible to ignore or avoid. And it raised the stakes in computer hardware by embedding the shopping experience right into the hardware, thereby making an App Store an essential feature in every connected device.

In the process, Apple succeeded in doing something extraordinarily difficult: it has changed consumer preferences permanently. Every person who uses an iPhone also uses the App Store, not just to download apps but also to obtain regular software updates that improve the function of the device and keep it running. This tightly bundled combination of device + software + content + commerce has actually transformed the end user, training Apple's customers to prefer the integrated experience. Apple customers have gradually lost their appetite for physical media, and with it, they've fallen out of the habit of visiting a music shop, talking to clerks, browsing the displays, wandering in the aisles late at night, and serendipitously encountering movie stars and recording artists. Customers have also discovered to their glee that they do not miss driving in traffic, waiting for a parking spot, dealing with weather, standing in line, and carrying bags and packages.

In the process of vaporizing entire product lines and retail categories, Apple hasn't just destroyed demand and annihilated companies. It has also managed to absorb vast amounts of revenue that previously resided in the physical economy. Today iTunes Software and Services is Apple's fourth-largest source of revenue after the iPhone, iPad, and computers. In April 2015, Tim Cook announced that App Store revenue grew 29 percent year over year. That was an understatement: analyst Horace Dediu of Asymco has observed that iTunes revenue growth averaged 29 percent a year for the previous six years.

In 2013, Apple's total software sales generated $23 billion in gross revenue, twice as much revenue as the entire iPod product line. That is comparable to Microsoft's total revenue for Windows or Office and equivalent to almost half of Google's core revenue from advertising. iTunes is a bigger business than several venerable leaders in the physical economy, including Xerox, Kimberly-Clark, US Steel, Union Pacific Railroad, and Kraft Foods. If iTunes were listed as a separate company, it would be included in the top 150 of the Fortune 500. What began as a loss leader to spur consumer adoption of the iPod has matured into a booming e-commerce business that grows in double digits each year.

The most profitable quarter in history

Apple ended 2014 on a high note, delivering holiday-season results that surpassed even the most aggressive forecast. The *Wall Street Journal* reported that Apple hit "an improbable trifecta" by selling more iPhones at higher prices and greater profit per unit than ever before. Apple is the only company to increase profit margins and sell more volume of an aging computer product line. During the last three months of 2014, Apple sold 74.5 million iPhones. That's like selling 34,000 phones an hour, twenty-four hours a day. The company earned $18 billion dollars in the quarter, and, according to market research firm S&P Capital IQ, Apple earned more profit in that one period than 400 of the 500 companies that S&P monitors have each earned in total profit in the previous five years.

The App Store propels this growth in several ways. Most significantly, the huge selection of 1.3 million apps acts as a bug light to attract customers. Consumers who want access to this immense candy store are willing to pay a hefty premium when they buy Apple hardware: the company's profit margins on devices are nearly ten times greater than those of other computer makers. And the App Store itself is also highly profitable. Apple's total billings from paid apps and in-app purchases rose 50 percent in 2014 to $15 billion. Apple shares most of that money with the developers who build the apps, but the company's own 30 percent take is a whopping $4.5 billion. Vaporization is a highly profitable business.

NOBODY IS IMMUNE, NOT EVEN APPLE

Nobody gets it right every time, and even Apple is vulnerable to the relentless process of vaporization. There's been a spot of trouble brewing in Apple's iTunes business model for several quarters. Namely, the business of selling music files for download is losing steam. Music sales at Apple's iTunes store fell 13 percent since the beginning of 2014. Audiences are migrating en masse to even more vaporized versions of music such as streaming radio like Pandora and subscription-based music-on-demand streaming services like Spotify and Deezer. Streaming music services are growing so quickly that they are on track to generate more income than downloads for independent labels like [PIAS] Recordings and majors like Warner Music Group. These services are easier to use and cheaper. The consumer owns nothing but has access to everything.

The erosion of iTunes music sales—in the middle of all the hoopla about Apple's epic quarter and the booming sales of mobile apps—neatly illustrates another aspect of the Vaporized Economy. Vapor is volatile. Those unbound bits move constantly. Therefore a vaporized business is inherently unstable, everchanging, and subject to disruption, just like atmosphere. Information empires built on air require constant pumping up, or they can collapse. For example, Apple struggled mightily to launch iTunes Radio but it was a rare flop. Similarly, the collapse of the music download business explains why Apple spent $3 billion to acquire Beats Electronics and its streaming music platform, Beats Music. In 2015, a revamped Beats Music will be launched as Apple's latest attempt to maintain its dominance in digital music.

Apple is hardly the only company to offer digital goods for sale in a virtual store. It built the template that every rival must follow, and now thousands of companies have begun a stampede to mimic the iTunes store. Today an online app store is an obligatory accessory for any digital device: ebook readers, digital cameras, smart televisions, game consoles, fitness trackers, lighting systems, and soon cars, medical equipment, smart appliances, and even smart diapers and bras. If it has a screen and a microprocessor, there's probably an app store lurking nearby. If there isn't, the device can likely be paired with an iPhone and an app downloaded from Apple's App Store.

Google, Amazon, Microsoft, and many other companies that compete with Apple are vying to control the landscape for vaporized business on their terms. Chances are, one of them is planning to come after your business. Your company may be a blip on their radar, a target for them. Your chief executive officer, chief financial officer, and senior management may have no idea how to contend with this challenge and may even be oblivious to this trend. Your career depends upon understanding these dynamics and mastering them.

THE SCOPE OF THE CHANGE IS IMMENSE

The process is not finished. On the contrary, this party has barely begun. The process of vaporizing physical things and replacing them with digital substitutes is the biggest trend affecting manufacturing, distribution, retail, and marketing in the twenty-first century.

This trend is happening worldwide, and as every nation introduces wireless broadband services, it is accelerating to mobile devices of every shape and size. What began with media and computer software has rapidly expanded to many other fields entirely unrelated to those industries: banking, retail, mapping, automobiles, travel, education, even government functions are subject to this process.

For startup ventures with no stake in the old physical economy, this is the modern Klondike, a gold rush of epic proportion. For old-school bureaucracies, it's a scary new world. Nothing is safe. The process of vaporization is not going away—in fact, it's speeding up. We all need to adapt if we plan to participate in this economy. To do so, we must cultivate a deeper understanding of the dynamics of vaporization, how it works, who wins, who loses, where value is controlled and extracted from the economy.

If you work in an industry that produces and sells any type of physical product or service, not only do you need to be familiar with the process of vaporizing things, you need to master this phenomenon by understanding every facet, including:

> **Pace:** The rate of innovation in vaporized markets is accelerating. This is a simple function of low barriers to entry combined with a sweepstakes mentality. Thousands of companies in hundreds of nations are now competing in a race to be the first in a winner-take-all economy that spans the globe.

> **Scale:** The Vaporized Economy already reaches every corner of the planet, including 2 billion people today and an estimated 6 billion by 2020, according to telecom equipment maker Ericsson. As old industrial systems are dismantled and replaced by software, billions of dollars are at stake. Vaporized products are placeless, leaping national boundaries with ease. Their expansion is thwarted only by countries whose protectionist industrial policies expressly block foreign software firms in order to foster a clutch of homegrown stalwarts.

> **Form:** As real-world products and retail experiences are translated to digital form, they can be reimagined in lots of useful and sometimes surprising ways. Today's vaporized startup companies are launching with customers long before they have a product. They are adept at using games (gamification), soliciting ideas and money from online communities (crowdsourcing and crowdfunding), and drawing on a broad range of other remote collaboration tools to engage consumers, thereby garnering crucial first revenue faster than any company in the past.

If you want to play in this space (and why not? It's early days and nearly everything is up for grabs), you'll need to rethink some of the basic principles that govern your business. By moving from tangible physical goods to virtual digital apps and services, we are moving away from many familiar aspects of the real world towards the slippery and strange attributes of the vaporized world:

- From solid to vapor;
- From heavy to weightless;
- From dense to diffuse;
- From concrete to abstract;
- From slow to fast;
- From energy-intensive to efficient;
- From expensive to cheap;
- From scarce to abundant;
- From paid to free;
- From fixed to flexible;

- From unchanging to versioned;
- From outdated to updated;
- From tangible to intangible;
- From visible to imperceptible;
- From steady to dynamic;
- From owned to shared;
- From exclusive to communal;
- From mass-produced to personalized;
- From centralized to decentralized;
- From controlled to democratic;
- From regional to global and transnational;
- From supply chain to ecosystem;
- From channel to marketplace;
- From literal to metaphoric.

> **Enablers:** The smartphone is not the only thing driving the process of vaporization: it's just the front end of a wedge of technology that will split us away from centuries-old habits and customs. That phone provides instant access to several new technologies that are reshaping the business landscape: Big Data, cloud computing, crowdsourcing, open software, and proprietary software platforms. In combination, they create a seismic force that is altering the structure of the consumer economy. We'll take a closer look at the implications of these changes in subsequent chapters.

> **Control:** New invisible empires are being established as the tide of commerce shifts towards digital platforms. These platforms are not the model public marketplaces described in classical economic theory: they are proprietary markets that exist within closed ecosystems governed by arbitrary business rules and bound to proprietary software systems and computer hardware.

THE SOFTWARE-DEFINED SOCIETY IS TRANSFORMING US TOO

And then there's the impact on us: the people doing the shopping, browsing, consuming, commenting, and reviewing. We play a role in constructing these virtual emporiums, explicitly with our commentary, our five-star reviews, and our purchase history, but also implicitly because every product or service we browse and explore, every minute we are in the virtual store, and every offer we notice and respond to is tracked, stored, and processed in a huge relational database.

It is very difficult for individuals to gauge the seismic shift underway in the consumer economy. This process is not just rapid and unstoppable, it's also so seamless and silent and all-encompassing that it's easy to miss. Most of us just click on the link to update our apps and agree to new Terms of Use without stopping to consider what, exactly, has changed. We have finally reached the time that so many pundits and futurists had predicted in the past. We've entered the Information Age.

For more than forty years, we have been hearing about this coming Information Age and its sibling, the Information Economy. We've heard these terms so frequently that most of us have grown rather numb to them. And now that we've finally arrived in this era of massive-scale data gathering and instantaneous transmission, we can't even see the changes around us. It is easy to miss the implication of computing power widely dispersed across society because, for the most part, these changes are invisible. Our information systems are so widespread that we take them for granted, like plumbing or electricity. We only notice them when our network connection isn't working properly—and then we complain bitterly because we suddenly realize how fiercely addicted we've become. When everything runs smoothly, we rarely stop to think about where the apps and services come from and how they are changing our lives.

Most people in North America, Western Europe, Japan, and Korea have migrated to high-speed, always-on Internet services via smartphones and smart appliances. Other countries, including China, and many in Latin America, Eastern Europe, and South Asia, are catching up fast. In some places, such as Africa, the telecommunications companies are leapfrogging into the mobile era, skipping the wireline broadband phase completely.

We haven't yet arrived at our final destination. In fact, we've only just reached the low foothills of the Information Age, and we barely glimpse the massive peaks that lie ahead. But we can start to discern the shape of things to come, and it's a pretty awe-inspiring sight, full of opportunity, imagination, and some rollicking shifts.

We are constructing a world that bears no resemblance and owes no allegiance to the forms and structures of the past. This tidal wave won't cease with commercial enterprises; it's going to roll right through the rest of society too, and in the process it will transform our schools, our government and civic institutions, our currency and banks, our army, and just about everything else—including us.

The Information Age isn't just about the sharing of information, or even about the devices and systems we use to share that information. It's about how we conceive of ourselves, how we are counted, and how our individual impact on the world around us is measured. It's not just a new way of sharing the information we've always shared. It's about capturing, synthesizing, selling, and utilizing information that has never been gathered before, but can now be gathered in detail and in depth, and then organized and optimized and refined in ways that were previously unthinkable. This process raises questions about the very framework upon which our society operates.

What lies ahead is a transformation so vast that it will represent a complete break with the industrial era that defined the twentieth century. Society will be so different from the world that we knew in 1999 that it will be nearly impossible to imagine a time when people had to drive in cars to shopping malls to buy movies and songs on disks, when citizens stood in line to cast a vote with a paper ballot, when human workers instead of robots served us in fast-food restaurants, when medicine and replacement joints and even organs were not custom-made for each individual, when a video call couldn't reach any place on Earth, when information was not available all the time, when it was possible to be out of touch or anonymous or beyond the reach of the law.

The soon-to-be vaporized world of physical products—slow, ponderous, scarce—and their big-box stores, shopping malls, warehouses, and manufacturing plants will soon seem as antique and quaint as the vanished world of the horse and buggy, steamships, telegraphs, and messengers.

⏭ THE DISRUPTION MYTH

There's a widespread myth about disruption, which is that it happens overnight. According to this myth, a previously unknown startup company emerges out of nowhere and upends an entire industry in a matter of months.

It's not surprising that this myth exerts such a powerful grip on the public imagination: everyone likes to fantasize that they, too, might someday launch a successful business that instantly reinvents an entire category. The problem with this myth is that it is mostly untrue.

The myth of the fast-growing disruptive startup is deceptive because it reverses cause and effect. The fast-growth startup company is a consequence, not the cause, of vast tectonic changes in the information technology that underpins an existing industry.

The MP3 was introduced as a digital audio format in 1991, eight years before the music-focused file-sharing service Napster arrived on the scene in 1999. Streaming media existed for nearly ten years before the video-sharing website YouTube debuted in 2005. Downloadable apps for mobile phones were a thriving business eight years before Apple launched the App Store in 2008.

Changes in the foundational technology are incremental and mostly invisible because they occur on the periphery. They take place over such a long period of time that few observers notice them. They are easy to dismiss because, in the early stages, the technology is clunky and the resulting product quality is subpar. But these changes accumulate and accelerate and gradually they alter the economics of the industry, shifting away from the scarcity dynamics of a mechanized era to become abundant information-based processes, which require new ways of working and new kinds of workers with different skill sets. By the time the rapid-growth startup companies emerge to take the spotlight, the landscape has evolved so greatly that the entire basis of the industry has been altered.

Until 2007, this process took a decade or more. That's why the myth of the overnight startup success is only mostly untrue. What's changed since then is that the technological foundation for change has become so ubiquitous and so well established that new ventures can launch much more swiftly with far less capital investment and grow to massive scale in much less time. Today it is common for a successful new mobile messaging app to add a million new users a day during a viral breakout.

Older established businesses are often hamstrung, unable to take advantage of technological changes. They have a responsibility to amortize massive investments in industrial-scale facilities made in previous years. They are bound to long-term contracts with suppliers and other partners. They operate in a slow-moving regulated environment. Although they have learned how to operate profitably within these constraints and, in some ways, these constraints have protected them because of the high barrier of entry they present to newcomers, these established businesses suffer as the entire economy shifts. The old constraints become a barrier to innovation inside the established company, and often these companies are blind-sided by technology startups that have learned to thrive in the harsh environment outside the protective barrier. In Darwinian terms, the incumbent firms are ill adapted to the new environment. That's why the leaders of established businesses often insist on bending new technology to fit old infrastructure.

The single most vexing question facing every chief executive officer of a mature company is, "When is the right time to put a bullet in the head of a stable business and switch to an unproven model based on new technology?" The consequences of making a wrong move can be catastrophic because investors have no patience for companies that miss forecasts or lose market share. Public companies are damned in the short term by the demands of the stock market and in the long term by technology.

Often it makes more sense to start a new venture from scratch. Unencumbered by commitments made in the past, a digital startup can easily adapt to the new technologically defined landscape. Responsible only to a small number of venture capital investors, the startup is immune to the demands of the stock market and can operate unprofitably for many quarters while it perfects its offering and acquires customers.

What makes a successful startup venture seem so brilliant is a combination of timing and execution. The trick is to consolidate a set of technological changes into one easy-to-consume package and deliver it at a much lower price made possible by the process of vaporization. It takes time and resources to get this right, and it is an iterative process of trial and error. When the combination works, the results are explosive.

The widespread adoption of mobile devices, social and digital media, cloud infrastructure, e-commerce, and related technology means that the foundation is now in place for digital disruption to occur in many fields simultaneously. Startup companies can engage prospective customers using digital devices much earlier in the process, sometimes before a product is even developed. Vaporized companies can launch with customers before they have products. Demand pull from customers speeds the innovation process, so smart companies are developing a way to listen to their audience, engage with them as early as possible, and design their offerings in response to the feedback they receive. Companies of any size could benefit from this practice.

The biggest impediment you will face as you attempt to lead your company into the vaporized era is cultural. You'll need profound charisma in order to persuade, cajole, convince, demonstrate, and lead others to accept the new technology and the new way of doing business. Be prepared for some resistance. Trust me, most of them won't want to go there with you.

ASK YOURSELF
> How might software provide a substitute for your company's product or service?
> Can software replace even part of the product made by your company?
> If your company provides services, how might these be delivered digitally?
> Is mobile software considered a vital strategic priority in your company? Or is mobile app development considered peripheral and non-essential?
> Are you aware of any startup companies in your industry that focus primarily on reaching customers on the smartphone?

2

FROM PRINT TO PIXELS

EVERYTHING THAT CAN BE
DIGITIZED WILL BE

Sooner or later, the leaders at every company will begin to realize that they face the prospect of vaporization. From health care to handbags, no industry is immune. At least some portion of every firm's activity will be transformed from the old-school physical industrial process into a vaporized state of information processing that occurs entirely in the digital domain. They won't be able to stop this process, but if they react soon enough, they will at least have the option to determine how and when they will respond.

This is obvious. And yet the leaders of many companies fall into the trap of repeating mistakes that other industries made years earlier. They don't see the parallels. Given the choice of embracing this trend or resisting it, the leading companies in any field opt to do everything they can to fight the future while starving their digital teams of the resources and freedom to reinvent the business. They resist vaporization with all their power, capital, and political clout, and they fail to think imaginatively about reinventing their business model.

After exhausting every possibility of thwarting the inevitable, they capitulate. And when they do, they face a shocking realization. They find themselves lost on a new playing field in completely unknown terrain, facing a new kind of competition that they are utterly unprepared to contend with. Their competitor, bred from birth for the mean new environment, operates by a completely different set of economics and harbors no sentimental attachment to the past or the heritage of the leading brands.

At that instant, some executives will realize that all of the time and money they spent shoring up the defense walls were wasted. Instead of using the advantage of time and scale to prepare for the transition, groom key talent, and invest in future capabilities, they squandered their market leadership position on a fruitless fight to preserve the past.

Executives are not stupid; they are human. Nobody likes to dwell on a grim topic like this. It's unpleasant to imagine a stable, mature, highly profitable industry degrading into a fiercely competitive, low-margin firefight in a highly volatile environment. It's much easier to deny that future scenario and focus on what worked in the past. After all, the future is uncertain and the past is crystal clear. But denial is fatal.

I know this because I've been working at the forefront of digital change in the media industry for twenty-five years. Media businesses are among the first to be transformed by digitization. The lessons from their painful transition should be studied by every industry, because the vaporization of media provides a useful template for every information-rich business. Any industry that undergoes a transformation from physical goods into information tends to operate by the same rules that govern digital media. What happened to them will eventually happen to you.

THE DAWN OF DIGITAL MEDIA

In the early 1980s nobody used the phrase "digital media." Mass media came in one flavor only: analog. Once digital media began to gain traction, however, the term became a way to distinguish old media from new. There were three principal forms of analog media: text and images on paper, broadcast signals in the airwaves, and recordings on vinyl or tape.

While the flameout of the music industry probably looms largest in the public consciousness, it really wasn't the first industry to be vaporized. The dawn of the digital media era began with hunks of melted lead in the printing industry. Today when we compose a document on a computer, we tend to use the word "font" interchangeably with "typeface" or even "type." This is sloppy diction. It's the equivalent of saying "MP3" instead of "song." One is the format, the other is the content. In its original meaning in the Middle French *fonte*, a font refers to "something melted," and the reason typecasting firms were called "foundries" is that they trafficked in molten metal.

A typeface consisted of an entire collection of metal fonts that represented every possible size and shape for each character in the face. In a letterpress shop, the capital letters were literally stored in the upper case of the typesetter's rack, and the small letters were stored below in the lower case, which led to today's metaphorical use of upper- and lower-case to describe majuscule and minuscule characters.

Until the 1990s, the terminology of the typesetting trade retained its literal meaning. However, today's computer fonts are vaporized versions of the lead letters used by printers for centuries. We've replaced chunks of metal with pure math.

I experienced this transformation firsthand. Fresh out of college in 1985, I was hired as a runner for a television production company in New York that specialized in making commercials and music videos. My job was to carry physical stuff across town: written budgets, sealed bids, storyboards, artwork, cans of film, props, photographs, wardrobes, even coffee. At $80 a day, I was cheaper than a messenger and better value because I was willing to work unreasonably long hours in the hope of advancement.

When we needed a special type treatment for a TV commercial or a title sequence, we had to create custom artwork that could be photographed. I'd ride the sweltering #4 subway, carefully guarding the wrapped handwritten instructions from the art director with my body so they wouldn't be bent or crushed by the crowd in the train, and then I'd exit in Midtown, find the street address of the typesetting shop, and ride the elevator upstairs. I'd enter the grubby lobby of an old shop with worn linoleum floors and a tiny window, where rattling somewhere in the back was the metallic din of typesetting equipment. I'd stand in line for twenty minutes until it was my turn to approach the clerk at the window, who was usually a lady smoking a cigarette. She would take my order, give me a written slip, and say, "Alright kid, come back in three hours." Later I'd return to pick up a white board with the perfectly set type stretched out on a precisely specified curve across a piece of latex rubber, ready to be photographed.

Typesetting was a commodity skill, but for a full century the entire printing ecosystem was controlled by a handful of firms that used proprietary equipment to maintain fat profit margins. The way to control value in the typesetting industry was to control typefaces, and certain shops had trademarked and copyrighted their typefaces. When the art director specified a special typeface, I had to go to one particular shop to get the job done. This is hard to imagine today, when every art director has a huge library of fonts stored on her computer, with tens of thousands more available to download as needed from the Internet.

I kept the catalogs for each foundry on hand. I studied the work of legendary type designers Frederic Goudy, Ed Benguiat, and Herb Lubalin whose designs were the intellectual property of their employers. Even though it was inconvenient, I liked it when the art director's instruction required me to travel to a certain shop in order to get type set exactly the way it was specified. I felt like I was part of a grand tradition that stemmed from Gutenberg and the Mainz printers and revolutionary publishers of the past.

This process of crisscrossing Manhattan with artwork sounds ludicrously inefficient today, but in the 1980s it was the norm. The 1980s were not the digital Dark Ages. Office workers were fully aware of computers, which were widely in use as word processors. Seen as a more sophisticated version of a typewriter, the computer was used for letters, memos, and contracts. Everything else—brochures, menus, instruction manuals, annual reports, posters, and cards—was the domain of the professional typesetter and letterpress printer.

Within five years, that perception would change dramatically, thanks to Steve Jobs at Apple.

DIGITIZING TYPE

In 1984, Apple was playing catch-up. The proliferation of cheap IBM personal computer (PC) clones forced Steve Jobs, the company's co-founder, to scan constantly for ways to differentiate Apple computers. Hewlett-Packard had already introduced its LaserJet printer for PCs. Apple needed to respond with a laser printer of its own.

Jobs met with the founders of Adobe Systems, two refugees from Xerox's Palo Alto Research Center (PARC) named Chuck Geschke and John Warnock. Geschke and Warnock had conceived of a new way to use a computer to describe and depict a printed page, but, like many researchers at PARC, they were unable to persuade Xerox to release this software language as a product. As a result, they quit Xerox and founded Adobe Systems, where they turned their invention into the PostScript page-description language.

With PostScript, graphic designs composed on the computer screen could be transferred precisely to a laser printer. Their breakthrough gave substance to the then-popular acronym WYSIWYG: "What you see is what you get." Jobs, perhaps the only executive in Silicon Valley with an understanding of the aesthetics of typefaces, immediately recognized the value of Geschke and Warnock's invention. As a college dropout, he had audited a course in calligraphy at Bard College that opened him up to the heritage and traditions that shaped the typesetting industry. He maintained this interest throughout his career.

Jobs persuaded the two inventors to embed PostScript in a new generation of laser printers that would be compatible with Apple's Macintosh computer. He also invested $2.5 million of his own money into Adobe Systems to ensure that the startup venture had the resources necessary to deliver on his vision. In 1985, Apple introduced the LaserWriter, the first printer powered by PostScript. The era of desktop publishing had begun, and with it began the demise of the professional letterpress shop.

The LaserWriter was more than a printer: it was a complete system comprising both software and hardware. It was expressly designed to make it easy and affordable for any small design firm to adopt; the system was also open to innovation by developers of new software programs and to manufacturers of devices. This combination of features attracted many companies that competed and innovated to provide better programs and equipment at a variety of price points. The variety attracted more users. It was a virtuous cycle. More users spurred more intense competition, which led to continuously improving tools and ever-increasing value in the initial investment. The result was the very rapid take-up of desktop publishing, especially Apple Macintosh computers.

THE BUILDING BLOCKS OF DIGITAL TRANSFORMATION

The story of PostScript is a neat illustration of the process of digital transformation because it encapsulates all of the ingredients into a single narrative: slow-moving incumbents, nimble startups, and an underlying technology landscape that improved gradually, eventually emerging as a platform for reinvention. Most important of all, the story of PostScript illustrates how an entire industry can shift to a new technology quickly when all of the pieces are aligned.

The key components of the PostScript system constitute the foundations of digital change for any industry and include:

> **Processing power:** Rendering PostScript files required an immense amount of processing power, far more than most desktop computers had at the time. The solution was to put a much more powerful processor in the printer, which meant that laser printers initially cost much more than the computer.
> **Connectivity:** Apple's LaserWriter debuted at a nosebleed price of $7,000. The only way to make the LaserWriter affordable to small design agencies was to include some means for many computers to connect to a single printer. So Jobs also bundled AppleTalk, which was Apple's proprietary means of connecting multiple computers in one office to the printer. That way the cost of the printer could be amortized across several different computers and thereby increase the value of the investment. By 1987, just two years after the launch of the LaserWriter, AppleTalk was the most widely deployed networking technology in the

world, with more than 100,000 installations. For many personal computer users, AppleTalk was the first time they connected any device to a digital network.

> **Device-independent software systems:** PostScript was an open system in three parts: a page-description language, a collection of fonts, and an interpreter that could be licensed by manufacturers of printers. Previously, image-setting and typesetting machinery were proprietary, which meant that to produce print-ready artwork, the entire system had to be purchased from one single vendor. A PostScript file, however, was "device independent," which meant that a design could be created on one computer, modified on another, and printed on a third from an entirely different manufacturer, as long as they were all PostScript compatible.

This novel combination of hardware and software spawned an entire industry, from tools for designing and managing fonts to clip art collections, image-editing software, and new printing devices in a range of resolutions and price points.

> **Software optimized for workflow:** The first desktop publishing program, PageMaker, was the best example of this new industry. PageMaker gave designers unprecedented ability to lay out pages, and it included many features that we take for granted today: drag-and-drop placement of images and type elements, tools for drawing shapes and for manipulating type, a way to import images from other software programs and scans. Pages designed in PageMaker could be printed accurately on laser printers via PostScript. The combination of Aldus PageMaker, Adobe PostScript, and the Apple LaserWriter very quickly established Apple computers as the preferred work environment for graphic designers and art directors, a market position that the company has never relinquished.

> **Network effects:** AppleTalk linked computers together within a single office, but PostScript benefitted from a second kind of network effect. Companies that provided services to design firms and creative agencies needed to have compatible equipment. Because fonts are copyrighted and trademarked intellectual property, designers were not permitted

to send the font along with the final artwork to the image-setting shop. Instead they would send the PostScript file, which contained a software description of the rendered text treatment but not the font software itself. This meant that, soon, every law-abiding image-processing shop and every design firm was obliged to purchase PostScript-compatible equipment in order to do business with its customers.

It had taken a decade to get all of the foundation elements in place at the right price: powerful processors, networking technology, advances in laser printing, and specialized software. Once these pieces were in place, the entire design industry rapidly converged on PostScript as the standard, and the hardware manufacturers soon followed. By 1987 more than 400 computer programs using PostScript had been created for Apple and IBM computers, and the standard was soon adopted by Microsoft as well as computer manufacturers Digital, Wang, and even rival laser print manufacturer Hewlett-Packard.

The impact on the traditional typesetting business was devastating—and surprisingly fast. In its heyday in 1900 there were 180 typesetting shops in Manhattan. By the end of the 1990s, just fifteen years after the debut of desktop publishing, most of these shops were gone for good. In 1998, the Typographers Association of New York held its last meeting to celebrate the end of an eighty-seven-year legacy.

Digitization of typesetting occurred just at the moment before it was common to network personal computers in office settings. Later, as the computers were networked and then connected to the Web and finally morphed into smartphones, the *entire process* of typesetting, pre-production, design, creation, publishing, and distribution of print was vaporized.

It took a century to create the modern printing industry and only a decade to wipe it out completely. From its beginning in Mainz in the 1450s, printing had always been a trailblazing technology: it was the first mechanized industry, the first mass medium, the first pure information product, the first mass-manufactured product. And in the end it was the first casualty of the digital media trend.

Today this story seems a little quaint in an age when every teenager has a smartphone a thousand times more powerful than the legendary PCs in the dawn of desktop publishing. That's exactly the point. The foundation technology never ceases to improve. On my smartphone today I have more than 100 apps, including twenty-two related to editing images, creating graphics and posters, using type design and typesetting. I can do everything on my phone from shooting a photo to writing an article, from designing the layout to creating the graphics, and publishing the final product to my blog or any other site. This content is never produced as a hard copy. It exists purely in digital form.

LINOTYPE'S EVOLUTIONARY LEAP

The story of the mass extinction of the typesetting industry also includes an example of how one traditional business made the evolutionary leap necessary to transition successfully into digital media. The Mergenthaler Linotype Company managed to survive by responding quickly and embracing digital dynamics, by vaporizing its legacy machine-age business into pure software.

The linotype machine was a classical mechanical system invented by Ottmar Mergenthaler in 1883. It consisted of a proprietary keyboard that required a specially trained typist to key in sentences, which were rendered into metal strips by the linotype machine. Without linotype it would have been impossible to set all of the pages of the newspaper in a single afternoon, and it was rapidly adopted by nearly every newspaper in the world. In fact, the firm dominated the typesetting industry for 100 years. By the late 1970s, the mechanical linotype machine was surpassed by newer photocomposing technologies and offset lithography. The company faced obsolescence.

But Linotype made a bold and visionary move that would ensure its survival while its peers perished: it migrated one of its core proprietary business assets to a digital format. This turned out to be an epic pivot. Like most companies in the typesetting trade, Linotype owned the copyright to several popular typefaces. The company was courted by Adobe because PostScript relied heavily on the availability of familiar fonts for its success.

A major turning point for both companies was reached when Linotype agreed to license thirty-five of its most popular fonts to Adobe to include in the PostScript system.

By migrating to software licensing and later jettisoning its hardware business entirely, the Mergenthaler Linotype Company managed to survive the decline of the traditional print industry. Today the company lives on as a provider of font software.

▶▶ THE RISE OF THE ACTIVATED AUDIENCE

The most revolutionary aspect of the story of desktop publishing is not about computers or other technology. It's about the people who use the technology. The proprietary systems of the mechanical era required trained specialists to operate the equipment. By wresting creative control from the hands of the closed-system shops and placing it in the hands of his customers, Jobs created—unwittingly perhaps—a nascent community that would increasingly gather momentum to become the defining force in the digital landscape: the activated audience.

Digital technology put the tools in our hands, in our computers, in our phones, and immediately this access to desktop publishing software yielded a profusion of work by amateurs. These were perfectly horrid compositions by people who had no design talent whatsoever: garish birthday announcements with ugly clip art, unreadable yard sale signs, clumsy attempts at personal newsletters. Jokes about unsightly desktop publishing disasters abounded. It was easy to laugh about these ham-fisted efforts.

But those who dismissed these amateurish attempts to master embryonic software programs missed a much larger and subtler trend towards activation, in which audiences ceased being passive consumers and began to engage meaningfully in the process of production. Admittedly, their first efforts were often cartoonishly bad, but many of these non-professionals ultimately did manage to master the skills. Over time the software was improved, and better templates and easy wizards were developed that provided guardrails to minimize aesthetic clumsiness. After that it was only a matter of time before the expert masters of the previous era became an endangered species.

The emergence of the activated audience is a new phenomenon that emerged with the advent of the personal computer. At first, it was just a bunch of computer geeks who were easy to overlook. Now, the activated audience—and its cousin, the activated consumer—has become a force that commands the attention of marketing executives in every industry. This group's habits, expectations, and always-on connectivity give it unprecedented power to shape trends, influence product development, and force the hand of major consumer product companies on matters that were once dictated by management, such as pricing, access, and even product design.

Consumers now expect to participate meaningfully whenever they wish, to decide how and when to consume, and to exert themselves in shaping their environment, including the political landscape. Back in the 1980s it was hard to envision this situation. Today, there's really no excuse for companies that don't see what is coming next.

ASK YOURSELF
> Does the story of the printing industry present a parallel to circumstances in your industry? How might your business get vaporized?
> Does any part of your business process consist of information embedded in a physical object, like the melted-lead type used in the printing business?
> How is value controlled in your industry? Is there one particular machine or system that everyone relies upon? Can this machine be replaced by software? If not, can the upstream or downstream business processes be converted to software?

3

TELEVISION AND INSTITUTIONAL DENIAL

EVERYTHING THAT CAN BE UNBUNDLED WILL BE

By the late 1980s, I had begun producing and directing television commercials and music videos. I did a lot of work for Music Television (MTV) because the company offered me more creative freedom than advertising agencies and music labels. In 1991 the head of MTV International, Tom Hunter, asked me to move to Hong Kong to serve as the creative director of the new affiliate channel, MTV Asia. I hesitated. By moving from New York, I felt that I was moving from the white-hot center of creative innovation to a distant backwater. I was in for quite a shock.

When I arrived, I learned that Hong Kong had the most state-of-the-art digital facilities for producing television in the world. In fact, these technologies were a decade ahead of the best editing shops in New York at the time. And in retrospect, I recognize this as another aspect of digitization: latecomers tend to leapfrog over established players. Technology improves constantly, doubling—or more—in power every two years. A company that starts four years later than its competitors has superior baseline gear right from the start, forcing the competitors to play upgrade catch-up.

On one occasion, I was marveling at the high-tech gear in the TV editing suite when the engineer in charge began to boast about the digital broadcasting system. He told me that the system was set up to allow data to flow in as well as out, which meant that by putting a phone line back into this facility, we had the potential to make the TV shows fully interactive.

"If we had a return path, anyone watching could interact with the television," he said, and then explained that a return path could consist of any connection to send a signal back, such as a standard telephone line.

Broadcast television is a one-way system designed to send a signal out to as many homes as possible. But it can't listen to or see audiences. If there were a way for the people watching at home to send a signal back, television could be interactive. A dialog instead of a monolog.

"You mean to tell me that someone watching our channel in a pub in Kathmandu could be playing along with a TV game show just by punching buttons on a touch-tone phone?"

"Sure," he said. It was technically possible in 1991.

This blew my mind. For months afterward I thought about how different TV would be if viewers could respond to it. And if it could respond to them. What kind of shows would we make? What kinds of stories would they tell?

When I returned to New York in 1992, I decided to investigate interactive technology with gusto. My office was right next to the research department: the latest findings showed me that teenagers were playing video games on consoles like the Super Nintendo and Sega Genesis and they were using a new service called dial-up bulletin board services. These devices had screens. I felt that MTV needed to be on every screen, not just the TV screen.

I called an emergency meeting of my colleagues at MTV and the heads of the other channels that MTV owns: Nickelodeon, HA! (a precursor to Comedy Central), and VH1, which at the time was kind of like MTV's little sister with a wimpier playlist. I opened the meeting by explaining that our audience was migrating to new screens. I shared data from our research department, and I told the group that we needed to develop a strategy for putting our brands on these new screens. While I thought it was a pretty exciting idea, nothing could have prepared me for the reaction that I got.

My counterpart, the head of on-air promotion at Nickelodeon, abruptly stood up and said, "This is a waste of time. I'm trying to run a cable network, not make video games. I don't know why we're having this meeting." He left the meeting, followed by his boss, Geraldine Laybourne, the head of Nickelodeon. The executives from HA! and VH1 followed shortly thereafter.

I was left in the room with Judy McGrath, the president of MTV, and Abby Terkuhle, the head of on-air creative. They looked at me sympathetically and Judy said, "That didn't go very well."

"Not for MTV Networks," I said. "But I know what I am going to do next." I had the courage of my convictions. It was clear to me from market research data that our audience, mainly young teenage boys, was heading towards interactive digital platforms. I wanted to get there first. Even though I loved my job at MTV and thought it was the coolest place to work, I decided to go for the future. Within six weeks of that meeting, I resigned from my job, packed up my possessions, and moved to Los Angeles, where I co-founded one of the first computer-game studios in the US, called 7th Level. There I made a series of hit game titles for CD-ROM, including the first animated multimedia programs for the personal computer. We had turned the computer into an entertainment device.

In 1994, 7th Level went public. Within eighteen months of leaving MTV, I had earned more than a million dollars at a startup software company. I never looked back at television the same way again. One-way broadcasting wasn't the future: it seemed like a relic of the industrial past.

When my colleagues at MTV looked at computers and game consoles, they saw something that was totally different from television. And that's as far as their imagination let them go. They couldn't possibly conceive of a computer with a color screen or sharper graphics on the game console. All they could perceive was the state of these devices at the time, which was so clearly inferior to television that they dismissed them without further consideration. They had no inkling of continuous incremental improvement in computers and that's why they assumed that tomorrow everything would be the same as it was today. What I did not know at the time is that this reaction is quite typical. Now after twenty-five years, I know better.

Most people tend to react to new ideas in exactly the wrong way. When they hear about something new, they say, "That will never happen" or "The customers will never go for it" or "There's no business model for that." The problem with knee-jerk reactions like this is that the brain immediately ceases to consider the proposition. It's like turning off a light switch, except that the thing that's turning off is the imagination.

Very few people have the imaginative capacity to envision the total transformation of their industry. Indeed, within any industry the most successful people have the hardest time imagining such a change because they have the most personally invested in preserving the current set-up. It's a side effect of knowing a system well enough to be able to exploit the weaknesses to advantage.

Every company has blind spots, and so does every leader. These blind spots can be lethal. The secret to success when technology is driving change rapidly in an established industry is to envision possibilities that are unthinkable: to make an effort to envision what that change might look like, and how it will transform the entire business process. That's easier said than done. To do that, a leader has to set aside everything that made him or her a big success and focus on the changes that will wipe all of that success away. This is not an easy exercise for anyone.

One after another, traditional media industries have seen the bottom drop out of their core businesses. Between 1999 and 2009, the newspaper and magazine industries were demolished by the Internet, their core sources of advertising revenue ripped apart into standalone sites like Craigslist and cars. com. The music industry, blindsided by the file sharing of MP3s, fought the process with every tool at its disposal. Playing defense couldn't save old industrial media companies. The newspaper industry attempted to participate online but most papers continued to prioritize the print edition (and arguably still do). As a result of their own entrenched attitudes and inflexible systems, these industries failed to make the transition and are today in a weaker position than ever. Half a century's growth was wiped away in a decade.

The last remaining stalwart in media is television, which has been remarkably resilient in the face of the Internet onslaught and remains stubbornly profitable.

THE BATTLE FOR THE DIGITAL LIVING ROOM

Television makes no sense. I'm not talking about the programming, which remains a delightfully eclectic mixture of smart scripted dramas and awesomely lowbrow voyeuristic reality junk. What I am referring to is the way those programs are presented to audiences. Think about it this way: in the future grandchildren are going to ask, "Is it really true that there was once a time when the entire country had to sit down in front of the TV at 8:00 to watch a show?"

It sounds funny when we put it like that, but that's how watching broadcast TV live still works. That fact has not changed in sixty years, although today more than half of all viewers have taken matters into their own hands by using digital video recorders or video-on-demand services to timeshift their favorite programs and skip the commercials. The activated audience is willing to pay extra for the privilege of evading the constraints of the television schedule.

Even when a show can be accessed on demand via a cable or satellite operator, the full series is often not available, or episodes sometimes randomly disappear from the menu. This makes no sense at a time when a thoroughly vaporized video service like Netflix has conditioned us to binge viewing.

And when consumers say, "I want out of this crazy system. I want to watch programs on my own terms on the screen I prefer at a time that I would like to watch," they get penalized. The most energetic members of the activated audience are branded criminals for infringing copyright. And then the broadcast industry sues them. The broadcast schedule has become the object of a tug-of-war for control between centralized programmers and decentralized audiences.

If we invented TV from scratch today, at a time when nearly every person in the audience has a smartphone or a tablet and is fully capable of responding and engaging and setting up their own playlists and recommendations, no sane person would propose anything like the current system. It's no longer a question of "Will television be disrupted?" Of course TV is getting disrupted. Every single inconvenience that the television industry insists upon imposing on audiences presents a golden opportunity for a challenge by a host of innovative startup companies. The startups didn't create these absurd conditions: the TV industry did, by forcing consumers to comply to its arbitrary programming schedule and adhere to an old-fashioned business model.

At the same time, new video aggregators have emerged on the Internet. YouTube now reaches a billion viewers a month offering more than a million niche video channels provided by a million content providers. Netflix blazed a trail by investing in original programming, thereby upping the ante for rivals Amazon, Hulu, and even Microsoft Xbox Video, all of whom followed suit. New channels are created every day, in every language on Earth, and they are available on any device that can display video. These Internet video "channels" cheerfully erase the old distinction between professional shows on the TV set and supposedly lower-grade fare on the Web. Netflix put an end to derisive comments about low-quality Internet video in 2013 by garnering sixteen Primetime Emmy nominations and two awards.

Today half of the TV sets in the United States are connected to the Internet to access "over the top" Internet video services like YouTube, Netflix, Vimeo, Break TV, MLB.com, Twitch, and many more. A geyser of video programming simply bypasses the convoluted mess of pay television and flows directly from the producer to the audience via the Web. As a result, the TV industry now must face something it has never confronted in the past—real competition. For six decades TV dominated the living room. Now, increasingly, there's an alternative that is bigger, faster, cheaper, and everywhere at once.

Unencumbered by legacy business models, infrastructure designed for a single purpose, and long-term contracts, the new video distributors are free to cater to consumer predilections in ways that old distributors never could. They facilitate new habits of consumption: binge viewing and season passes, like an unlimited all-you-can-eat smorgasbord with no linear channels or fixed schedules to constrain viewers. They've established new revenue models that rethink advertising and direct-to-consumer sales and subscription. No middlemen like cable or satellite companies are involved. They operate profitably in a strange, new, lean financial model, balancing low margins with low overheads and low marketing outlay. Fans and talent do most of the marketing themselves. And these new video giants prioritize immediate delivery to all devices instead of being bound by the old rule of TV-first, followed by a slow sequential release over months to other screens.

The reaction among TV networks has been a kind of gobsmacked denial, pretending that digital alternatives are not valid substitutes and dismissing them as cheap and inadequate. Denial is dangerous. Instead of studying the economics of the new platforms and making the adjustments necessary to meet them head-on as competition, the TV industry has squandered the past decade in denial. Its inaction left the category wide open, which enabled newcomers to gain a strategic foothold among digitally savvy consumers and earn some early revenue. By hesitating, the TV companies created the gap in the market that permitted alternatives to thrive.

In 2014 the big TV giants finally snapped out of their stupor when they realized that Internet distribution is a real business that they don't own or control. In October 2014 Home Box Office (HBO) announced plans to offer a direct-to-consumer subscription service over the Internet. The next day, CBS announced a similar plan, followed by Spanish-language giant Univision. Suddenly every channel is scrambling to work out the logistics of delivering its programs directly, outside of the pay TV system.

They'll find plenty of competition waiting for them. Quietly a new digital distribution business has emerged on the Internet, and it's nothing like traditional TV. None of the big new digital distribution systems are owned by traditional media companies: Apple owns iTunes, Google owns YouTube, Amazon owns Prime, and Netflix stands alone. Facebook video views are surging, Twitch is booming. Collectively these companies reach billions of viewers who account for the vast majority of video consumed on the Internet, and that's why they garner the lion's share of the revenue generated.

WHO'S IN CHARGE OF REINVENTION?

Despite the competitive pressure, television has managed to resist the Internet. In fact, we might say that TV has been too well defended. In the desire to maintain control and preserve the business model of the past, TV has lost the ability to innovate and adapt to the future.

In 2013 I ran a series of workshops at Turner Broadcasting in Atlanta, Georgia, and I asked the attendees to raise their hands if they worked in digital media. Half the people in the room raised their hands. I then asked, "What do the rest of you do?" They told me they worked on "traditional TV" in programming, marketing, and distribution. I asked them to consider that every step of the TV production process is now digital, from the scripts and budgets written on computers in the very beginning, to principal photography on high-definition cameras, to digital post-production in state-of-the-art editing bays, and finally to the signal that is sent to a digital uplink and transmitted digitally to a satellite. Even the home equipment is digital.

All of television is now digital media. While the executives weren't looking, digital media snuck up and infiltrated their stronghold. The main problem inside the old television companies is that there is no one in charge of the innovation process. In every TV network, development and programming executives create and manage the shows while sales and marketing people sell the stuff on the truck and build up the audience. Not one of these people has the responsibility of doing something different. Sure, they launch plenty of new shows each year (and most of those new shows fail). But there is no one in the entire organization tasked with the job of rethinking its business from scratch.

Instead, most television executives are incentivized to do the same thing year after year, which is the old formula of driving up ratings and raising advertising rates. If they succeed, they get a bonus. If they fail, they will probably get fired. Fear is a factor. Few are willing to make a mistake or try something different. The stakes are too high, the consequences of failure far too great. And there's no reward for changing the formula. As one senior vice president told me confidentially: "In the TV business today, we're all playing musical chairs. There are fewer chairs every year. Nobody wants to lose their seat when the music stops."

We might expect that task of innovation to fall to the Internet department or digital media team at the big TV companies. After all, they are the people on the front line of change, competing against the bold Internet companies. But no, reinvention is not really their job either. Until 2009 the primary mission of most digital departments was to drive viewers back to television! Today they do have a mandate to build a business on the Web and in mobile, but never at the expense of the television business. They are allowed to experiment around the margins but they cannot mess with the core. The one thing that the digital departments of TV networks are never, ever permitted to do is to rethink the primary business model of television. This is true of the digital mobile teams in every company. In banking, retail, publishing, and even major universities, the digital teams dance in an awkward waltz with the legacy business, looking down, not up, to make sure they don't step on any toes.

The old guard is not wrong to be wary. Given the unpredictable nature of Internet businesses and the high rate of failure for new ventures of any type, compounded with the high rate of failure for TV shows in particular, the odds of failing to finesse the transition are very high indeed.

THE PERILS OF DEFENSIVE INNOVATION

Actually, it's not entirely accurate to say that the TV industry doesn't innovate. During the formative years of the Internet and mobile industries, the pay TV industry did quite a lot of innovation in one particular area: packaging and pricing. What cable TV innovated was bundles.

First, a number of TV channels were offered together. This bundle grew from 50 channels to 100 to 200 to several hundreds. Then video on demand was added to the bundle. And then residential telephony was added, and broadband too. The bundle kept getting bigger and more expensive. Yet, nobody really needs or wants the bigger bundle. It's just like buying a supersized Big Mac that comes with too many fries: the big bundle sounds great until you eat it, and then you feel bloated and nauseous.

The cable TV business is the greatest supersizer in the history of consumer products. It figured out a way to get 50 million households to pay $100 a month for something nobody demanded. Bundling is a great way to prevent customers from downsizing or cutting the cord with the company. Asking the cable provider to disconnect the TV subscription service usually results in the price of residential broadband being doubled. Huh? Why are these two things connected? The bundle makes no sense to consumers, but from the cable operator's perspective it's a superb way to lock the customer in.

Television is pursuing a classic strategy. Described by Harvard Business School professor Clayton Christensen in his book *The Innovator's Dilemma*, *sustaining innovation*, as he called it, is the process of making incremental tweaks to an existing and well-known business model. Every company in the world practices sustaining innovation as part of its ongoing marketing efforts. But then there's the other flavor of innovation, which Christensen called *disruptive innovation*, that renders the old business model irrelevant by offering a stripped-down version that costs far less and thereby connects with an enormous underserved audience. It's a formidable threat. I describe this contrast as *defensive innovation* versus *offensive innovation*. No team has ever won a game by playing defense. In other words, sustaining innovation can never trump disruptive innovation.

One of television's bolder attempts at innovation was Hulu, the television industry's own attempt to build a competitor to video channels YouTube and Netflix. At first it seemed like a smart move. A joint venture of the big networks, Fox (owned by 21st Century Fox), ABC (owned by The Walt Disney Company), and NBC (owned by Comcast), and a private equity firm, Hulu was a great product built by a visionary launch team. The studios provided a broad selection of television content not available elsewhere. But the tension between the three TV companies made it impossible for Hulu to achieve its full potential. Each partner imposed arbitrary and inconsistent restrictions on its content: some shows were available the day after they aired on broadcast TV, others were available after a one-week delay, and still others were not available at all. The result was utterly bewildering to TV fans. In spite of offering high-quality video, Hulu remains an also-ran compared to nimbler rivals, even those with inferior technology.

Apart from Hulu, not one US television company has managed to launch a successful digital business from scratch. It's no accident that YouTube, Snapchat, Vimeo, Instagram, Pinterest, and Vine were all developed outside the traditional media industry.

A concise example of defensive innovation in TV is the scheme called TV Everywhere. Developed cooperatively between the channels and the cable and satellite distributors, TV Everywhere was announced with great fanfare in 2009 as the TV industry's plan to migrate programming to every digital device while preserving the subscription TV business model.

The reality falls far short of that goal. The program selection in TV Everywhere is spotty and inconsistent because some networks can't obtain the Internet rights from the companies that supply the programs. Some sports leagues refuse to sell digital rights because they want to compete by selling digital subscription services direct to consumers.

TV Everywhere apps are a pain to use. Each channel relies upon a completely different interface, which is a headache for consumers. And users must log in twice, once with the channel and once with their cable or satellite company.

Worst of all, TV Everywhere does not generate much revenue. It costs the channels millions to produce and operate the service, but they offer it for free just to keep their customers subscribing to television. And TV Everywhere actually *reduces* advertising revenue for the channel websites because it siphons audiences away from video on the Web, where it can be monetized with advertising. It is a money-losing sinkhole.

An obligatory loss leader with a feeble revenue model, TV Everywhere must represent the worst fears of all companies wary of wading into digital initiatives—that they will be both costly and ineffective—a terrible double whammy.

HOW THE TELEVISION INDUSTRY IS DEFENDED

The US television industry consists of two cozy interlocking oligopolies:

> the six big media giants that own 90 percent of the electronic mass media in the United States. Comcast (which owns NBCUniversal), 21st Century Fox (which recently split off from News Corporation), The Walt Disney Company, Time Warner, Viacom, and CBS operate most broadcast and cable channels, plus the major movie television and film studios.
> the telecommunications giants such as Time Warner Cable, DirecTV, AT&T, and, again, Comcast, that distribute the TV signal. These include cable system operators, satellite broadcasters, and telephone companies that distribute TV programming through fiber-optic cable.

There's plenty of friction between these two groups, as evidenced by the frequently acrimonious negotiations between programmers and distributors, but they have an overriding common interest to preserve their proven business model. These companies have so much at stake that they usually set aside their differences in order to defend the entire business from interlopers. Just like old-time pioneers circling the wagons in the face of an onslaught, these companies rely upon a combination of proprietary technology and legal defenses to protect their industry.

Technology barriers
> An exclusive broadcast spectrum owned by the television networks.
> Signal-decryption devices required by all viewers but owned by the cable or satellite providers.
> Proprietary billing systems that control the customer relationship.
> Closed distribution networks that block newcomers.

Legal barriers
> Intellectual property laws that keep content out of the public domain.
> Legislation and regulation that favor incumbent companies.
> Litigation that can cripple a startup venture with huge expenses.

All of this defensive action has a weird side effect. It paralyzes the TV companies. Instead of innovating, they pour all their energy into defending an outmoded service that no longer conforms to consumer behavior. TV has failed to adapt to the preferences of an evolving consumer.

MOBILE VIDEO AND THE SHIFT FROM CONSUMER TO CONTENT CREATOR

"Freedom of the press is guaranteed only to those who own one," quipped A.J. Liebling, the editor of the *New Yorker,* in 1960. Thanks to desktop publishing and the Internet, this quip has been relegated to a droll artifact of the linotype era. Today everybody with a smartphone owns a publishing system. Now mobile video and YouTube are doing the same to television as PostScript did to printing with breathtaking speed.

The first time I saw mobile video was in 1999. I was senior vice president of Digital Media at Sony Pictures Entertainment (SPE), and my job was to figure out how to make a business out of Sony's vast library of great TV shows and movies on the Internet, interactive TV, and mobile. My colleague Tim Chambers had come across a company called PacketVideo Corporation at a trade show. "They claim they can stream video to a mobile phone," Tim told me, so we invited the company to visit us at the SPE campus in Culver City, California.

I'll never forget that meeting. The two founders, Jim Brailean and Jim Carol, arrived carrying a big duffle bag from which they pulled out a pile of electronic components that they set on the gleaming mahogany conference table in our offices. There lay a long green circuit board, the color screen from a dismantled Compaq iPAQ handheld computer, the antenna of a wireless Sprint PCS phone, and a small set of speakers from a laptop computer. The entire mess was held together with alligator clips and wires that curled all over the conference table. It looked like they had spilled the random contents of a nerd's high school locker in front of us. But when they turned their funky assemblage on, something magical happened. A movie trailer flickered across the screen. It was a Sony Pictures film! It wasn't loaded on the device, but, using the cell phone antenna, they were able to receive data at the very thin rate of 14.4 Kbps. They were streaming video live from the Internet over the air.

The quality of the video signal was not great. In fact, it was atrocious, but I was hooked anyway. I knew exactly what was going to happen next: the components would eventually be miniaturized and embedded into a future chipset for mobile phones, the chips would get more powerful, and the radio signal would be faster. Color screens and tiny speakers would be embedded in phones too. It was immediately obvious to me that every mobile phone would eventually play video. We were going to turn the phone into an entertainment device, just like the computer a decade earlier.

In 1999 it seemed laughable that anyone could be excited by these video clips. In the earliest days, the video was grainy and would freeze, and sometimes the phone would overheat or crash. Occasionally, during demonstrations, we had to use a cable to connect the phone to a handheld computer because the phone didn't have a color screen that could refresh fast enough to display video. In retrospect it was hilariously bad. It took heroic amounts of imagination to envision mobile video as anything other than a novelty.

Most of my friends in the TV business thought I had lost my marbles. They said, "TV belongs on a television, just like music belongs on a stereo." In their opinion, judging from the standards of broadcast TV, the video quality on mobile phones was terrible. It was too hard to get a signal, too hard to use, and too grainy to bother watching. Besides, mobile data was expensive. They couldn't imagine how it would ever improve. Who was going to pay for such a service?

What no one could have imagined at the time was just how big the change would be, and how fast it would occur. In a way it was a repeat of the digital transformation that had swept through the typesetting industry. In 1980 nobody used computers for typesetting or page design. By 1990 the entire advertising, publishing, and design industry had adopted it. Similarly, in 2000 nobody was using mobile phones for video. Just a decade later, everybody did.

The TV industry may not be entirely aware of it yet, but a sleeping giant has been roused. The activated audience will behave in ways that are completely different than the passively programmed audience of yesterday. Already we are becoming our own individual broadcasters. We post and share video on social networks so routinely, we take it for granted. We are making our own shows, telling our own stories, documenting our own experiences. In the process we are erecting something that will soon overshadow mass media and transmit massive change rapidly through society.

The greatest TV networks in the world are limited in their reach to one single nation, one language, one audience. In contrast, digital media can easily transcend the traditional barriers of language, culture, geography, and even state censorship. And social media is the fuel in the mobile rocketship. The versatile smartphone puts a printing press, a camera, a personal TV station in one device that is always accessible to capture any incident or inspiration. The social network is the personal broadcast system to transmit information to friends and followers, who retransmit. We are exchanging ideas faster than any previous society on Earth.

As I write this, more than one-quarter of humanity belongs to a social network, according to research firm eMarketer. Seventy percent of the adults in industrialized nations own at least one smartphone. Of those smartphone users, more than 75 percent use the device to watch video. And, even more amazingly, more than 70 percent use their smartphone to create content: to record and share video and photos on social networks. That's more than a billion people creating, sharing, and watching video on their phones. Among the youngest cohort, the percentage using and creating video is significantly higher. In the span of a single decade, a billion people have taught each other a brand new way to communicate.

Many professionals in the television industry hold a negative opinion of user-generated video. They dismiss it. They reject it as below TV quality and therefore unworthy of their attention. Television executives have told me that "YouTube video is Web junk. It's not important." Just a few years ago, I would have agreed that Internet video and especially video shot on mobile phones was generally of poor quality. That's no longer true. Just like desktop publishing, people are learning to do it better.

It doesn't really matter, however, if the video is good quality or bad according to broadcast standards. On the two-way digital network, *relevance equals quality*. And TV programming that comes from a broadcast network seems so detached from our normal daily experience that it is often significantly less relevant than other mobile video. Broadcast TV programming is no more or less pertinent than my niece's video from her trip or my best friend's video of her son's wedding. If I am interested in learning to play a piece of music or master a particular cooking technique, a homemade YouTube video can be far more relevant, and therefore higher quality, to me in that moment.

We create more video than ever before, and the rising flood of this user-generated content (UGC) contains a certain percentage of high-quality clips. It may be a small percentage of the total, perhaps less than 10 percent, but that percentage will remain constant even as the volume grows exponentially. In other words, the sheer amount of quality UGC video is growing exponentially too, but from a smaller base. It may take longer, but eventually just the high-quality segment of UGC itself will dwarf the output of the Hollywood studios.

What's also interesting—or terrifying if you are employed by a television network—is that YouTube's total video library appears to be growing at an exponential rate, doubling every eighteen to twenty months. In 2007 users uploaded eight hours of video to YouTube each minute. By 2008 the number had nearly doubled to thirteen hours, and by 2009 users were uploading twenty-four hours of video each minute. In 2011 the figure doubled to 48 hours uploaded per minute, and the following year it spiked to seventy-two hours per minute. The amount of video uploaded increases geometrically.

As of 2014, YouTube reported that people now upload more than 300 hours of video every minute of the day to YouTube. That's twelve days of video uploaded every minute. The equivalent of Hollywood's entire annual output of movies and television shows is uploaded to YouTube in an afternoon. And within two years, this figure will double again. By 2020, at this rate, YouTube fans will be uploading sixty-six days of video per minute. That's more than *ten years'* worth of video every hour.

THE MOBILE PHONE IS NOW THE PRIMARY SCREEN

These numbers are staggering but they are not fiction. There is a simple reason that explains why we can be fairly certain that this doubling will occur, even though these numbers may seem preposterous and hard to achieve. The mobile telecommunications industry is banking on the fact that the number of people using their smartphones to connect to the Internet will also double and double again, from the 1 billion in 2013 to 2 billion in 2016 and 4 billion two or three years after that.

Every year for the rest of this decade, the mobile industry expects to sell at least a billion smartphones. Some of them will be replacements for existing phones, but about half of them will be sold to first-time users. That's 500 million new Internet users each year. What's more, in addition to uploading video and photos, these new users will use their smartphones to buy groceries, obtain financial services, and gain an education. The smartphone is the first and last stop for most information searches. It will support the world's largest transactional marketplaces.

These new users won't be using a $600 iPhone. They will probably be using ultra-cheap smartphones like the Firefox phone, designed by Telefónica in partnership with the Mozilla Foundation. Versions of this phone, which uses an open-source operating system, can be purchased for one-tenth of the price of an iPhone. That price will surely drop as the volume of users rises, which means we're rapidly approaching an era of the $25 smartphone. The global phone. The free phone. The everybody phone. Maybe someday soon, the disposable phone. The more people who connect and communicate, the more video will be shared.

It's really hard to envision this rate of growth, particularly in the beginning. But today every person who uses video, and especially every advertiser, marketer, or producer who deals with television, must recognize the fact that the mobile computer is about to transform the media landscape so completely that everything we have come to call "television" is about to be reordered. Professionally produced TV programs are a tiny and dwindling percentage of a vast ocean of video that continuously expands at an exponential rate.

WHAT HAPPENS TO TELEVISION WILL HAPPEN TO YOU

If you don't happen to work in Hollywood, you may think this tale does not pertain to you. Why should you care about what happens to TV? You need to care because not only is TV the dominant medium of our contemporary culture and the most valuable marketing channel, it's also how we communicate and share ideas as a society. More importantly, what happens to TV companies will eventually happen to every company faced with vaporization.

Pause for a moment and consider what might happen to your business if it, too, is vaporized. What happens if your product can be delivered digitally by anyone? What happens when you or anyone else can sell direct to consumers? When every customer your industry touches can suddenly respond, contribute, add to, explain, ask questions, answer them. When peer-to-peer sharing renders your services obsolete. How will your marketing evolve? How will the experience of consumption change? How will you cope with the flood of incoming content?

THE FUTURE OF TELEVISION

It's easy to predict the future of TV. Vaporized video will grow. Consumer-generated video will grow. Mobile video will grow. Advertising dollars will follow audiences to the new platforms. Traditional TV is in long-term decline. The oligopoly of distributors and channels will unravel when, one by one, channels bust out of the pay TV bundle and go direct to the consumer with digital offerings.

In April 2015 Daryl Simm, the chairman and CEO of Omnicom Group's media operations, a firm that manages $54 billion of advertising spending globally, was quoted in the *Wall Street Journal*: "We are counseling our clients to move between 10 percent to 25 percent of TV dollars to online video."

TV won't collapse overnight the way music did. TV remains the most cost-effective way to reach mass audiences and it will remain well defended behind its barricades. But the famous walled garden of pay television is beginning to resemble France's Maginot Line, a planned strategic defense that never served its intended purpose but instead became a massive liability by tying down troops in a battle that required mobility and speed. By attempting to stave off innovation, the Big Media companies have cut them-selves off from the vital source of new ideas that would guide them towards the future. Increasingly isolated, TV will slowly decline in relevance and fade into the background. It will linger long and someday go out with a whimper, not a bang.

BEWARE OF BLIND SPOTS

The great irony of the story of television is that the TV industry anticipated all of this. It should have been the one to dominate this space. In 1991, just as the print industry was being dismantled by desktop publishing, an analyst named Peter Miller gave me a report titled "Delivering Interactive Services Over Cable" that he'd prepared for the pay TV think tank CableLabs. In it Miller envisioned nearly every digital service that we enjoy today, from local auctions to travel services, from online classified ads to dating, from distance learning to home shopping, from games to gambling to banking, video on demand, porn, and even social media.

In retrospect it was a brilliantly accurate forecast. Except for one thing. Miller predicted that the services would run on top of the cable TV system to the TV screen, not the personal computer. Looking back twenty years later, the scale of the missed opportunity is breathtaking. The TV industry had the blueprint for online services. It could have owned the Internet. But the cable industry never took action to invent new services, even when dial-up service providers AOL and CompuServe demonstrated that consum-ers were willing to pay ample amounts for such a service. Even when AOL succeeded in acquiring Time Warner a decade later, the other TV companies *still* did not act. Even when the cable companies began to lay high-speed broadband pipelines to homes, they were complacent, satisfied to rake in juicy access fees without making any serious effort to build value-added services on top of their pipelines.

Instead, tiny new startup ventures seized the opportunity and got big-ger as digital media grew. Everything anticipated by the CableLabs report actually became reality by 1999, but not on the cable system. Because that system was closed and the owners were not interested in digital services, the startup ventures decided instead to set up shop on the new fledgling World Wide Web. Smart move. Consumers craved the Web so badly that they voted with their checkbooks to pay for an additional phone line so they could go online to experience these new services, including every one of the concepts envisioned in Peter Miller's cable industry manifesto.

The new Internet companies defined how the new media marketplace worked; they set standards and wrote new rules about advertising and monetization. The new video distribution systems are here today and yet not one major media company controls any of them. TV—and every vestige of old media—is now just another app on someone else's platform.

ASK YOURSELF

> Do the leaders in your company embrace the transition to mobile software? Or do they persist in denying it?
> Who is in charge of reinventing your company's business model and operations? Does anyone in your company have such a broad mandate?
> Does your company rely on barriers such as proprietary technology, arbitrary business rules, and regulations or litigation to stifle competition?
> Are you aware of any startup company in your industry that focuses solely on getting the job done with digital or mobile software? What does it do differently? What can your company learn from the competition?

4

SWITCHBOARDS, MARKETS, PLATFORMS, ECOSYSTEMS

EVERYTHING THAT CAN BE INFRASTRUCTURE WILL BE

I n the early days of telephony, competition was lively. Although American Telephone and Telegraph (AT&T) would later emerge as a federally sanctioned national telephone monopoly in the United States, during the late 1800s it was busy fending off feisty rivals. The companies were racing to wire the major cities along the East Coast.

Meanwhile, in the far western US states, something entirely different occurred. Ranchers began to experiment with building their own networks. They had no choice. The telephone companies refused to do so because investors who provided funding for the first wave of telephone expansion preferred the safe bet of building networks in densely populated industrial cities on the East Coast. They eschewed the risk of pouring precious capital into vast reaches where ranchers and farmers were far-flung and few in number, because the business case was unclear.

Self-reliant ranchers took matters into their own hands. They realized that they already had a network right in their backyards. By 1900, millions of miles of barbed wire had been strung up across the western states to keep animals and crops apart. It was easy to transform this fencing into a ready-made telephone network. All the farmers and ranchers needed to do was cut the tops off a lot of beer or whisky bottles to fashion crude insulators atop fence posts and then wrap the wire around the glass. The final step was to order a telephone from the Sears or Montgomery Ward catalog. When it arrived, the telephone could be connected to the barbed-wire network, and then each household would string a line on high poles across the road to connect one barbed-wire network to the next neighbor's fence. Today we'd call this a crowdsourced network. Back then they called it a party line. And what a party they had.

The barbed-wire party line was the first instance of social media on a telecommunications network. There was no central switchboard facility, just a peer-to-peer connection relayed from one ranch to the next, and as a consequence, there was no privacy. Officially every family had its own personal ringer sequence, like a proto-ringtone, but in practice anyone on the network could listen to everyone else's phone calls. And people did it all the time. Conversations were understood by all participants to be quasi-public, even if private matters were being discussed. Eavesdropping by nosy neighbors was not only common, it was expected and grudgingly tolerated. News of births, deaths, disease, and disaster spread rapidly through the community thanks to the total transparency of the party line.

Some creative thinkers took advantage of this transparency and idle hours to experiment with novel forms of entertainment: those who had access to the telegram dispatches at the local train station could read the news over the party line. Others played musical instruments and sang songs. Some told funny stories.

The barbed-wire networks lasted a surprisingly long time: some holdouts continued until the 1970s. In the end, the old party line simply couldn't compete: it lacked the dimension of long-distance calling. To connect with the wider world, it was necessary to hire a switchboard operator who could patch the barbed-wire network to a line connected to the national telecom system. The convenience of private, switched phone calls, long-distance connections, and eventually direct dialing lured the ranchers to sign up for the telephone company service. The barbed wire network was dismantled as individuals were absorbed into the network run by the major phone companies.

▶▶ MOORE'S LAW AND METCALFE'S LAW

If you've ever read a book on the Internet Economy, then you've already heard of Moore's law and Metcalfe's law, the two fundamental concepts that underpin the Vaporized Economy. If so, skip to the next section. If not, read on—you really need to know this stuff.

Moore's law is named after Gordon Moore, the co-founder of Intel Corporation, who observed in 1975 that the amount of computing power on a chip tends to double every eighteen months while the price remains constant, leading to a doubling of price performance. Although there is no scientific principle that makes this law inevitable, it has been a remarkably durable prediction, holding steady and governing the pace of improvements in computer microprocessors for forty years. As Kevin Kelly wrote in *What Technology Wants,* it may very well be the case that Moore's law has so accurately predicted the pace of improvement for such a long time that the entire semiconductor industry now routinely gears the pace of innovation to meet that expectation. In other words, the rule drives the market expectation that in turn drives the behavior. A self-fulfilling prophecy.

Moore's law tells us that devices will continue to grow ever cheaper and smaller even as they grow more powerful. This explains why ultimately every person on Earth (and every car, watch, television set, appliance, home, office, streetlight, etc.) will be connected to the Internet. Every year someone comes out of the woodwork to tell us that Moore's law is bound to fail eventually by running into the limits of physics. This year is no exception. Quoted in *IEEE Spectrum,* Gordon Moore himself said, "I see Moore's law dying here in the next decade or so." But magically each decade, engineers manage to come up with yet another way to push past the boundary and continue to squeeze out more performance from ever-smaller chipsets.

Metcalfe's law pertains to computer networks and telephone networks. It states that the value of the network equals the square of the number of people connected to the network. According to Metcalfe's law, a network with four users is worth four times what a network with two users is worth, and a network with ten users is worth 100 times the two-user network. It's not just a matter of "the more users, the more valuable the service," but rather that an increasing number of users drives a geometric increase in the value of the service. Metcalfe's law suggests that services that grow to global scale on the digital network will become immensely valuable. This explains why three-year-old companies in the Vaporized Economy can be worth billions of dollars.

What's most important to understand is that these two laws reinforce and compound each other's effect. Moore's law makes devices cheaper, which makes it possible for more people and devices to be connected—which, in turn, makes the network more valuable. Moore's law multiplies the impact of Metcalfe's law. One law makes devices cheaper; the other law makes companies richer.

These two laws govern everything that happens in the Vaporized Economy. This magic occurs at the intersection of two distinct technologies: the telecommunications network and mobile computers in the form of smartphones, tablets, and soon smartwatches and a range of other smart devices. Everything in the Vaporized Economy runs on chips and networks, and that means everything in this economy is subject to the dynamics expressed in these two rules.

Sometimes traditional, old-school companies that plan to enter the Vaporized Economy make the mistake of attempting to recreate their existing business in this new environment. They believe they can transpose their supply chain and impose their economics from the real world into the mobile telecommunications ecosystem. That approach never works.

The companies that succeed in this new arena are those that have mastered the dynamics of telecom networks and mobile computing. This is a relatively new field and it continues to evolve, but the companies that master the process of planning their businesses to take advantage of Moore's law and Metcalfe's law tend to succeed, sometimes wildly. Those that don't, miss completely.

EVERY SUCCESSFUL DIGITAL BUSINESS IS A SWITCHBOARD AND A MARKET

Our story about the barbed-wire party line illustrates the power of Metcalfe's law in action. It turns out that the wires stringing the houses together were not the key to controlling the network: they ultimately proved to be a cheap commodity. The switchboard emerged as the far more important control point. The fatal weakness of the homegrown barbed-wire network was the inability to scale beyond a small local community. The switchboard made it possible for a single caller to connect with another individual home or business on another network far away in a city or town and, eventually, for the network to function at national scale for a population of millions. The switchboard is the first of four basic concepts that describe the key value points of businesses operating in the Vaporized Economy. Together, they are: switchboards, markets, platforms, and ecosystems.

At the center of every telecommunications network is a switchboard that routes messages to their intended recipient. What makes the telephone company such a powerful monopoly is the ability to make connections, which is why control of the switchboard is so valuable. And to succeed as a vaporized company, you need to own the switchboard part of the business, not necessarily the wires (or channels or supply chain). How does your business make connections?

The Vaporized Economy runs on top of the telecommunications network, and any number of businesses can be built there. However, the essence of every successful vaporized business is a virtual switchboard that can scale to connect millions of users simultaneously. Instead of patching together two parties on a phone call, the vaporized company does something even more powerful: it matches buyers and sellers. It creates a *marketplace* on top of a telecom switchboard.

Every successful online company is a switchboard connecting not just people to people or people to information providers, but, crucially, buyers and sellers in a virtual marketplace. Put another way, markets in a network economy are switchboards that connect buyers and sellers. Even if no money changes hands between them, these people are exchanging valuable information that will eventually be monetized. Whoever controls the switchboard market also controls the flow of value.

Google is a switchboard: Google's powerful search engine connects those who seek information with the sites that provide it. As one Google executive said, "If it's not on Google, it doesn't exist." Google search is the most efficient mechanism for connecting people who seek information with those who provide it.

eBay is a switchboard: the auction site matches independent merchants of collectibles and goods with a huge base of geographically dispersed customers in search of specific items they can't find in their local stores. Its sheer size and scale and global reach ensure that eBay offers more selection and unites more buyers and sellers than any other marketplace.

Amazon is a switchboard: the Earth's biggest bookstore has become North America's biggest emporium for goods of all sorts. Amazon connects millions of goods from an extended network of independent retailers and merchants with the customers that want them.

Craigslist is a switchboard: by ripping the classified ad section out of the local newspaper and putting it on the network, Craigslist simultaneously scaled up and unified the offerings of buyers and sellers and provided an easy, consistent way to navigate among them.

WhatsApp and other messaging apps are switchboards: these apps connect two parties that want to communicate, just like the manual telephone switchboard of yore but way faster and much cheaper.

YouTube is a switchboard: more than 1 billion people turn to YouTube each month to find videos, and many of them search for specific video clips on YouTube first and look no further. If you produce video and want to connect with a global audience, you cannot afford to remain outside of YouTube.

The switchboard concept teaches us how to extract value from digital information. The switchboard enables a company to control the flow of information from one participant to another and see every single transaction. The switchboard operator harvests data from every transaction: it knows who is shopping, what they are seeking, which items are selling and which aren't, and a host of other details that individual marketplace players can't possibly be aware of. This confers a decisive strategic advantage on the company that manages the switchboard.

It is possible to build a network without a switchboard, but it is impossible to scale a digital business without one. This explains how a vaporized startup can come out of nowhere and, four years later, be worth more than most of the incumbent companies in the category.

THE LAW OF INCREASING RETURNS TO MARKET LEADERS

Many economists have noted that the Internet tends to favor a "winner-take-all" economy, whereby the leading company in a category tends to dominate the market utterly until the next cycle. W. Brian Arthur of the Santa Fe Institute identified this dynamic in his 1996 paper "Increasing Returns and the New World of Business," published in the *Harvard Business Review*. He wrote: "If knowledge-based companies are competing in winner-take-most markets, then managing becomes redefined as a series of quests for the next technological winner—the next cash cow." That's why today's Internet giants never cease in their efforts to crack open new markets.

Several factors tend to reinforce this phenomenon in the Vaporized Era: global reach to two billion smartphones makes it possible for one company to compete in many regional markets, abundant information keeps customers well informed about market leaders, social media amplifies and accelerates dominance because friends tell friends where they found a good deal. The result is that a fast-growing startup in a new category can grow very swiftly to massive scale, serving a huge number of customers in multiple markets, even as the cost—in terms of computing power and bandwidth—diminishes. No brick-and-mortar business could ever grow this swiftly or as efficiently.

The success and longevity of an Internet switchboard business depends upon two things: speed and scale.

> **Speed:** The customer asks one primary question: "How quickly can I find what I seek?" The merchant asks, "How quickly can I generate revenue?"
> **Scale:** The seller wants access to the greatest number of buyers. And in turn, the buyer wants access to the greatest range of products or pieces of information.

Driven by the quest for speed and scale, both buyers and sellers naturally gravitate towards the site that provides the largest customer base and the greatest selection of products with the greatest ease of use and the least friction. By operating purely in the realm of digital data, freed of the constraints of physical inventory and tangible products and premises, vaporized companies can accomplish this much faster and at much greater scale than any traditional incumbent possibly could. Amazon even manages to achieve this with physical goods by bending the rules of distribution to conform to the Internet.

Whereas traditional markets are governed by geography, language, national borders, and currencies, vaporized markets have no such limitations. And because the Internet knows no national or geographic boundaries, there is no upper limit on its scale except "everyone on the network," which, thanks to Moore's law, will eventually mean "everyone in the world." That in turn means that there is practically no upper limit on the valuation of the best-performing switchboard marketplaces. Well, okay, according to Metcalfe's law, that theoretical upper value would approach the square of 7 billion people on earth. Which explains why investors tolerate outsized valuations for startups like the accommodation booking service Airbnb.

Airbnb: A switchboard marketplace for vaporized accommodations

On the surface, Airbnb's valuation just doesn't seem fair. It is a startup venture that owns no property, no hotels, and no physical hospitality facilities whatsoever. It doesn't employ any chambermaids or concierges either. And yet, the value placed on the company in a recent round of investment exceeds the stock market value of major hotel chains Hyatt Hotels Corporation and Wyndham Worldwide, which manages 7,500 hotels including the Ramada and Wyndham brands. In March 2014, the *Wall Street Journal* reported that TPG, a private equity firm, led a round of investment in Airbnb at a valuation of $10 billion, making the six-year-old venture one of the world's most valuable startup companies, and more valuable than all hotel chains except the biggest three: Hilton Worldwide Holdings, Starwood Hotels & Resorts International, and Marriott International, Inc.

What's the secret to Airbnb's success? The company has redefined the hotel marketplace for the Vaporized Era. In fact, the company doesn't offer hotel rooms at all because that's not necessarily what its customers seek. Airbnb provides "room nights" in private homes and apartments, all made available via a photo-rich website and mobile app. What Airbnb offers is information about these private accommodations that often cost less than one-third of a typical business hotel room. It's a good example of information replacing physical infrastructure. Airbnb doesn't own hotels; it owns a switchboard marketplace for room nights. Poof. Airbnb vaporized hotels!

Airbnb is often cited as the poster child for the "sharing economy" in which individuals connect with each other directly to share goods and services, eliminating the need for a purchase—and eliminating the role of a merchant. But the company also happens to be a terrific illustration of what happens when an entire market gets vaporized. Remember, the primary principle of the vaporized concept is that information can be a substitute for physical products. If you can get the job done profitably by providing an information service instead of a tangible product, you're on the right track. Airbnb undercuts every hotel chain on price and often provides a much better product, particularly for travelers who want an adventure or a big discount.

When Airbnb first came to the attention of investors in the early days, around 2010, many people assumed that the company was confined to the category of vacation rentals, which isn't such a tiny niche: the US vacation home rental market is a cool $23 billion a year, according to market research firm Phocuswright. Then Airbnb experienced a surge of explosive growth in 2012, zooming from 5 million rooms booked in January 2012 to 10 million less than six months later, and doubling every six months thereafter. Airbnb has outgrown the seasonal holiday market and now competes directly with major hotel chains for business travelers, offering accommodations in every country in the world except North Korea.

As a vaporized startup, Airbnb enjoys several advantages that established hotel chains lack. None of Airbnb's operating capital is tied up in physical hotel infrastructure, meaning there are no sunk costs to recover and no capital outlays for ongoing maintenance and upgrades. The upshot is that the company is nimble, unencumbered by physicality, and free from the constraints of geography. Currently operating in 190 countries and 34,000 cities, Airbnb is immune to the ups and downs of various destinations due to the economy, weather, politics, crime, or any of the other factors that influence traveler behavior. And unlike a traditional hotel chain, Airbnb can be somewhat detached about its inventory because it doesn't have a stake in the fate of any one particular property.

Switchboard market owners are neutral; they don't play favorites and they don't pick winners. Instead of investing money marketing and promoting a particular set of properties, Airbnb enables individual homeowners to compete for customers on a level playing field, providing an easy set of tools that allow anyone to list their properties with photos and enticing descriptions. Listing is free, though the company takes a 6 to 12 percent commission on every transaction associated with the more than 1 million individual properties posted on its site.

However, by operating virtually and by representing an unimaginably vast inventory of accommodations, from spare sofas to castles and houseboats, Airbnb can appeal to a much broader base of customers than any single hotel chain. Yet it simultaneously provides the most personalized experience possible. This apparent paradox is a function of greater choice and better filters. Nearly every traveler can find a suitable accommodation at an attractive price. There is room for improvement, naturally, and some shoppers quibble about the hassle of sorting through too many options. But Airbnb can afford to invest the time and effort to continuously improve its filters and recommendations because these are the company's only asset.

The reason investors place such a high valuation on the company is that the growth potential is vast, and although it has been steadily doubling the number of transactions every six months, the company is still nowhere near the theoretical limits of market saturation. The advantage of the vaporized approach is that Airbnb can focus its precious startup capital at a narrow set of tasks that will bring the biggest result: the best tools for listing properties and the best tools for browsing, discovering, and booking accommodations.

NEVER UNDERESTIMATE THE POWER OF HUMAN LAZINESS

At the heart of the Vaporized Economy is a virtuous cycle that accelerates growth. Just as the molecules in a vapor move much faster than molecules in a liquid, transactions in the Vaporized Economy will continue to move faster and faster as more buyers attract ever more merchants which in turn will attract more buyers, or information seekers and information providers. This process explains why one company typically emerges as not just the segment leader but the absolute category dominator. Faster, cheaper, and better means more people come in every year, and the leading sites will attract them. There's no reason to visit the second-best site in a category.

Moreover, once the market leader has been established, it is very hard to displace because it enjoys not only an enormous knowledge advantage but also the benefit of human laziness. Force of habit is the most powerful retention mechanism in the Vaporized Economy: once we've developed a habit, navigating to our favorite sites becomes a mindless default behavior (by using a bookmark, by typing a URL, or by launching an app), as does using the tools. In contrast, overcoming that inertia to master a new user interface and new set of tools is a hassle for most people because there is a learning curve associated with every app and every website. Most of us prefer to stick with what we know and use already, and this "groove-in" process is the ultimate in experience branding. Once we become addicted to a brand, we don't even see the alternatives.

PLATFORMS SUPPORT—AND LOCK IN—MANY BUSINESSES

Successful digital marketplaces tend to attract other players too, not just buyers and sellers. When a market reaches a certain scale, suddenly all sorts of new services and business concepts emerge: promoters, marketers, customer acquisition experts, packagers and merchandisers, advertisers and campaign managers, data brokers, and vendors of tools to manage the bidding process and tools to search across multiple marketplaces. In order for everyone to participate, they must speak the same language, use the same currency, and abide by the same laws. These disparate parties demand a standardized way to transact. When this occurs, the switchboard market evolves again. It becomes a platform.

We use the term "platform" because the market quite literally provides a base for others to build a business. Platforms are different from basic switchboard markets because they are multi-sided. They connect many different types of companies transacting with many different types of customers, and many ways to get paid or exchange value of some kind.

This is not a new idea. Computing platforms have existed as long as there has been software. Personal digital assistants (PDAs) and game consoles are types of platforms. The first and most fundamental digital platform is the computer operating system.

In the early days of mainframe computers, when instructions were hand-fed into the computer via punch cards and later magnetic tape, there were no operating systems. Instead, each program contained a complete set of instructions to the machine. But as computing proliferated and many more users began to demand a variety of software programs for specific purposes, this arrangement quickly grew inefficient. The solution was to write a set of instructions that provided general-purpose commands to the computer that were consistent across every program. This was the genesis of the operating system (OS).

The OS emerged as a kind of buffer layer between the central processor and the software programs. While running in the background, it enabled all of the applications to work smoothly and consistently, and so provided a valuable service both to developers and the people who used computers. Then, during the era of personal computers (PCs), operating systems evolved into a proprietary wedge of software between the hardware and the applications. This gave Microsoft, the leading provider of operating systems for personal computers, a measure of control over the application developers. Developers' software couldn't talk to the machine without going through Microsoft's proprietary OS, Windows. In order to get access to the core function of the computer, developers had to deal with Microsoft. That's one way that Microsoft managed to exert control over the PC business.

The combination of applications and operating system made the PC much more useful to the end consumer. And that meant that the combination was also immensely valuable to the companies that made the hardware: without an operating system and a rich array of applications, there would be zero demand for the personal computer. That's another way that Microsoft exerted control over the PC business: it was able to extract huge license fees from the companies that made computers.

The operating system became a software platform. In essence, the Windows operating system served as a switchboard market that connected computer manufacturers with application developers. Microsoft turned the operating-system-cum-platform into a value control point and extracted monopoly rent from both sides for decades.

With the smartphone, this platform concept goes into overdrive—more than a million apps are no further away than a pocket or a purse. Every day, no matter the situation, there is an app to help. And every one of those apps adds to the perceived value of the software platform in the mobile device. To reach customers and provide that value, the app maker must go through the company that controls the operating system on the mobile device.

It can be risky to expose the operating system to outside parties: in the hands of an incompetent or malicious coder, the computer could be damaged. For this reason, an OS provider like Microsoft will typically provide developers with a set of tools called application programming interfaces (APIs). These tools act as a buffer, providing a way for applications to talk (interface) with the operating system safely without opening the computer up to harmful commands; APIs also serve as the glue that binds all of the creative activity to the platform. When developers use the API and toolkits to write their apps, the end result is hardwired to the OS: if the APIs are cut off, the app simply won't work. The APIs enable the platform owner to aggregate the collective efforts of lots of developers. That makes the platform more valuable to the end user, and the platform owner in the middle can then rake a fee or tax off all transactions.

BUILDING A STICKY DIGITAL PLATFORM BUSINESS

Switchboards compete by being the most efficient connection mechanism. An entire industry really only needs one: the one that matches sellers the fastest and most efficiently with the market they seek. This is the first step towards winner-take-all. When it works, this switchboard blocks the second-best by locking in the best customers.

Marketplaces compete on efficient transactions; by having the biggest collection of buyers and sellers, or seekers and providers. The most efficient market crowds out the others as it attracts more participants and reduces the time to revenue.

Launching a platform business means thinking carefully and imaginatively about pricing, specifically where to charge and how much, and who to charge. Who gets in free? Who pays? And how much? Every day, startup ventures attempt to become platforms. Many fail because they don't master the switchboard + market principle first.

It's a game of "attract 'em and keep 'em." To attract customers, a business must offer better value for the money, time, or effort invested and superior ease of use. To attract developers, the platform owner must offer well-documented, stable APIs; a scalable software platform with superior performance; the shortest time to revenue; and the greatest base of likely prospects.

To keep them, the platform owner must make it painful to switch to another system. The term "switching costs" is used to describe tactics that lock both sides of the market into the platform. One switching cost is the time it takes a new customer to learn how to use the platform. The consumer's learning curve is an investment in learning how to use the service; if she switches to another service, she must sacrifice the time and effort invested in learning. Likewise, the merchant's investment in building up a presence in the marketplace is expensive in terms of time and effort: if it were to switch to another platform, the process would be quite painful.

Unless the marketplace fails spectacularly, the twin forces of inertia and stickiness tend to keep users locked in. Generally consumers don't switch until somebody builds a much better mousetrap. And if that happens, be prepared for a mass exodus.

STRATEGIES FOR MIDDLEMEN

In many industries, intermediaries control most of the transactions. Digital networks are different because they tend to push the levers of control from the middle out towards the ends of the value chain: to creators and consumers. In offline markets (what we sometimes call real-world markets), there is often information asymmetry that reinforces the power of the middlemen. Agents and brokers, the middlemen in a transaction, tend to know more than any buyer or seller what is happening in the broader marketplace, which gives them the ability to influence and control individual transactions. For instance, the Multiple Listing Service (MLS) of properties for sale was previously available only to real estate agents: this inside information enabled brokers to control transactions in the real estate market. Similarly, market makers who control trading on the NASDAQ Stock Market are another example.

The information asymmetry advantage enjoyed by middlemen is a kind of inefficiency. But in the vaporized world, the switchboard is designed to remove inefficiency. Free-flowing information is available to all participants. As a result, switchboard marketplaces tend to erode the power of middlemen, brokers, agents, and bundlers, sometimes eliminating them entirely. In the end there is only one big middleman: the platform owner, who extracts a toll on every transaction.

What if your business is a broker-type of business? Can you still play a role? Sure. You just need to find a new way to add more value when customers have access to the same information you do. Brokers still have expertise, experience, insight, know-how, historical knowledge, and pattern recognition: they may end up offering a different service but that can be valuable in a noisy, complex market with lots of diverse offerings that are hard to compare.

One middleman survival strategy is to *complexify the market or the products* so that only experts can play the game. That's what Wall Street bankers managed to do with derivatives, a financial instrument whose price depends upon one or more underlying assets subject to changing conditions that are nearly impossible to predict. Wall Street brokers lost their information advantage when the Internet made it possible for day traders to execute simple trades on desktop computers at home. So Wall Street began to create products like derivatives that were so complex that the punters at home couldn't play.

Another strategy is to *use government*. Regulations distort markets. Many regulations are written or influenced by insiders: these tend to favor incumbents who write the rules. For example, real estate brokers still manage to get paid nowadays when everyone has a mobile house-hunting app. That's because the law requires that a lot of complicated paperwork be signed by both parties. Although these piles of paper are mandated by regulations, ostensibly to protect consumers, they have the side effect of making it harder for people to do their own real estate transactions without a broker.

Sometimes regulations can *force a digital transaction back into the physical world*. For instance, a customer might shop for a car online, work out all the details on price, and then learn that she still must drive to the dealership to sign the lease. The idea is to force the consumer out of the digital world back into the old physical world where the incumbents still have an advantage. The same thing happens when a customer shops for a loan on the Internet: typically she is obliged to visit the bank in person to complete the transaction.

But these tactics are anti-consumer. They go against the grain of freedom and flexibility characteristic of digital media. And they are inefficient. In the long run, they are doomed because the benefits of operating efficiently in the Vaporized Economy are so much greater that some innovator somewhere will devise a way to bypass the roadblocks. In Chapter 8 we'll explore some of these innovations.

There is an alternative to complexification. It's a pro-consumer strategy: offer better service, solve a problem, find something unique or different, deliver a much better price than the consumer can find on her own, or sort through all of the many confusing options for him. When I book my air travel, I tend to get a better price or a better seat through my travel agent than I am able to find online. As a result, I am quite happy to pay her commission. It takes a lot of hustle, but it is possible for a broker or agent to thrive without ripping off consumers.

ECOSYSTEMS EMERGE WHEN BUSINESSES THRIVE ON THE PLATFORM

As platforms grow, they tend to evolve more complex mechanisms for value generation. When this happens, we say that an "ecosystem" emerges on top of the platform. For example, the mobile app ecosystem enables a diverse group of content providers, app developers, marketers, and retailers to co-exist because there is a source of nourishment that supplies the whole ecosystem. Namely, there is a revenue stream that feeds each player so that it can continue to survive and grow and add value to the overall ecosystem.

The term is a biological metaphor to describe an environment just like a pond or a tidal pool or a coral reef that supports a diverse population of fish, plants, birds, and crustaceans. This metaphor is apt because digital ecosystems are so complex and have so many participants that they begin to resemble living systems. Ecosystems have life cycles. They thrive only when a delicate balance is maintained. If one party begins to cut off the supply of nutrients, the ecosystem can wither and die. This dynamic is true in the metaphorical sense in the digital economy.

Successful ecosystems grow on top of switchboards, marketplaces, and platforms. Those elements are the infrastructure that support the life cycle of the inhabitants of the ecosystem. An incident from the past five years illustrates how vitally important this ecosystem concept really is in the vaporized world. For more than a decade, Nokia reigned as the most powerful and most successful maker of mobile phones in the world. In nearly every market it commanded the leading market share. The company pioneered new devices that were ingenious, bold, even visionary. It introduced new services. By 2005 Nokia had created the smartphone market and dominated it in the early days, commanding 50 percent of the market around the world. But that was before Apple and Google entered the game.

For the launch of the iPhone, Apple leveraged the vast media ecosystem that had already been established for the iPod during the previous five years. The availability of so much content as well as the novel design of the iPhone and the brilliant ease of use of its touch interface were the primary factors that caused a mass migration from mobile phones to smartphones. Suddenly, instead of being a power tool for geeks, the smartphone was the new object of desire for millions, a personal media terminal, a mobile Internet browser, and a cool new phone.

Nokia, the reigning smartphone champion, was suddenly in trouble, but the company underestimated the threat. Apple's iPhone did not work on the advanced third-generation (3G) networks at the time, and the Nokia executives, comparing their smartphones to Apple's, felt they were safe. What the executives missed was the rich ecosystem of content that was bundled in the iPhone. This ecosystem conferred a decisive advantage on Apple, even though the computer maker was very late to the smartphone game.

In 2011, shortly after Stephen Elop joined Nokia as CEO, he published a now-legendary memo that was leaked and widely published on the Web. In it he likened Nokia's position in the smartphone market to standing on a burning platform. He wrote:

> There is intense heat coming from our competitors, more rapidly than we ever expected. Apple disrupted the market by redefining the smartphone and attracting developers to a closed, but very powerful ecosystem...
>
> And the truly perplexing aspect is that we're not even fighting with the right weapons. We are still too often trying to approach each price range on a device-to-device basis.
>
> The battle of devices has now become a war of ecosystems, where ecosystems include not only the hardware and software of the device, but developers, applications, e-commerce, advertising, search, social applications, location-based services, unified communications and many other things. Our competitors aren't taking our market share with devices; they are taking our market share with an entire ecosystem. This means we're going to have to decide how we either build, catalyse or join an ecosystem.

Just like the ranchers who were peeled off, one by one, from the barbed-wire network to the telephone company's switchboard networks, Nokia's customers were weaned away, one by one, to the superior ecosystem offered by Apple. Within two years of this memo's publication, Nokia's share price crashed. The company was later acquired by Microsoft, which, according to the pundits, was like an airplane crash-landing onto a sinking ship.

What Stephen Elop experienced at Nokia will soon be experienced by companies in many industrial fields, such as those who make home appliances, consumer electronics, medical equipment, lighting systems, and automobiles. It's no longer a battle of one product against another. It's now a battle of ecosystems.

VALUE CONTROL IN THE VAPORIZED ECONOMY

Most industries operate on a standard supply chain model as defined by economist Michael Porter in his 1985 book *Competitive Advantage*, whereby various participants in a linear sequence contribute to the process of assembling a product. Each step in the sequence adds a little more value to the final product. At the end of the process, the finished item is packaged neatly, delivered first to a shop, and then into the hands of a delighted customer.

Sometimes one or more players in the supply chain can exert control over the rest by seizing one key choke point. We call this a *value control point*.

The crucial difference between traditional business and big Internet platforms such as Apple, Google, and Amazon is that they are not managing a simple linear supply chain. Instead, they run a multi-sided platform business on top of a digital network, where they deal with many intersecting supply chains at once. They host a bewilderingly large range of buyers and sellers on all sides simultaneously.

It would be impossible to attempt to manage the conduct of millions of developers, publishers, marketers, retailers, and others who participate in the vast vaporized ecosystems, and it would also be prohibitively expensive. Instead, the big platform giants concentrate their efforts on maintaining control of just a few key functions that enable them to extract their share of value from all of the transactions on the platform and also manage the behavior of other participants according to the terms of use.

The platform giants bring order to the marketplace by maintaining strict control. The trick is to maintain just enough control over the entire marketplace to ensure that the merchants and providers—and especially the buyers—continue to rely upon your platform, but not so much control that you drive key players elsewhere. By controlling key features in the platform, value can be extracted from every transaction, and sometimes from both sides of the transaction. Value is not just monetary: it may consist of marketing value in the form of word of mouth or endorsements or favorable positioning; it may consist of content that is produced in a proprietary format that is captive to your platform; and value might exist in the form of communications and messages that are sent through your platform from one participant to another.

The major Internet platforms have massive distribution power not only because they reach enormous global audiences, but also because they control a range of marketing and communication channels that every participant in the ecosystem must use to reach those audiences. The big platforms control the way offers are presented, found, and paid for. Finally, the big platforms also control the screens, browsers, and media players that people will use to access digital products.

There are four primary value control points in the Vaporized Economy:

1. Tools for creation: How participants create content on top of the platform

The users of any digital platform generate several kinds of valuable content.

> **Primary content:** My writing, my photos, my reviews, my lists, my videos, my chats.
> **Ambient content/session data:** Details of my visits: how long, how frequent, time on site, time on page, page velocity, shopping cart, purchase history. This is sometimes called "data smog" because we generate it unconsciously through our actions.
> **Secondary content:** My likes, my bookmarks, my favorites, my lists, my shares, my forwards.

> **Tertiary content:** My friends and their comments, my groups, my comments.

Each of the big platforms provides its own set of tools and services to make it easier for audiences to generate, save, share, and display the content they produce. For instance, Apple offers *free tools* like iPhoto, Photos, iMovie, and Mail. Google offers Gmail and Picasa, plus a full suite of video-creation tools at YouTube. User-generated content is a cheap way to foster engagement that adds up to a significant investment of time and effort by users, and that creates a switching cost. Amazon pioneered the use of user reviews and curated lists to differentiate itself from other online booksellers, and the company built upon the long-standing tradition of threaded discussion forums to build a lively community on top of commodity content such as ISBN numbers and book descriptions.

Of course, consumer audiences are not the only source of content. Successful platforms also offer tools expressly designed to encourage professional developers to create content and apps. Every giant platform, including Facebook, Google, Apple, Amazon, and Microsoft, runs an active global outreach program to recruit developers. Each of them provides its developers with training and access to application programming interfaces (APIs) and sample code. Some companies offer custom tools for publishing in a proprietary format, such as Amazon's Kindle Direct Publishing tools or Apple's iBooks Author. Some platforms collaborate with companies that sell licensed software for professional creators, such as Pro Tools, Logic, and the Adobe image-editing and illustration software. Apple also publishes professional software tools for content creation, such as Final Cut Pro.

2. Tools for discovery and communication: How participants discover content and services and communicate about them
How do users sort through a million apps to find the one they are looking for? That's an important question. Making it easy to find content and apps is just as critical as making it easy to create content. That's because most people are not primarily content creators. The old rule of thumb on social

media sites was 1:10:100, which is a short way of saying that for every one person who writes an article or posts a video, there are ten people who comment on it and 100 who simply watch or read it without leaving a response. Facebook and Twitter have made it much easier to respond and share. But every major platform must invest hugely in making tools for discovery.

Google dominates this field with search, of course. Microsoft Bing, Apple's Siri, and Facebook's newsfeed (which itself was derived from the Twitter newsfeed) can all be considered attempts to design a better way for people to discover fresh content. This is a field of unending invention and ferocious competition. Social discovery systems such as friend recommendations, lists, likes, favorites, and five-star ratings are public tools for content discovery. One-to-one systems, like email and messaging apps, provide private channels to share information and content directly. As video grows in popularity and gets easier to create, apps like FaceTime, Hangouts, and Skype offer another avenue of discovery and communication.

3. Systems of monetization: How participants get paid for their contributions

Money is like oxygen. Cut it off and the ecosystem withers. While consumers may be pleased to share their information for free, developers must get paid. Otherwise they have a habit of going out of business. A crucial ingredient in the ecosystem, then, is money. Platform operators must ensure that money flows through the systems to developers in a timely way or they risk losing them to a rival platform.

There are two primary ways to get paid: *consumer transactions* or *advertising*.

The Apple App Store and iTunes, as well as Google Play and the Amazon Appstore, are mechanisms for collecting payments from consumers and sharing revenue back to the developers and professional content publishers. Tens of billions of dollars flow through these stores: they are a primary source of revenue for content publishers in digital media and therefore this is a crucial value control point. The process of submitting content to these stores is a related value control point, as is digital rights management (DRM) software, which is sometimes bound to one particular platform. User identity and customer accounts, and especially credit card information, are yet another related means of controlling value: Apple has nearly 1 billion credit cards on file from customers.

Google utterly dominates the digital advertising industry with the biggest ad server, DoubleClick for Publishers; the biggest ad networks (AdSense, AdMob, and the Google Display Network); the largest ad exchange (DoubleClick AdX); and the largest demand-side platform (DoubleClick Bid Manager, formerly known as Invite Media). It is almost impossible for digital publishers to avoid doing business with Google and its DoubleClick advertising brand.

Most recently, the big Internet platforms introduced *subscription content services* akin to Netflix and Spotify. Amazon offers Instant Video as part of its Prime subscription program. Apple offers streaming iTunes Radio and the Beats streaming music service and is expected to announce a Netflix-like subscription video-on-demand service in 2015.

Implicit in transactions and advertising is another lever for value control: user identity and user profiles. The information we provide when we use the platform is collected, organized, and associated with our identities and user profiles; this information is used to optimize purchase recommendations and targeted advertising. Each of the major platforms exerts control over hundreds of millions of user identities.

*4. Devices and software for content consumption and storage:
How information is packaged and presented to end users*
The final set of value control points for managing a digital ecosystem consist of all the tools and devices used by consumers to get access to the content and display it.

The original software control point for consumption was the *browser*, which functions like the lens through which the Web is pulled into focus. Examples of browsers include Google Chrome and Apple Safari. Microsoft's old browser was Explorer and the new one is called Edge.

Hardware as a value control point began with computers, then shifted to smartphones and tablets and now includes a range of accessories for devices like televisions. This progression charted a decisive shift away from using digital technology to *create and do* things towards using digital devices to *watch or listen* to content produced by others. Apple began with computers and laptops, then introduced a series of iPods, followed by the iPhone, the iPad, the Apple TV, and most recently the Apple Watch. Apple is clearly moving in the direction of consumption; creation is a lower priority. Google now sells hardware too, in two flavors: Android devices like the Nexus smartphones and a set of laptop computers running the Chrome operating system, plus a smart TV dongle known as Chromecast. Google's acquisition of Nest puts it in the home with a range of smart thermostats, smoke detectors, security cameras, and other so-called smart devices. Amazon offers the Kindle ebook readers and tablets as well as a Fire TV accessory. Microsoft also offers Surface tablets, smartphones, and the Xbox game console.

Finally, *cloud storage* is a new value control point that functions like a storage locker for personal media like documents and photos. Just like the Roach Motel, it's easy to check in but a lot less easy to check out. Amazon is the leader with Amazon Web Services, and every competitor follows: Apple iCloud, Google Drive, Microsoft OneDrive. One way to think about cloud storage is as a new form of bundling. Unlike the pay TV bundle, which consisted of subscription access to channels of content provided by television networks, the new bundle consists of subscription access to the content created by consumers themselves, which is stored in the cloud. Think of photos taken with a smartphone and saved in the cloud drive. It's a far better business model because the cloud companies pay nothing to acquire the content, and few subscribers are willing to let their subscriptions lapse, lest their memories and their documents be deleted. Cloud storage of personal content may be the stickiest subscription product ever invented.

Beneath these tools lie the proprietary layers of software that link the entire platform together, such as operating systems, search engines, recommendation systems, provisioning platforms, data analytics, and user tracking systems.

HOW WELL DOES YOUR COMPANY MAP TO
THE VALUE CONTROL POINTS?

It's obvious that Apple, Google, Amazon, Microsoft, and, to a lesser extent, Facebook offer the full suite of value control points. They can't afford not to. Some of them are stronger in one area than another: for instance, Apple's App Store generates twice as much revenue as Google Play, even though there are hundreds of millions more Android devices in use. Conversely, Google dominates advertising. Facebook is dominant in social media and discovery but lacks a range of devices for consumption.

When you contemplate how your company will thrive in the future Vaporized Economy, it makes a good deal of sense to think about not just who controls the ecosystem but also how they do it. Business owners who plan to launch a platform business must ensure that their product offering conforms to, or improves upon, these four value control points. What you may find is that some companies do not map very well to these four points at all.

Consider your value control points carefully as you evolve your own business in the future. Are you building a business for the new information economy or are you stuck in the old mechanical one?

ASK YOURSELF

> In your field, is there one central switchboard to connect buyers and sellers? How efficient is it? Can you do the job faster and cheaper, with less friction, using software?

> Has a winner-take-all effect happened in your industry yet? If so, can you identify the points of lock-in? Are there weaknesses, such as inefficiency or a high entropy bill that starves ecosystem participants?

> Does your company invest in physical inventory or in software tools to enable others to market, manage, and promote their inventory?

> What are the value control points in your industry? How well do these translate to the digital domain?

5

BIG BULLIES IN
THE APP DICTATORSHIP

EVERYTHING THAT CAN
BE COMMODITIZED WILL BE

Best-selling author James Patterson addressed the audience at the 2014 Book Expo America, the largest gathering of book publishers, bookstore buyers, librarians, and writers in North America, with a blistering rant about online sales. "Right now, bookstores, libraries, authors, publishers, and books themselves are caught in the crossfire of an economic war between publishers and online providers.

"To be a teeny, tiny bit more specific," Patterson continued, "Amazon seems to be out to control shopping in this country. This will ultimately have an effect on every grocery- and department-store chain, on every big-box store, and ultimately it will put thousands of mom-and-pop stores out of business. It just will, and I don't see anybody writing about it, but that certainly sounds like the beginning of a monopoly to me. Amazon also, as you know, wants to control book selling, book buying, and even book publishing, and that is a national tragedy."

What's remarkable about Patterson's rant is that it is so *unremarkable* in the Vaporized Economy. Sooner or later, nearly every participant in the app economy has said or felt something similar about the company that controls the underlying ecosystem.

When everything is running smoothly on digital platforms, most participants barely notice the environment in which their content and services exist. But sometimes a change in the app ecosystem chokes off one of the species. And that's when people like Patterson begin to complain. The creators, publishers, developers, and designers chafe when they become too aware that their content, their products, and their services exist entirely at the whim of the company that owns the underlying platform.

Patterson's complaint is at once specific and broad. On the one hand, he was referring to his own personal situation: as a top-selling author, he was the one caught in a crossfire between his publisher, Hachette, and its biggest retail channel, Amazon. Patterson's own book sales suffered because negotiations between these two giant companies had broken down. To gain leverage in the negotiation, Amazon removed Hachette titles from the Kindle store, suppressed the search results for Hachette titles, and delayed the shipping for many hardbound books published by Hachette. At one point in the battle, Amazon posted a notice for customers, encouraging them to shop for Hachette books elsewhere. Patterson, like all of Hachette's authors, felt the pain. Amazon was acting like a schoolyard bully, pushing the other kids around in the playground. It was easy because Amazon owned the playground.

But Patterson's complaint was not limited to books. In his Book Expo remarks, the author pointed a spotlight on an ugly situation that extends far beyond books and disputes between publishers and booksellers. Patterson's point is that every company in the Vaporized Economy will exist at the pleasure and sole discretion of a platform owner like Amazon. In other words, books are the canary in the mineshaft. Every company that has built a software platform demonstrates a tendency to bully independent artists, publishers, developers, and other companies that create content, apps, or services on their platforms. What's true for media will be true for the rest of the digital economy.

Pretty soon, your industry—and every industry that generates a huge volume of data—will go through the same meat grinder as Hachette.

THE FIGHT FOR SUPREMACY IN THE VAPORIZED WORLD

Already it's not hard to find examples of bullying by a variety of the biggest digital platforms. Consider the following incidents that were widely reported on tech blogs:

> According to *Digital Music News,* in early 2015 YouTube threatened to block long-established channels and remove music videos by independent artists unless they agreed to provide music on most-favored-nation terms to Music Key, the new ad-free subscription music service from YouTube.

> Several big Internet platforms, including Twitter and LinkedIn, have curtailed developer access to APIs. Netflix has cut off access to its public API entirely. Twitter in particular has come under scrutiny from TechCrunch, Mashable, and other tech blogs because the company has shifted from an open ecosystem to much greater centralized control, limiting access to apps that don't comply with its display requirements, and cutting off the full stream of tweets and metadata to firms that compete with Gnip, a data analytics firm acquired by Twitter in 2014.

> According to TechCrunch, Facebook applied intense pressure on Zynga, the leading game publisher on the Facebook platform, during a negotiation in 2010. An anonymous email cited by TechCrunch said that Facebook threatened to cut off Zynga services on the Facebook platform.

> As I write, Apple is rumored to be in the process of applying pressure to the major record labels to cancel the licenses that enable Spotify to stream free ad-supported music. That move is intended to help drive paying subscribers to Apple's own Beats Music streaming-audio service by eliminating the free alternatives. The *New York Post* reported in April 2015 that the European Commission's Directorate-General for Competition has begun querying music labels about their dealings with Apple,

and in May *The Verge* claimed that the US Department of Justice and the Federal Trade Commission have begun a parallel investigation.

What makes the Amazon story so interesting is that eventually the US Department of Justice actually did get involved, but not in the way most people expected. The DOJ intervened to protect Amazon from the publishers!

The backstory reveals just how ferocious the competitive dynamics in the Vaporized Economy can be. Shortly before the 2010 launch of the iPad, Steve Jobs decided it was time for Apple to get into the ebook business to compete with Amazon. At the time, Amazon was firmly established as the dominant Internet bookseller and its Kindle e-reader device was already a major hit.

Amazon's success in the ebook category was attributable to a vaporized feature: Whispernet. With this 3G wireless plan provided free of charge by Amazon, consumers could download ebooks over the air at the touch of a button, any time, any place. This feature proved to be a significant advantage over competing devices from rivals like Sony where books could only be transferred to the reader by connecting to a PC via a cable.

Then, to stoke greater demand for its ebooks and drive further adoption of the Kindle, Amazon insisted on pricing best-selling books at $9.99, far lower than the retail prices suggested by the publishers, and even lower than the wholesale price paid by Amazon. In other words, Amazon was losing several dollars every time a Kindle owner purchased a bestseller on that device.

Crazy? Nope, brilliant. It was a pre-emptive strike against Apple's eventual entry into ebooks. Amazon sought to make it impossible for any competitor to profit from ebook sales if it attempted to match Amazon's prices; and yet, if bestsellers were offered at higher prices, no customer would consider purchasing the devices. Amazon was building a perfect moat around the Kindle, and it was prepared to go hungry just to ensure that incoming rivals starved.

What was Apple's plan to compete with Amazon Kindle? Collusion, according to the US Department of Justice. In order to launch its iPad with a wide selection of digital books for download, Apple's Eddy Cue held a series of secret meetings with six of the world's largest publishers to fine-tune the proposed business model and sign contracts. Steve Jobs personally intervened, contacting Lachlan Murdoch, the scion of the News Corp dynasty, to ensure that its book publishing company, HarperCollins, would participate.

But Jobs' plans were undone by an idle boast to longtime tech journalist Walt Mossberg. When Mossberg asked the ailing Jobs how Apple expected to sell ebooks for $12.99 when Amazon was undercutting that price by three dollars, Jobs smugly announced that all the prices for ebooks would be the same. That careless remark put Apple and its book industry partners into hot water.

Amazon complained to the US Department of Justice, which began an investigation into the suspicious synchronicity and uniformity of the publishers' negotiations. Ultimately, five of the six biggest publishers in the US were investigated for conspiracy to fix prices. The publishers, including Hachette Book Group, HarperCollins Publishers, Penguin Group, Simon & Schuster, and Macmillan, settled with the Department of Justice, agreeing to pay $166 million in fines in the form of credit to the customers who overpaid. As part of their settlement, the publishers lost all of the bargaining leverage with Amazon. And that's what gave Amazon the power to crush Hachette in the next round of negotiations in 2014.

But Apple didn't settle with the Department of Justice. Instead, insisting it had done no wrong, Apple decided to duke it out with the federal government. Despite a brilliant legal defense, described in *The Battle of $9.99* by Andrew Richard Albanese, in the end, Apple lost, undone by internal email messages that documented Steve Jobs' hubris.

Roadkill on the information highway

The story of ebooks illustrates that big Internet platforms are expanding so fast in every direction that they sometimes collide with each other. All bullies harbor a deep-seated insecurity. They know their dominance won't last forever, and out of fear of losing it they jealously guard their turf, throwing their weight around while they still can. So it is with the giant Internet platforms that bully their content providers, developers, publishers, and other partners. Amazon's collision with Apple on digital book downloads is similar to Google's collision with Apple over smartphones, and Facebook's collision with Google over social networking, and Amazon's collision with Google over e-commerce. When giants clash, they use the value control points to govern the flow of resources, traffic, money, support, and marketing exposure. Smaller companies and unlucky individuals like James Patterson tend to get squashed.

Most consumers are oblivious to the intensely competitive business dynamics and technology strategies that occur to make legal paid downloading possible. Behind the scenes of any friendly app store an intense battle is being fought between Amazon, Apple, and Google, who own and control rival platforms, and the rest of the participants in the ecosystem who feel strongly that their profits are being devoured by the platform owners. At the same time, the Internet giants are under constant pressure from telecommunications companies whose networks deliver their services. It's a multi-sided struggle for control. Any empire built on air is, by definition, unstable and evanescent. To maintain an empire in such turbulent conditions, it takes a lot of willpower, bravado, and cold-blooded willingness to choke rivals out of existence.

Some observers misinterpret what happened with Amazon, Apple, and the book publishers over ebooks. The frequently aired complaint that Amazon is a monopoly is demonstrably untrue. Amazon faces plenty of competition both on the Internet and also from brick-and-mortar retailers in the real world. Plus the company continually seeks to lower, not raise, prices. The Internet giants are not monopolies, but inside their own private empires they do act like tyrants.

The book publishers did not like the terms offered by Amazon, so they turned to Apple for help. In doing so, they willingly became pawns in Apple's game. In the end, the publishers lost all leverage. The ebook saga is just a repeat of the previous decade's digital rights management fiasco. In the late 1990s and early 2000s, record labels turned to the technology giants for help securing their digital products with a special kind of encryption called digital rights management (DRM). Far too late, the labels realized that it was a mistake to allow companies like Apple to write proprietary DRM code because it glued their content to the iPod, the only device that could decrypt Apple's code. The labels had foolishly given the keys to distribution control away to the big Internet companies.

So what's the lesson? In mature industries, when the threat of vaporization appears on the horizon, the incumbent players tend to turn in desperation to a big technology company for help instead of building their own solution. That's like a small rural village asking Attila the Hun to protect the place from marauders. The big Internet platforms are not here to help; they are poised to suck the profit out of your old industry as it gets vaporized. The lesson is that when you relinquish control over your business and migrate to a digital platform that is owned by someone else, your business will continue to exist only at the whim of the company whose system you are riding on. Let's take a closer look at life in the App Dictatorship.

ROUND ONE WAS MOBILE GAMES

As more physical products dematerialize and are turned into invisible downloadable software, and as more of the information locked up in traditional businesses is freed and turned into digital vapor, it is increasingly likely that much of the value in the equation will pass through mobile devices, where a toll can be extracted by the big Internet giants.

Mobile ecosystems are neither open nor free. I learned this lesson the hard way, along with thousands of colleagues, in a completely different industry and in a completely different way than James Patterson. The rules of the modern App Dictatorship were set in the mobile game business in the early 2000s.

For several years, I had served on the board of directors at the Game Developers Conference (GDC), the oldest and largest gathering of game designers and publishers in the world. Most of the GDC is focused on games for computers and consoles, but I was attracted to games on other devices like televisions, phones, and the Internet. In particular, I had been interested in the rapid growth of mobile phones, and so in 2002 I created a special event at GDC focused on the fledgling industry of publishing games for mobile phones.

At the time, the games on mobile phones were so feeble that they were viewed with contempt by my GDC colleagues who built games for the Xbox and PlayStation. The critics had a point. Most mobile phones in 2002 did not have color screens, and very few could connect to the Internet to download data. Many of the early mobile games consisted of text, crude bitmapped graphics, or blinking black dots on a green screen. However, I had lived through this phase a decade earlier with games on PCs, and I knew that color screens and 3D graphics were coming soon to the mobile phone. It was clear to me that the games would improve as the devices improved, and that's why I wanted to hammer out the structure of the marketplace for this industry.

My objective was to gather all of the competing game developers together with the big phone manufacturers and the mobile network operators in a neutral forum so that we could all meet, discuss, and work out the issues facing the industry. The timing was good. Between 2002 and 2007, the mobile phone went through the equivalent of four generations of game console upgrades, from black-and-white to color to 3D to touch screen. GDC Mobile, my little game conference, swiftly emerged as the leading event devoted to the fastest-growing category of entertainment. We thrashed through the issues facing the industry with a lot of gusto and some lively debates. Attendees established software standards and normalized business practices between regions. We solved design challenges with the keypads and the size of the screens. We hammered out how to deal with different hardware configurations so the games would play whether the phones had powerful processors and plenty of memory or whether they were underpowered and weak.

The entire industry yearned for a single mobile device that was optimized for games.

Perhaps the biggest issue was the way that games were presented and sold to end users. The mobile networks, huge telecom companies like Vodafone, Telefónica, Verizon, and AT&T, insisted on being the only face to the consumer. Their common goal was simple: they knew that mobile Internet was going to be big, and they wanted to control the on-ramps. They wanted to train the consumer to come through their portals to purchase games and music and other kinds of content. Each network operator dreamed of being the mobile equivalent of AOL in its heyday during the dial-up internet era, circa 1997: the all-inclusive, unavoidable access point to the Web.

The problem was that the telecom companies were not very adept at designing this experience. The early mobile app stores were inelegant, cumbersome, slow, ugly, unimaginative, and generally horrible as a consumer experience. Smart users were already devising ways to bypass the mobile operator's clumsy virtual shopping malls. Worse, the telecom companies refused to listen to complaints or suggestions and they jealously refused to share performance data with any publisher. As a result, developers were flying blind, producing games for an audience we could only understand by convening focus groups. Any company that dared to go around the carrier to establish a direct relationship with the end user was banished from the telecom's closed ecosystem. Even at this early stage of mobile content, the platform owners acted like big bullies.

By 2007, in spite of these issues, demand for mobile games was heating up. Games were consistently the most profitable sector of mobile entertainment. Total revenue for mobile games crossed the $1 billion revenue threshold in 2006. Millions of real customers demanded better games, publishers were ready to deliver them, and decent smartphones were finally available at reasonable prices. The timing was perfect for Apple's entry into the market.

ROUND 2: MOBILE GAME DEVELOPERS VS APPLE

Given Apple's legendary design prowess, and its remarkable success reinventing the music business with the iPod, most of my peers in the mobile industry were excited about the much-rumored debut of the iPhone. Would Apple open the iPhone up to games? And would the company be the savior that might counterbalance the big mobile network operators?

I had some misgivings. In my opening remarks at GDC Mobile 2007 in San Francisco, I warned the audience of game publishers: "Be careful what you wish for. When Apple comes to mobile games, you may be exchanging one harsh master for an even more controlling one." This prediction turned out to be accurate.

In March 2008 Steve Jobs announced the Apple App Store for the iPhone and iPod Touch and invited third-party developers to participate. In July that year, the App Store launched with 500 applications. It was an immediate success: in the first weekend 10 million apps were downloaded, and within the first year Apple broke the 1-billion download mark. Although Apple didn't invent the app store, its improved version allowed users to manage apps offline and make purchases in the iTunes Store, with integrated one-click billing and a simple login process. This was an enormous improvement on the telecommunications companies' version of an app store. The sexiest innovation was the touch screen (an idea borrowed from Nintendo), a much more natural way to control a game than tapping on a phone keypad. The iPhone transformed mobile phones into an all-purpose computing platform, and the touch interface allowed it to double as a great handheld game console.

The verdict came quickly: the iPhone was a terrific device, and the App Store was a vastly better shopping experience than any mobile operator's download store. As consumers traded in their old Motorola and Nokia phones for Apple iPhones and the App Store, the old telco app stores closed. By 2010 the game publishers were left with just a few dwindling alternatives to Apple's App Store. There was no meaningful competition until March 2012, when Google converted its lackluster Android App Marketplace into Google Play. That's when the App Dictatorship began.

To say that Apple cracked the code on mobile content sales is an understatement. By mid-2014, Apple had more than 800 million credit cards on file in iTunes and the App Store, more than twice as many as Amazon, making it by far the biggest mobile media emporium, according to market intelligence site 9to5mac.com. Tim Cook, Apple's chief executive officer, acknowledges that app sales are the fastest-growing part of the computer giant's total revenue. Apple got there by carefully tuning the value control points in the iOS ecosystem.

The iOS mobile app economy sits on top of the Apple iTunes billing system, which gives Apple the power to impose the rules of engagement and restrictions on all apps sold. The problem for everyone else is that iOS is a closed ecosystem. Every developer must submit its work to Apple's review board for approval before it can be presented to consumers. If one doesn't comply, Apple can simply cut the miscreant out completely.

Arbitrary policies and capricious business rules, some written and some not, seem to determine the fate and fortune of every company that participates in this ecosystem: for the past five years, several tech blogs including Gizmodo, TechCrunch, and TechHive have posted reports of apps rejected after the App Store's "mysterious and seemingly arbitrary process," as TechHive described it in 2009. The App Store Review Guidelines, posted on Apple's site for developers, run to twelve pages of single-spaced type. Some of these rules are intended to protect consumer data and privacy. Other rules protect Apple trademarks and brands, but the logic of many rules seem capricious and vague to many developers.

According to the guidelines, an app can be rejected by Apple's review board for a variety of subjective reasons, including being "creepy," "amateur hour," "primarily marketing," "mean-spirited," "inflammatory," "objectionable," "crude," "over the line," or for the most sweeping reason of all—"less than good." Apple bans pornography—fair enough, there are a lot of kids using the App Store, and Jobs was determined to keep smut off the iPhone—but even apps that are merely vulgar, like fart apps, have also been rejected. In 2010, the App Store purged 5,000 apps that featured boobs, babes, and bikinis. Reporting on the incident, ZDNet's Jason O'Grady had fun mocking Apple's "thought police" before raising a valid question about whether this issue could be better handled by providing parental controls instead.

The policy is inconsistently applied: the games Video Strip Poker and Manga Strip Poker were removed but Sexy Poker remained. Apps from *Playboy* and *Sports Illustrated* were not removed. Also purged were a range of non-sexy but tasteless products such as the religious parody app Me So Holy, political satire apps like My Shoe and Obama Trampoline, a radiation detector app called Tawkon, and the functionless app for wealthy showoffs called I Am Rich. Likewise, games like Dope Wars that are deemed to "encourage excessive consumption of alcohol or illegal substances" have been banned, even though Apple sells plenty of pop music and movies that tout sex, drugs, and booze in the iTunes Store.

Sometimes, rejection appears to be motivated by a desire to stifle competition: for instance, apps that attempt to use any billing systems other than Apple's in-app purchase mechanism are rejected. So are apps that don't conform to Apple's rigid guidelines for user interface (UI), as are those that attempt to "create alternate desktop/home screen environments," according to the Guidelines.

These guidelines make it efficient for a small team at Apple to manage a huge number of outside developers. And in their defense, this team is reportedly inundated with low-grade apps and a torrent of blatantly obscene submissions. That's the unavoidable result of a huge developer network. In April 2014, at the company's Worldwide Developer Conference, Tim Cook boasted of 9 million registered developers who are seeking a piece of the action, a 47 percent increase over 2013.

What Cook did not mention, however, is that vanishingly few of these developers generate significant profit. "Our analysis shows that most mobile apps are not generating profits," reported Ken Dulaney, an analyst at the technology market research firm Gartner. He continued, "This is only going to get worse in the future when there will be even greater competition." In the Gartner report *Predicts 2014: Mobile and Wireless,* Dulaney forecasts that by 2018, fewer than 0.01 percent of consumer mobile apps will be considered a financial success by their developers.

The 2014 *Developer Economics: State of the Developer Nation* report from VisionMobile revealed, based on responses from 10,000 app developers in 137 countries, that half of iOS developers and 64 percent of Android developers generate less than $500 a month from their wares. Only 12 percent of development firms generate more than $100,000 a month. And there's a classic power law effect here. The more developers there are, the fewer actually make money: the top 1.6 percent earn between $500,000 and tens of millions of dollars a month. "More than 50 percent of app businesses are not sustainable at current revenue levels," the report concludes. "A massive 60–70 percent may not be sustainable long term."

Apple can afford to be indifferent to the fate of the individual players in this community because of the unique revenue model of iTunes and the App Store, which is known as the "agency model." Unlike the wholesale business model, whereby a retailer first pays a low-bulk price to a supplier and then marks up the final price paid by consumers, the agency model involves sharing revenue on transactions. Rather than paying an upfront wholesale price, Apple earns a flat percentage on every sale, peeling its commission off the top of each sale regardless of whether the app developer sells one or 1 million units. As long as Apple's App Store generates plenty of downloads, Apple will continue to thrive no matter which apps sell. Apple is immune to the hit-and-miss spikes of the traditional content publishing business. That's great for Apple, but it shifts the risk entirely to the developers.

Apple rakes a fee of 30 percent off every transaction, large or small, that occurs inside of its iOS ecosystem. In 2014 that 30 percent cut amounted to more than $4.5 billion for Apple. This was a business that Steve Jobs repeatedly vowed to run at a "break-even" basis, as recently as 2008 during an interview reported in the *Wall Street Journal*. At first Apple's 30 percent cut was only taken from the initial sale of an app. Then in 2011, Apple changed the rules: it now takes 30 percent of all transactions on its platform, including in-app purchases on free software.

For the companies that provide the apps, however, it is a very different story. With no viable alternative to reach paying customers on iPhones and iPads, the publishers and developers have no choice but to accept Apple's terms without negotiation. They've lost the power of price, positioning, and packaging. By opting into the App Dictatorship, their wares have been commoditized.

ROUND 3: APPLE VS THE MOBILE NETWORK OPERATORS

Apple preserved many of the core features that made the earlier mobile content systems work. For instance, the mobile networks maintained a firm grip on their billing system, exiling those who attempted to introduce alternative payment systems. Apple emulated this policy and deepened it with in-app purchases inside of free apps. However, the most important lesson Apple learned from mobile operators, who learned it from video game console manufacturers, is the agency fee. The game industry model is sometimes referred to as "razors and razorblades" because the game console (or mobile phone) is typically provided to the consumer at or below cost: profit is made when the end user buys content and other services.

In February 1999 the Japanese mobile operator NTT Mobile Communications Network (now NTT DOCOMO) launched the first truly successful mobile data service, called i-mode. It took a maximum of 9 percent as a share of revenue from the sale of content and apps, leaving 91 percent of the earnings to developers. When I asked about this relatively low fee, Takeshi Natsuno, the executive director of i-mode, told me that his team deliberately chose the business model that most favored content providers and developers rather than the network operator or handset maker. This humble approach worked: i-mode's low fee attracted a vast number of creative developers whose ingenuity and apps distinguished it as the most innovative platform in Japan, and, arguably, in the world at that time. And that is precisely what enabled the company to crush rival telecom companies, by signing up huge numbers of new customers. I was working in Tokyo in 2000 and witnessed long lines around the block outside the DOCOMO shops as customers rushed to switch to i-mode-capable mobile phones.

What the launch team at i-mode understood is that this fee, or "rake," as the house vigorish (or vig) is known in the casino industry, introduces friction in a transactional marketplace. Lower fees = lower friction. And low friction means greater velocity. If the goal is to grow quickly, low friction is the way to go. But other mobile operators who emulated DOCOMO missed the point.

In 2002 I spoke to the team that was preparing to launch AT&T's mobile data services in the United States. An executive told me that AT&T had studied i-mode closely but had decided to double the 9 percent fee to 18 percent in order to cover bad debt incurred by American customers. Ultimately,

AT&T rounded up this figure to an even 20 percent and then, later, bumped it even higher.

In 2003 an executive at Sprint Corporation informed me that its rake for mobile apps and services would be 25 percent, which was similar to the path fee charged by Sony PlayStation. When Verizon Wireless launched its mobile content service, it set the rake at 37 percent, and later raised it to 50 percent for some music products. In some European countries, the rake was 50 percent or higher. That was too much: developers tend to go out of business when the platform siphons off half of the revenue. Greed and a lust for faster return on investment compelled the mobile operators to skim ever-higher fees off content transactions. This was unwise: they were taking money from the wrong end of the platform. In so doing, they generated friction that would ultimately doom their efforts.

By settling on a flat fee of 30 percent of revenue, Apple chose a financial model that split the difference between DOCOMO and the greediest mobile operators. The 30 percent vig made it possible for app developers to remain in precarious existence, but it also ensured that most would never be so profitable that they could grow independently powerful. Most others app stores, like Google Play and Microsoft's Windows Phone Store, have followed Apple's precedent of taking 30 percent. There is nothing about the 30 percent rake that is set in stone: Apple—or any rival—could charge 50 percent or 9 percent or nothing at all. Given the fact that Apple has nearly $200 billion in the bank, the high commission on content transactions is puzzling. A 10 percent commission would still generate $1.4 billion for Apple, which would surely cover the cost of running the store.

Apple further improved upon the game console and mobile operator model by charging full price for its devices. Whereas the mobile operators subsidized the initial purchase price of the smartphone in order to get customers on the hook, Apple double dips, taking its full profit on the sale of the hardware and also collecting the agency fee on the sale of content and apps.

Apple also tweaked the original mobile operator formula in some very important ways. For instance, when customers purchase a new iOS device, Apple enables consumers to transfer the content and apps that they have already purchased from the old device to the new one. This encourages consumers to upgrade their devices more frequently. Most mobile operators were unable to do this because they offered such a wide range of handsets and could not guarantee that all content was available on all devices. So the content was stuck on the old phone. Net result: their most avid consumers of content were often the slowest to upgrade their phones, reluctant to retire a device that was loaded with $100+ of content.

Apple changed this dynamic by giving consumers accounts in the App Store where all of their purchases were recorded and available for downloading to a second, third, or even a fifth device. Giving consumers the freedom to manage their content across multiple devices is one way that Apple reduced friction en route to huge scale. Apple's best customers tend to buy more content and they upgrade devices more frequently. Most important, they remain loyal to Apple devices. Transferrable content is the glue that binds consumers to Apple's ecosystem. When a user has dozens of apps, hundreds of songs, and thousands of photos shared across an iPod, an iPhone, and an iPad, that customer is highly unlikely to switch to an Android device.

When Apple opened the iOS developer program to all comers, it broke with the mobile operators' usual practice of engaging with only a small number of preferred vendors. Paradoxically, by diversifying and expanding the suppliers of apps, Apple grew more powerful. The intense competition among millions of developers ensures that none will ever become powerful enough to challenge Apple. And though iOS is not exactly an open platform, it is certainly more open than its predecessors. The more open the platform, the cheaper the content. Opening up the App Store to millions of developers actually increased Apple's control over the ecosystem because it reduced the bargaining leverage of any single app developer. Openness leads to commodity pricing. (Android is even more open than Apple, and the content in the Android ecosystem is more commoditized: Android monetizes apps at about half the rate of iOS.)

Finally, Apple crushed the mobile operator portals by focusing all effort and ingenuity on a single device, instead of dissipating effort across thirty-five different handsets. This concentration of marketing power enabled Apple to accomplish what the mobile operators failed to do: create a scalable network effect. More users attracted more apps, which in turn attracted more users. This upward spiral is great for users. But when the network is privately owned, it's also an immense win for the owner of the platform because massive user adoption lifts every part of the business. In Apple's case, the upward spiral led to the surge in sales of iPhones that continues to this day. Surging demand keeps prices high and margins fat. Every platform aspires to achieve the upward spiral of Metcalfe's law.

THE KNOCKOUT: WINNER TAKES ALL

As we've seen, the winner-take-all phenomenon means that, in every digital category, just one company emerges as the overwhelmingly preferred option for hundreds of millions of users. And the more users who participate, the larger the leader's market share and the more valuable the service becomes for all of them. With the worldwide adoption of smartphones, Metcalfe's law now operates at global scale making the big companies even bigger. This phenomenon isn't exactly common but it does seem to repeat itself each time a new Internet giant rises.

The companies that master this dynamic become so dominant that we can't even think of a competitor. What's the #1 search engine? Google, of course. Can you name the #2 search engine? Most people would guess Bing or Yahoo or Ask.com. They would be wrong. The #2 search engine, in terms of traffic and search volume, is YouTube, which also happens to be owned by Google.

Facebook is a textbook case in the evolution of a winner-take-all company. In the early days, from 2004 to 2006, the fledgling online social networking service was small and tightly focused on a growing number of college campuses. Later Facebook expanded from students to alumni, and by 2007 it opened up to anyone over the age of thirteen. Opening up the site to more people made Facebook more useful to its existing members. Still, as recently as 2007 there were dozens of rival social networks—and many of them, including Myspace, were much bigger than Facebook.

That year Facebook made a crucial decision: just as Apple did with the iPhone, Facebook made its closed system available to third-party developers by offering a suite of tools to build apps on top of the social network. This move transformed Facebook into a platform that aggregated apps and games and other services. Instead of competing with thousands of little social networks, Facebook absorbed most of these projects and all of the creative energy of their developers, thereby extinguishing a generation of rival websites.

Seven thousand apps were published by November 2007; just one year later, at the second annual F8 Facebook Developer Conference in San Francisco, Facebook announced that the number had nearly quintupled to 33,000. These apps added value to the platform by giving the members many more ways to connect and share and communicate. They also generated new revenue streams from the sale of goods like virtual gifts and stickers and boosts in games. Most important, they added immense value to Facebook at minimal cost because they increased the level of engagement and the amount of time its members spent on the site.

Facebook's next move was equally bold and strategically decisive. By 2008 nearly every publisher on the Web was seeking to build communities on its own site. Vendors sold custom social networking systems that could be integrated with an existing news or entertainment website, but in December 2008 Facebook introduced Facebook Connect, which was free of charge to publishers. By allowing web publishers to add the Facebook login to their own site, Facebook spared them the considerable hassle of developing and maintaining complex social software systems. And with just the click of one button, visitors to those sites could effortlessly log in via Facebook without the hurdle of setting up a profile account and password. This made life easier for the publishers, but it also left them dependent upon Facebook.

By leveraging the creativity of developers and the reach of publishers, Facebook surpassed Yahoo in early 2010 to become the second-most visited site on the Internet (after Google). When Facebook filed for an initial public offering in 2012, it revealed that more than 9 million apps and websites had integrated Facebook Connect. In a few countries, particularly China and

Russia where Facebook was banned or discouraged, homegrown local variants managed to take root. But in most parts of the world, rival sites like Bebo, Friendster, Myspace, and Orkut swiftly faded into irrelevance as Facebook emerged as the undisputed champion in social networking.

In the process of growing from 100 million members in 2007 to 1.4 billion in 2015, Facebook made yet another strategic pivot, focusing on smartphones as the key driver to future growth. In 2012, Mark Zuckerberg, Facebook's chief executive officer, declared a "mobile first" strategy that began to yield results remarkably fast: less than one year later, mobile ad sales were on track to account for half of Facebook's revenue. By October 2012, Facebook Mobile had surpassed Google Maps as the most popular mobile app.

Most smartphone owners spend 80 percent of their phone time on apps, and more than 20 percent of that time is spent on Facebook. Naturally, mobile game publishers want to reach those users, and they're spending advertising dollars to do it: from 2013 to 2014 Facebook's mobile advertising revenue grew a staggering 150 percent. It contributed more than 60 percent of the social network's total advertising revenue of $2.7 billion in the second quarter of 2014, and that revenue is largely derived from mobile app developers who are trying to gain some visibility for their products in the App Store. The upshot: a big percentage of the money earned by mobile app developers who publish games on iOS and Android ends up in Facebook's pocket, because the game developers spend everything they can on advertising in Facebook Mobile in order to acquire more customers.

So who is the winner? In the Vaporized Era, the App Dictators are. Whoever controls the ecosystem can pick winners, crush would-be rivals, and continuously tweak the revenue-sharing formulas and percentages in their favor. However, the benefits of participation in this ecosystem can be enormous for those who comply. Apple, Google, Facebook, and Amazon can help the publishers in their ecosystems to reach hundreds of millions of customers rapidly, with easy access to built-in monetization. Successful apps routinely attain tens of millions of users within weeks of launch. Developers can communicate directly with their end users and get feedback and suggestions for improvements, which are seamlessly pushed back down to the end user's device. This instant feedback loop makes it possible for companies to iterate rapidly and keep their customers satisfied.

But success in this environment requires absolute compliance to the rules set forth by the owner of the ecosystem. As unappealing as the dynamics of the app economy may be when compared to the business models of the twentieth century, most companies acquiesce without a fight for the simple reason that the alternative is total annihilation. Your choice is to comply or be rendered irrelevant.

HOW TO LIVE IN THE APP DICTATORSHIP

Content creators face many long-term risks in the mobile ecosystem. These include a loss of pricing power, a reduction of the product's value to commodity level, and a never-ending proliferation of available substitutes. Developers in the app ecosystem—none of whom are willing to speak on the record—variously describe life in the app ecosystem as "tyranny," "misery," and "a living hell." Certainly, the App Dictator has a number of tools to wield power to keep its subjects in line:

> **Banishment:** The platform owner can remove any app for seemingly arbitrary reasons.
> **Displacement:** The platform owner may decide to get into the same business as a successful app developer, forcing the app out.
> **Disruption:** The platform owner can provide access to free or nearly free alternatives that undermine a successful app's business model.
> **Suppression:** The platform owner can manipulate search results to bury an app under other competing products, making the app hard to find. That's what the Federal Trade Commission determined that Google had done, skewing search results to favor Google apps and products. This treatment puts app developers on the profit-eroding treadmill of spending endless marketing dollars to maintain visibility.
> **Bait and switch:** The platform owner can arbitrarily change the business model long after a developer has garnered a big audience.

> **Addiction:** The platform owner can put in place so many constraints that developers, publishers, and other participants who adapt find themselves inextricably hooked as the revenue grows. They discover they cannot afford to leave because it requires too much time and effort to retool their business process in order to pursue an alternative strategy.

Closed economies are rife with strange distortions, and the App Dictatorship is no exception. With more than 1.3 million apps jockeying for visibility and some kind of advantage in an app store, it's no surprise that the overwhelming majority of apps are free. Developers are willing to slash prices in order to attract customers. And how do consumers find the app they want to download in a store that has famously poor navigation?

Developers will often hire a marketing company on a cost-per-install (CPI) basis, which means that the marketing firm gets paid every time a player downloads and installs the app, whether or not the developer makes money. According to market research firm Chartboost, the average cost per install ranges from $1.00 on Android to $2.30 on the iPad. This is like paying another company to give your product away for free. Every serious developer and publishing company does this, sometimes spending hundreds of thousands or even millions of dollars on CPI marketing just to move the needle on its download volume, hoping thereby to catapult a new title onto the Top 100 list and thereby become one of the lucky 1.6 percent whose apps generate millions of dollars. The most successful game publishers on iOS are hooked on paid installs, spending hundreds of thousands of dollars every day on this peculiar form of marketing just to preserve their position on the list. And if you want to make money as a developer in the App Store, getting on a Top 100 list is a matter of life or death because that's the way consumers will find your product.

Appeals to Apple won't do much good. The company is famously aloof to developer concerns. Every developer I spoke to is hesitant to complain for fear of retaliation. After all, Apple sets forth a warning explicitly in the App Store Review Guidelines: "If you run to the press and trash us, it never helps." Developers would rather take their lumps in the mosh pit, hoping that their next app breaks out. Occasionally Apple will grace a compliant developer with featured placement in the store, but the rules that govern this kind of favor are murky. Tales of secret payoffs, lavish gifts, and other attempts to grease the wheels are often told but hard to verify. Most developers and publishers end up spending the bulk of their profit (after the 30 percent tax) on paid installations or other forms of marketing for mobile apps.

For all but a lucky few titles it is a profitless exercise, the vaporized version of sharecropping or tenant farming, whereby all the cash earned by those workers is spent on provisions at the company store. The egalitarian—or indifferent—nature of the vaporized marketplace presents a sobering reality for many, and the same dynamics pertain regardless of the size or nature of the business.

The agency model immunizes Apple from the fate of the publisher: Apple gets the same cut whether the app makes $1 or $100 million. In one sense this is fair, but it may come as a rude awakening to the big-box retailer, global consumer product brand, or major media company that finds it has no greater leverage than a basement startup. In an app dictatorship, there is no negotiation at all.

Broadly, the App Dictatorship should be a concern for everyone who cares about free speech and the sharing of ideas. For years, civil liberties advocates and supporters of the open World Wide Web have clashed with those who seek to impose controls on the Internet, such as conservative political groups, religious organizations, copyright owners, and even authoritarian governments. Whether they frame the issue as copyright infringement or hate speech or political dissent, what unites these disparate groups is their goal of imposing some form of control over free expression on the Web. Civil libertarians resist this fiercely because they know that once a mechanism for censorship is established for any reason, it will inevitably be expanded and ultimately abused. It is not a huge step from banning bikinis and racy fare to banning political speech, satire, parody, criticism, and negative product reviews. From the perspective of civil libertarians, each constraint chokes discourse a bit more until free speech no longer exists.

In mobile, the battle has already been lost. There is no concept of free speech inside the App Dictatorship, and that's exactly why we should all be concerned. In the United States, only government entities are required to support free speech. Private companies have no such obligation, which is why there are no political protests at the local shopping mall. But in the Vaporized Economy, there is no public commons. There is no open forum for the free exchange of ideas; it's all private enclosures. Mobile apps are not like web pages: they are built from proprietary toolkits, not open standard software, and they are inextricably linked with a closed system.

This closed environment is the fastest-growing medium in history. Mobile Internet usage is soaring, surpassing desktop Internet and even television as the primary media activity in most industrialized nations, and the overwhelming majority of that usage occurs within apps. According to the market research firm Flurry, US consumers spend two hours and thirty-eight minutes a day on their smartphones, and more than 86 percent of that time is spent inside of highly controlled apps, not on the browser on the open Web. The constraints imposed on app developers matter to everybody.

For Apple, this represents a strange reversal of an inspiring heritage. The company sprang from the Homebrew Computer Club, a movement based on the free exchange of ideas and open access to the fledgling personal computer ecosystem as a tool for free expression and creativity.

STRATEGIES FOR SURVIVAL

Once a company begins to participate in an app ecosystem, it is extraordinarily difficult to pull out. The more time, energy, and marketing resources are invested into mobile apps, the more they tend to be bound to the platform. And developers invest heavily to promote awareness of their products in the app stores of Apple, Google, and Amazon. Of course, these campaigns tend to benefit the platform more than the developer since telling customers to "find us in the App Store" just worsens the developers' dependency on them.

Most mobile developers yearn for the adoption of HTML5, a new version of the page-description language that democratized publishing on the Internet. If it works as promised, it will give developers the opportunity to create app-like Web experiences that look and feel like iOS apps but that can live outside the App Store. However, HTML5 is not quite ready for prime time.

Despite all the present friction and restriction, somehow thousands of companies do manage to operate in these environments. So, what can you do? Which strategies are used by developers to survive and thrive in the digital ecosystem?

1. Sell a digital service along with your product; transact outside the App Store. The ideal business model is to establish a direct-to-consumer service that enables you to bill the customer directly. You'll want to provide a free app in the App Store that gives subscribers mobile access to the service. This is easier said than done. It's very hard to convince consumers to sign up and provide credit card information but it is worth the effort.

2. Be on every platform. Port your app; in other words, optimize it for all the leading platforms. Learn to tolerate the low-margin lifestyle after the 30 percent revenue split. Compensate for low profit by aiming for vast reach. Cultivate a preferred relationship with Apple, Amazon, Facebook, Microsoft, and Google to ensure the best possible placement of your product.

3. Offer an app for free. With this strategy, you give the first taste of the product, service, or game away for free, get users hooked, and then convert as many as possible to paying customers. Basically you use the App Store to develop distribution and marketing channels that reach a large number of consumers who use the app for free, and then upsell a percentage of users to a premium tier or premium features. It's called monetizing usage. The business model was perfected in the highly competitive mobile game industry, where game developers have evolved a suite of sophisticated product design features and highly addictive game mechanics to manipulate player behavior. In 2013, free games with in-app-purchases zoomed from 77 to 92 percent of all mobile game revenue, reported the mobile analytics firm Distimo. It is a highly effective—if sometimes coercive—approach, as the top-grossing mobile games with in-app purchases generate hundreds of millions of dollars a year. For instance, market intelligence firm ThinkGaming.com reports that Candy Crush Saga, one of the top-grossing free-to-play apps on both iOS and Android, generates $907,000 a day in the US, earning $330 million in the year.

4. Roll your own. Some companies build their own marketplaces and distribution platforms outside of the App Dictatorship or a meta-marketplace that spans the big Internet platforms. This step is the hardest of all to master but it's not impossible, especially for those with vision and stamina who are the first to define a new category. Netflix did it. Amazon Kindle did too. Uber and Airbnb are in the process. To accomplish this ninja move, you must provide the most efficient switchboard marketplace in your category and remain studiously neutral about all of the offerings. Be prepared to fight like hell to maintain your position and preserve your direct relationship with the customer.

5. Most important of all: study the platform. If you are going to operate in the Vaporized Economy, you must be a student of Apple, Google, Amazon, and the other Internet giants. If you're familiar with these dynamics you'll need to pay attention, but if you're coming from a brick-and-mortar industry where these tactics are virtually unknown, redouble your efforts. Even the slightest tweak to their ecosystem can determine your fate or your fortune. And if you rely upon external vendors to manage your mobile apps and your relations with the Internet giants, you are about to get blindsided. Ignore this information at your peril.

Google's approach: mimic Microsoft

Of all the Internet giants to study, pay especially close attention to Google. Although Apple is a formidable player, the Apple strategy centers squarely on the iPhone. Google is less concentrated on a single value control point or physical product and therefore provides an alternative example that is a bit more vaporized. A big chunk of Google's strategy seems to be based on tactics from the Microsoft playbook. No surprise: Google debuted at a time when Microsoft dominated the computer industry, and since then Google has hired thousands of former Microsoft employees.

The Seattle software giant always understood the value of a thriving developer ecosystem. For twenty-five years Microsoft enjoyed an enviable position as an ecosystem overlord by maintaining tight control over Windows OS, which drove a wedge between the PC and the applications that made the personal computer useful. Those applications made Windows more valuable, and Microsoft leveraged that fact to extract more money from the hardware companies. At the same time, the company continually expanded the value of its software by absorbing and bundling more and more features: often what were previously stand-alone applications from independent software vendors became part of the platform, or part of the Office Suite, in Microsoft's next release.

Microsoft set the template for domination that many big Internet companies have followed:

> Starve your rivals by bundling free products with your core product.
> Enlist a huge army of developers to support your mission.
> Extract as much value as you can from the ecosystem.

Google has modified this template to succeed in today's Vaporized Economy.

1. Commoditize your complements. Complements are products that must be bought together in order to be useful, like hot dogs and buns, cars and tires—or an operating system and a computer. If you want to increase the value of your core product, one smart tactic is to drive down the price of all complementary products. That tends to drive up demand for your product. As software programmer Joel Spolsky wrote in a widely-cited blog post titled "Strategy Letter V," Microsoft commoditized the PC, which made Windows incredibly valuable. Similarly, because Google's core search and advertising business grows linearly with every additional person on the Web, it makes sense for Google to commoditize anything that will attract more users to the Web, including formerly valuable content such as news, headlines, books, maps, video, and music. Google offers an ever-growing suite of free services (like email, browsers, productivity apps, creativity apps) and they deftly utilize open-source software projects like Android to disable the revenue engine of their biggest rivals. No wonder competitors and producers of complementary goods struggle to achieve profit inside Google's domain.

2. Seize the value control points. To maintain their invisible information empires, the leading companies seek to exert control over the value network surrounding their products. Each company manages these control points in its own unique way, but no leading company ever relinquishes control of the essentials. The app economy enables Amazon to pursue a different strategy than Apple or Google, but all of these companies maintain a firm grip on their primary value control points. No company has more value control points than Google, which spans advertising, e-commerce, social media, video and mobile, as well as a full suite of hardware products.

3. Own the path of progress. Microsoft was late to the Internet and it missed mobile completely. As a result it lost control of the path of progress. Google is not about to make the same mistake. That's why it is buying or investing in everything that might emerge as the next frontier of computing when the desktop browser and PC decline completely. We'll take a closer look at this strategy in Chapters 6 and 7.

Also, to fend off threats from the Internet service providers and mobile operators upon whose networks Google relies, the company is building its own ultra-high-speed broadband network in the US and a floating one suspended from balloons in the skies over New Zealand. Search is still at the core of Google's business, enabling a dynamic marketplace of bidders who want their information to be findable, and encompassing several gushing geysers of user-generated information and a huge pool of third-party developers, vendors, merchants, and apps that rely upon Google data. By controlling this rich and complex ecosystem, Google is in the enviable position of being able to choose where to take its profit margin. This is a conscious choice among known alternatives. In other words, Google chooses to be hugely profitable in advertising, so that all of its other businesses can operate on thin margins or no profit at all while reinforcing the core data asset and attracting creative developers whose apps pull in ever-more users who generate ever-more data for Google to mine.

What all of these initiatives have in common is data. Google's mission is to organize the world's information, and the company interprets that mission rather broadly. If there is information attached to it, Google will find a way to seize it, control it, and build a moat around it. As a result, I would not want to be an old-school manufacturing company, publisher, insurance firm, transportation company, or educational institution facing off against Google without a solid understanding of how to control the data flowing through my industry.

Information is certain to grow faster than anything else generated by human beings far into the foreseeable future, and I expect to find Google at the center of that growth for a very long time to come.

ASK YOURSELF

> What is the primary business objective behind your participation in the App Store? To reach consumers directly on their preferred device? To offer content in the fastest-growing medium in history? To make money? To displace a rival? Each goal will require a different strategic approach.

> How much are you willing to sacrifice in order to reach that goal? Are you okay with zero profit, or even losing money, to gain exposure and mindshare? Are you willing to pay a marketing firm to give your product away for free?

> Which value control points can you maintain? Is it possible for you to enjoy the benefit of distribution via the App Store in order to build a direct channel to consumers and extract the benefit elsewhere?

6

BIG DATA AND THE
EVERYTHING GRAPH

EVERYTHING THAT CAN BE
MEASURED WILL BE

"What is your proprietary data asset?" In the Vaporized Economy, no question is more important. This question was first put to me by Brad Burnham, one of the founding partners at New York's leading venture capital firm, Union Square Ventures. At first I was stumped and I fumbled an improvised answer. Afterwards I realized that having a large bank of specific, aggregated data is the key to success for every vaporized business.

This chapter is about the value of data to businesses in the Vaporized Economy. As ever more industries evolve by replacing physical infrastructure with pure digital information, it's crucial for every person in the organization to understand the value of data assets owned and managed by the company.

I had visited Burnham in 2006 to pitch a new startup venture, an opportunity that he politely but promptly declined. Most venture capitalists are not in the habit of explaining their decisions when they decline an investment, so I was pleasantly surprised when he offered to share his reasoning.

At the time, a new generation of Internet companies were building web services that generated fresh data as a by-product of normal use. The more users, the more data. The task for such a company is to manage the flood of data, organize it, and give it structure so that it can be archived, searched, and analyzed. In many cases, this data will eventually emerge as the most valuable asset owned by a company. Hence the term, "proprietary data asset." Those are the kinds of businesses that Union Square Ventures preferred to invest in.

The startup project that I presented to Burnham failed to meet this criterion. My plan was to produce content, which certainly is a type of proprietary data, but my team intended to do it the old-fashioned way by hiring editors and writers and freelancers to supply articles. The audience's role was to consume the content, but these consumers would not contribute much information themselves. That was an old-school approach to a new medium.

The problem with this model is that on the Internet, content produced by professional writers is likely to be consumed much faster than it can be generated. It's like a sink that drains faster than it can be filled. Moreover, it's expensive to hire professional writers, editors, and videographers, and there's no guarantee that audiences will like their work. If they don't, the project is doomed. That's a risky bet for a publisher let alone a venture capitalist!

But even if the audience loves the content the publisher is on a treadmill, diverting income into hiring ever more writers and editors to meet growing demand. Most digital news outlets today have greatly expanded their video features to attract high-margin video advertising; however, back when I visited Union Square Ventures in 2006, video ads were scarce. They are still no guarantee that a publisher can break the cycle of the consumption treadmill. It's incredibly hard for even established news brands to break out of this low-margin cycle.

From an investor's perspective, these factors make it quite unappealing to invest in creating original content. And that's why Union Square passed on my proposal.

What kind of companies exhibit the characteristics that Brad Burnham and his partners seek? Union Square's portfolio of investments has included Twitter, Tumblr, Foursquare, SoundCloud, Disqus, Kickstarter, Shapeways, and many others. It's a diverse collection with a surprisingly high percentage of monster hits. Studying these companies provides insight into an entirely different business dynamic. These companies operate in a wide range of categories, from digital music to three-dimensional (3D) printing to local city guides and even crowdfunding and microblogging. What they have in common is that they provide a platform for users to do more than *consume* content: the users *generate* a specific type of data just by participating.

The type of data generated by each Union Square portfolio company is unique. On SoundCloud, users create original music tracks; on Twitter, they post 140 character tweets; via Disqus, users might share a comment or opinion in response to an article. That's one reason why it is proprietary. Nevertheless we can discern a single unifying dynamic: what these services share is a generative quality quite unlike the treadmill cycle of traditional publishing. On these sites, the unique data asset grows geometrically and much richer as more and more users participate, engage, and respond to each other. Interaction creates a compounding effect. More begets more. Both quality and quantity increase without additional cost as new users join the site and participate.

Instead of a *content sink*, the Union Square companies have created a *data geyser:* an inexhaustible wellspring of original content which they then manage, annotate, organize, and make available to the next round of visitors who react, reply, respond, and thereby produce even more content. It's a virtuous cycle. User-generated data is the closest thing to a perpetual motion machine ever devised. It is free and unlimited. And despite the abundance, the result can be highly valuable. These companies are not in the traditional "content" business. They are in the data-generation business.

On digital networks, companies have a chance to do something that was never previously possible or even imaginable in the physical world. They can track every detail of a customer encounter, from the first impression right up to the moment when the consumer decides to make a purchase and even afterwards, throughout the life cycle of the product. In fact, an entire business model called free to play (F2P), in which consumers are offered a free version of a networked product by registering and agreeing to the terms of service, gives companies the ability to upsell later by offering to unlock premium features for a fee. Using this strategy, companies bet that they can be more profitable, reach a bigger audience, and, by keeping a dialog open with end users, obtain more data.

Data collection is not limited to retail businesses. Any company that maintains a dialog with its users can track information. And in aggregate, this information reveals patterns of behavior that can be immensely valuable: it can help guide companies towards better decisions about their product design, the preferred components of their offers, and their most effective strategies for communicating with a particular segment of shoppers.

THE GRAPH CONCEPT (OR HOW TO IDENTIFY YOUR DATA ASSET)

Ever since Facebook founder Mark Zuckerberg borrowed a mathematics concept called graph theory to coin the phrase "social graph," it has become fashionable to classify Internet sites and mobile apps by the kind of graph of data generated by their users.

Think of the "graph" as a grid or spreadsheet in three dimensions. Facebook's social graph consists of a matrix that captures each individual's relationship to friends and contacts, cross-referenced by their mutual interests, affiliations, associations, and locations. At the intersection of friends and interests lie the attributes that marketers crave most: passion, commitment, priority, aspiration, and identity.

The social graph provides another way to understand the value of the data generated by Union Square's portfolio of venture-funded startups. The graph concept reveals the primary purpose of each company. For example,

> Foursquare generates a "location graph" that maps a user's behavior by location.
> Kickstarter yields a "crowdfunding graph" of passion projects indexed by the people involved, such as creators, followers, and funders.
> SoundCloud generates a "listening graph" of musical compositions indexed across members who produce and listen to them.
> Twitter pioneered the "interest graph" that cross-references discussion topics by participating members and followers.

Each company in the portfolio presents itself as a unique marketplace matching those who seek a certain type of information with those who provide it.

The graph makes the market even more efficient by solving a problem that is unique to two-way digital networks. Every website and app that invites users to participate faces a fundamental problem of scale. That is, as the number of participants scales to millions and tens of millions, they generate so much content that it soon becomes impossible for the average person to navigate using traditional organizational principles like curated lists, indexes, and directories. Classic Internet search engines are often inadequate under these circumstances unless the user knows exactly what he or she is seeking, and standard navigational concepts like categories and menus begin to break under the sheer volume of content. The solution is the graph. The graph is a new way to make the content navigable for all visitors.

The brilliance of the graph concept is that the *data itself* is used to make other data findable. As author David Weinberger remarks in a blog post called "Metadata and Understanding" on KMWorld.com: "The solution to information overload is more information . . . so long as that more information is metadata." Here's how it works. The social graph cross-references one type of data with another to instantly generate a list that is relevant to a specific context. One topic becomes a lens that pulls the other information into focus. Naturally, depending upon the site or service being used, the lists vary by subject matter such as the most popular coffee shops sorted by location, recently published books with the most reviews, the blogs with the most followers, today's most-shared articles, the crowdfunding projects with the most supporters, and so on.

These are not static lists or fixed navigation elements hard-coded by engineers: they are dynamic, which means that they respond instantly to the activity of other users on the site. The lists are not curated by human editors: they are generated automatically by algorithms. Continuously refreshed lists fed by real-time data have enabled Foursquare and Yelp to deliver superior results compared to a site like Citysearch. Whereas Citysearch relies on its editors to research, assemble, and publish information about the businesses

in each city—which means it is often out of date by the time it is posted—
Foursquare and Yelp receive constant updates from their users.

There's more. User engagement makes the service more valuable, not
less valuable, than a site with professional editors. That seems like a paradox
if we consider user-generated content as inferior to professionally produced
information, but it becomes clear in practice. For instance, suppose you and
I are both active members on a restaurant review site. We're both foodies, and
we love to discover great new gastropubs and sushi joints. Your participation
on the site makes the content more relevant to me, and vice versa.

The most active users automatically become navigational guides for
their followers, whether or not they consciously choose to play such a role.
Their activity on the site, such as posting comments, reviews, and rankings,
will eventually pull a wide range of disparate content into focus, making it
relevant for millions of others who join the site later. And conversely, even
the most obscure content can serve as a way to discover like-minded users
with shared interests, even if those other users happen to live on the opposite side of the planet.

The social graph could never exist on paper or in fixed media. It would
be frozen and swiftly outdated. Traditional manual editorial processes and
library systems are incapable of organizing vast information flows in real time.

The generative approach pioneered by the companies that Union Square
invested in around 2006 offers a sharp contrast to traditional businesses that
produce information by hiring experts. In the traditional approach, the value
of the content diminishes with time and use and is eventually depleted as
more and more people consume it.

WHY TRADITIONAL COMPANIES MISS THE MARK

Movie studios, record labels, and book publishers invest huge sums in original content. So do advertisers and their agencies. It's a risky business.
Sometimes it works and the result is a big hit. More frequently, this approach
fails to deliver the expected economic return. Most traditional media businesses are vulnerable to the cycle of hits and misses, with a few big hits
offsetting a string of misses. It's impossible to make every film a box-office

success or every book a bestseller. Even a hit factory like Pixar Animation Studios, which has produced such high-grossing, award-winning films as *Toy Story, Finding Nemo,* and *Monsters, Inc.,* will occasionally release a dud.

In 2013 I was invited to address the executive team at Turner Broadcasting System. In the cable TV industry, this team is the reigning heavyweight champion. Along with sibling HBO, the Turner channels deliver the majority of the revenue and nearly all the profit to parent company Time Warner. But these firms still operate on the old model of investing in content in the hope of making a hit show. My mission was to shake up the team's thinking a bit.

The topic of my session was "Thinking the Unthinkable." Inspired by Brad Burnham's criterion I asked my audience to compare Turner Broadcasting's proprietary data asset, TV shows, with the data asset generated by social networks. Specifically, I drew their attention to the following comparison:

	Pay TV Networks' Data Assets	Social Networks' Data Assets
Type of data	Original TV production or licensed TV series	User-generated content such as photos, videos, posts, comments, status updates
Production cost	Expensive	Free
Marketing and promotion	Expensive	Free (viral word of mouth)
Consumer fee for access	Expensive subscription	Free
Availability to end user	Scarce (limited to certain windows of time and territory)	Abundant, forever, globally available
Access by third party	Exclusive access under distribution contract	Freely available to all via API and developer program
Life cycle of data	Quickly depleted	Evergreen and continuously replenished

In my comments to the executives at Turner I used the television business as the example to make my point, but this comparison is hardly limited to media companies. It's valid for *any company* that participates in the networked economy, including manufacturers and retailers and their advertising agencies. Every business relies upon media to communicate with customers, partners, suppliers, and employees, and that means every company needs to understand how the dynamics of media change when business migrates to the two-way network.

If your company produces information by hiring staff and investing in the production of data, the inevitable outcome is that you will perceive your data as expensive and therefore precious. You'll strive to keep it scarce, locked in a vault. If, instead, you focus on investing in the tools and infrastructure that enable others to generate data on your platform and make it findable, such as the application programming interface (API) that we considered in Chapter 4, you can reap an endless harvest of free data that can be shared, mingled, remixed, commented, replied to, and thereby compounded.

Every company that I consult with is aware of the opportunities in data but most of them confess to being overwhelmed. They find themselves swamped by the sheer volume of the data and they lack the technical skills to sort through it and make sense of it. They don't have a history of partnering with others or sharing their proprietary data, which means they often can't extract the full value of their data asset. As more and more parts of our physical economy are vaporized and replaced with digital data, massive new business opportunities exist in the collection, recording, organization, analysis, storage, indexing, and retrieval of information. Companies that streamline their business process around the collection and management of data will benefit by finding new ways to improve products, invent new ones, and keep their customers satisfied. These are crucial survival skills in the Vaporized Era.

HOW THE MONEYBALL EFFECT CAN HELP

An increasing number of companies *are* finding ways to use the feedback loop of real-time data to optimize their business performance. I liken this process to the theme of *Moneyball*, the best-selling book by Michael Lewis that recounts the tale of a perennially losing baseball franchise that was saved by data. Aided by a young quantitative analyst, the head coach of the Oakland A's began to track and study player performance data and apply the insights to optimize the lineup and improve overall team performance.

Moneyball isn't really about baseball: the story is a hip allegory for management by data. The narrative includes a dramatic showdown between the coach and his old-school talent scouts who reject the data-driven approach, preferring to rely on instinct and intuition. Spoiler alert: in the end, the old-school dullards depart and the quantitative approach prevails, not just by transforming the team into winners but also by reshaping the management structure of the Oakland A's. Ultimately the Moneyball approach has been adopted by the entire professional sports industry because once one team adopts a data-driven approach to optimization, its rivals have no choice but to respond in kind. Rigorous quantification of professional athletes' training, rest, nutrition, supplements, and performance has now become a universal norm.

Today companies in every industry have begun to adopt a Moneyball approach to data-driven decision-making:

> Wall Street bankers use automated high-frequency trading software to scan the market for buying patterns.
> Media buyers rely on automated bidding programs rather than gut instinct to buy advertising in specific target markets.
> Doctors in health maintenance organizations (HMOs) use checklists derived from broad surveys of best practices to treat patients.

All companies generate information. Whether you produce marketing data or how-to guides or retail SKUs, it's a good idea to consider how you manage your data. Does your business create a proprietary data asset? Is it stored in a useable format or locked in a vault? Does that data asset grow or diminish with use? Does that asset grow or diminish with time? Do your partners contribute to its growth or subtract value? Does your business model depend upon the value of your information asset being depleted or constantly regenerated?

The answers to these questions will help you determine whether your company will sink or surf in the Vaporized Economy.

THE VALUE PARADOX: ACCOUNTING FOR INTANGIBLE ASSETS

"Information wants to be free," writer Stewart Brand famously quipped in his book *The Media Lab: Inventing the Future at MIT,* in 1985. "Information also wants to be expensive . . . That tension will not go away."

Brand's gnomic aphorism has emerged as the central paradox of the Vaporized Era. We're awash in information. It fills our inboxes and laptops, clogs our networks, and leaves us feeling chronically overworked and unfinished. And yet we are instinctively aware that this torrent of data is valuable, so we spend an ever-increasing amount of time and money managing the tide. Of all of humanity's various milestones in these tumultuous early years of the twenty-first century, one achievement stands out. We are champions of generating new information.

Every year since 2005, EMC Corporation, a data storage company, has sponsored the *IDC Digital Universe Study,* which estimates the amount of information generated on digital networks. We are doubling the amount of data every eighteen months and, according to the report, in 2010 human society crossed an important threshold. We collectively generated a zettabyte (1 ZB) of data.

Most people are familiar with smaller units of measurement, such as kilobytes and megabytes, because we get reminders from our email systems to limit the size of attachments. One thousand megabytes is a gigabyte, and 1,000 gigabytes makes a terabyte. If you've backed up your family photos on an external hard drive lately, you've probably used a terabyte drive. Now imagine 1,000 of those terabyte hard drives and you've got a petabyte. A thousand petabytes is an exabyte, which until recently was the biggest measure used to describe data.

In the 2000s the data storage industry measured the total output of human information generation in tens of exabytes. Now we're going to the next level. A zettabyte is a thousand exabytes; in other words, it's 10^{21} bytes.

To put it in perspective, open your desk drawer and fish out a one-gigabyte USB flash drive. It's just about one inch long. A decade ago, a gigabyte was more information than the most powerful desktop computer had on board: today we give away one-gig flash drives for free at trade shows. Now imagine putting 100 similar flash drives in a line and then making 100 more lines. You'd end up with a 100 × 100 grid of flash drives, which would make a rectangle approximately ten feet by six feet (depending upon the exact size of your flash drive). That rectangle is a terabyte.

Suppose that you stacked 100 more rectangles exactly like this on top of each other to form a cube of flash drives. The cube is a petabyte. Now picture 1,000 such cubes. It would cover a football field. That's an exabyte. Finally, imagine a million such cubes! That's a zettabyte. We're talking about city blocks covered with flash drives stacked 100 deep. A zettabyte is one *million million* gigabytes.

To illustrate how much data is in a petabyte, the authors of the IDC report, John Gantz and David Reinsel, wrote: "Picture a stack of DVDs reaching from the earth to the moon and back." One zettabyte is a million times greater than that. That's how much information human society produced in 2010. And we keep creating more. By 2011, the IDC report says, we nearly doubled that amount to 1.8 ZB. And by 2012 we generated 2.8 ZB. In 2013 we generated 4.4 ZB. Every year the estimate in the report is revised—upwards. At this pace, we've already outstripped IDC's prediction of 40 ZB by 2020. The authors recently revised their estimate, to 44 ZB. At that point, Gantz and Reinsel's stack of DVDs will reach halfway to Mars.

According to Chuck Hollis, the former chief technology officer at EMC, that means in 2020 at least 1.7 megabytes of data will be generated for every person on the planet—*every second of every day*. There will be 5,200 giga-bytes of data for every person on the planet. That data is not all photos and videos that we share on social networks. In fact, far more data is generated about us than we generate directly via sharing. Each year we are connecting more and more machines to the Internet, and they will begin to contribute even more information to the data pile than humans do.

In economic terms, this absurd oversupply suggests that information should be incredibly cheap. The information is often freely available—even if it takes some effort to gather it and organize it—but it's not really free, as in cheap. In the right organization, data is incredibly valuable. Yet, today very few chief executives can cite how much their data assets are really worth.

INFONOMICS TO THE RESCUE

This value paradox lies at the heart of a new theory called infonomics, or how businesses determine the economic value of their information, a term coined by analyst Doug Laney of Gartner Research. He points out that information behaves like no item on a corporate balance sheet, and that, lacking a generally agreed means to measure data's worth, accountants typically don't include it in the company's books as an asset. As a result, insurance companies explicitly exclude coverage for data assets, which means that if your server crashes and your corporate data is wiped out, don't even think about submitting a claim!

This challenge to account for the value of data leaves companies teetering in a precarious spot as ever-greater chunks of their business process and products are vaporized into pure digital information. Moreover, Laney points out that there is a gap between the *potential value* and the *realized value* of information assets. Unless it is managed effectively, data is a liability, not an asset.

It costs a lot of money to collect and archive data, and it's even more expensive to process that information in order to arrive at useful insights. Experts must be hired, and expensive equipment and software are required. Some databases must be licensed or purchased; others are obtained via barter or exchange with partner firms. These costs add up quickly, which makes it necessary for managers to quantify the value of data in order to justify these outlays. That's easier said than done.

Laney proposes several methods of establishing the value of intangible corporate data assets: the estimated cost to replace it, the potential price it might fetch in the open market, or the amount it contributes to a revenue stream. Another approach is to measure the impact on internal business operations.

But arriving at consensus on the value of data as an asset is just the first step towards measuring the total value of the Vaporized Economy. The standard methods of measuring gross domestic product (GDP) do not contemplate the process of replacing physical goods with information. A new smartphone comes loaded with dozens of vaporized substitutes for the camera, video recorder, game console, MP3 player, map, compass, alarm clock, notebook, and dozens of other products, but the only item recorded in the national GDP is the smartphone. The rest of those products just disappear off the balance sheet. As the vaporized portion of the economy grows and expands, it could lead to a paradoxical outcome: a shrinking GDP.

Our collective inability to measure and account for the value of the rapidly expanding intangible portion of the economy is the biggest self-imposed obstacle on the path to the Vaporized Economy. As more and more portions of industry, commerce, society, and culture migrate to digital vapor, the quantity and value of information assets will continue to increase but our ability to measure them and invest adequately to manage them languishes. Closing the valuation gap will emerge as a major priority for business leaders.

The biggest conceptual challenge to traditional companies and conventional thinkers will be to perceive their intangible data asset as their most valuable property. It's difficult to break the habit of prioritizing tangible, physical stuff. However, as the process of vaporizing things proceeds, those physical assets may be sold or written off as junk. Proprietary systems and processes may be upgraded and replaced, but information will reign supreme as an ever-growing asset and the primary driver of profitability.

Those who already see this opportunity can position themselves for a data-driven future. They can develop internal expertise at managing and analyzing huge data sets, and they will gather data from as many sources as possible. Many managers fail to see this future, however. Blinded by old-fashioned accounting practices and a sentimental attachment to physical facilities and tangible products, they will miss the opportunity to convert their business, as Linotype did, to an entirely information-based enterprise.

They continue to underinvest in data systems and the skill sets to manage them, falling further behind and quite possibly riding their physical infrastructure into obsolescence and obscurity.

As Laney wrote in the *Financial Times:* "Ultimately, executives who just continue to talk about information as one of their company's most critical assets, yet continue to eschew measuring and managing it as one, are doomed to continue having underperforming information assets. It may mean underperforming businesses as well."

USING SENSOR NETWORKS TO MAKE THE INVISIBLE VISIBLE

The notion that the entire world can be measured and described with numbers may be as old as the Greek philosopher Pythagoras, but until recently we lacked the means to measure *everything* with sufficient precision to be useful. Today we find ourselves on the brink of that fascinating possibility.

It's an axiom of business management that whatever is measured can be improved: for the better part of a century, business managers have been measuring what they could, optimizing where they can, and taking an educated guess at the rest of the operation. There remained a big gap between theory and practice. But that's changing fast with the introduction of cheap sensors, ever-more powerful microprocessors, and always-on wireless connectivity. The combination of these low-cost components makes it possible to measure millions, even billions, of micro-actions that were previously unrecorded. Data analysis tools make it possible to convert that information instantly into useful charts and gauges that provide a vivid visualization of those millions of actions.

This new information brings clarity to business management decisions that were previously based on murky perceptions or pure gut instinct. Measuring exactly the number of cars that drive past two particular parcels of real estate each day helps tell a developer which is the better location for a new shopping center. Counting precisely the number of coho salmon that escape upstream to spawn each day helps the boards of the Alaska Department of Fish and Game manage stocks in the coastal fisheries. Recording the level

133

of pH in the water surrounding coral reefs constantly provides evidence of the impact of climate change on undersea life.

Sensors are everywhere today: on oceangoing buoys to measure ocean current, temperature, and even sub-sea seismic activity; on cattle to measure location and temperature, even bovine methane-gas releases (I am not making this up!); and in Asian airports to measure the body temperature of passengers to spot the outbreak of severe acute respiratory syndrome (SARS) and other communicable diseases.

We are gradually moving into an era in which everything that can be measured will be. What's driving this change is the combined impact of Moore's law and Metcalfe's law on the technology for data collection. As we've seen with semiconductors, computer memory, and other computer components, Moore's law tells us that as demand rises, the prices don't rise; instead, they fall dramatically even as the performance increases. In other words, sensors will continue to become smarter, smaller, more energy efficient, and cheap enough that they will be deployed everywhere. And Metcalfe's law tells us that as these tiny devices are connected, the value of the entire network of deployed sensors will continue to grow exponentially as more are added.

Measuring everything means optimizing everything. With real-time data, firms can lower their costs, eliminate inefficiency, reduce spoilage, and deliver products where they are most needed in a timely way. However, Big Data isn't exclusively for Big Business. The law of increasing returns means that the first company to enter a category has an unprecedented opportunity to achieve a winner-take-all effect. How is your company positioned? There's plenty of opportunity in data for feisty startup companies.

How SteadyServ is using data and smart devices to reinvent brewing
The prospect of measuring what was previously unmeasurable opens up unexplored terrain. That's the kind of opportunity ideally suited to nimble startups that don't have a legacy business to defend. For imaginative entrepreneurs, vast networks of cheap sensors will give them x-ray vision akin to a comic book superhero, the ability to see what was previously invisible. That's an insanely unfair first-mover advantage. Such x-ray vision makes it

possible to find opportunities in even the oldest, most traditional industries. Even in a truly ancient industry like brewing.

Apart from the addition of stainless steel brewing vats, the process of brewing beer hasn't changed much in the past 1,000 years. And yet Steve Hershberger, a technology entrepreneur who built systems for tracking industrial manufacturing and distribution, uncovered an opportunity in the beverage industry. As a hobby, Hershberger once invested in a micro-brewery based in his hometown of Indianapolis, Indiana. From the outset he applied the tech-geek discipline of measuring everything: borrowing from his experience in Silicon Valley, Hershberger developed a set of key performance indicators (KPIs) for the brewery to track every measurable aspect of the brewing process.

As the fledgling brewery began to win awards and prosper, Steve shifted his attention to the distribution business. He wanted to learn about the data systems used by the beer distributors and their customers. He was mildly stunned to realize that there were no such systems in the entire beverage industry. Zilch. Zip. Nada. What Steve learned about the beverage business was shocking to an info-tech geek.

How does a bartender know how much beer is left in a keg? He lifts the metal canister by one edge, swirls the contents inside, and makes his best wild-ass guess. Sometimes the bartender guesses right and sometimes he is wrong: if he's wrong, the bar will run out of a popular brew on a busy night. Unhappy patrons won't stick around for another round. Multiplied across the 500,000 bars in the United States, this rudimentary technique leads to billions of dollars of lost income.

How does a beverage company find out which beers customers are ordering? Today it sends college students equipped with clipboards and pencils to ask patrons in bars. It's hard to imagine a less reliable source of information for a mature $100 billion industry than the alcohol-saturated memories of a partying crowd after happy hour.

The beverage and hospitality industries lacked a system for tracking the consumption of draft beer in real time. To Hershberger this was a golden opportunity to apply everything he knew about information technology to the ancient brewing business. In 2012 he started a new company called SteadyServ.

To solve the data problem in the beverage industry, SteadyServ created a product called iKeg that consists of a metal ring loaded with sensors and a wireless transmitter. The ring is attached to the bottom of a keg of beer and provides a steady stream of information based on the weight and pressure changes. The information is relayed wirelessly to SteadyServ's cloud, where it is converted into usable structured data. This information is then streamed to specialized mobile apps designed to optimize decision-making all the way through the brewing value chain:

> SteadyServ's mobile apps enable a bartender to keep track of all of the inventory in-house and order fresh beer with a single touch on the screen.
> Another app alerts the distributor automatically when a keg is nearly empty, thereby ensuring that a replacement will be on the delivery truck.
> The app for bar owners enables the proprietor to monitor the sales—by the glass, in real time—of every keg of beer in-house.
> A single integrated data feed in the app allows bar owners who manage several establishments to manage them all remotely, so they can compare the performance of one bar against another.
> More broadly, the aggregate data generated across all participating bars in a given city or region can provide beverage marketers and distributors with useful insight into breaking trends in different regions, even neighborhoods.

Ultimately, brewers will be able to use the data generated by SteadyServ to test and fine-tune marketing campaigns and promotions and to improve their product lineup.

The SteadyServ story is a microcosm of the Big Data trend that is sweeping across every mature manufacturing business in the world. Entrepreneurs in every field are using connected sensors to discover and analyze new fields of information, converting it from random data smog into useable insight to drive old-school manufacturing and distribution companies to greater efficiency.

With SteadyServ, Steve Hershberger developed a new technological tool to collect data that allowed him to run his business more efficiently. This isn't the only way that a traditional business can develop a proprietary data asset. In some cases, no invention is necessary: the data that can transform your business and give you a critical competitive edge in the Vaporized Economy might already be in your pocket. But you need to figure out how to unlock it and utilize it before your competitors do it first.

WHAT GOOGLE KNOWS

In its quest to organize the world's information, Google has scoured vast troves of data to amass the greatest accumulation of information assets on the planet, including the billions of search queries on google.com and YouTube and the billions of interactions on Android, the dominant operating system for most mobile devices. Google also controls an ever-growing index of the world's websites and the browsing history of more than 2 billion users, three types of maps of the Earth's surface and traffic patterns, a real-time list of trending topics, the largest archive of discussions in Usenet groups, the entire contents of 20 million books, a huge collection of photographs, the largest collection of video on the planet, the largest online email repository, even the largest archive of DNA data.

As the leading information company in the world, Google is converting its entire Internet business to a data platform. Google's audacious goal of organizing the world's information means converting more and more of the activity, resources, and systems on the planet into data. Google, more than any company, is driving towards the Vaporized Economy. It has no choice. As Internet usage on mobile devices soar ahead of desktop or laptop computer access to the Web, Google's core business of desktop search and advertising is in jeopardy.

The company is banking on data, converting its entire collection of Web and mobile properties to a unified platform to capture information created by users. To accelerate that process, Google announced at its I/O conference in June 2014 a suite of APIs to enable third-party developers to write applications on top of Google services. Simultaneously, Google reportedly shuffled more than 1,000 workers from the Google+ social network to focus on mobile apps built upon Android and Google services-as-a-platform. The move to jettison G+, Google's lame clone of Facebook, and convert its entire suite of services into a platform, suggests that the company intends to leapfrog Facebook's social graph by creating a Total Information Graph. Call it the Everything Graph.

This strategy builds on an earlier decision in January 2012, when Google integrated all user accounts and merged more than seventy different privacy systems into a single unified system. Now users no longer need to sign into YouTube or Gmail: they simply sign into Google to gain access to huge swaths of the Internet. Any mobile device running Android is automatically logged into Google. Ditto for computers running Chrome OS. Just logging in to Gmail, YouTube, or Google Maps personalizes those services for the user.

During daily use of the Internet, it's almost impossible to avoid being tracked by the search giant. Robert Epstein, a senior research psychologist at the American Institute for Behavioral Research and Technology, wrote a column for US News & World Report entitled "Google's Gotcha," in which he inventoried fifteen ways that Google tracks users online, including:

> Android operating system for smartphones
> Behavior predictive analytics
> Gmail, the world's largest email provider which keeps a copy of every message received, sent, and deleted
> Google AdWords and AdSense ad-serving systems
> Google Analytics, the most widely used system for tracking visitor behavior on the Internet, now used by 55 percent of the most-visited 10,000 websites
> Google Chrome browser
> Google Glass augmented-reality system
> Google Maps

> Google Search, which completes nearly 12 billion search requests each month
> Google Street View, which gathers 360-degree images from streets and trails around the world and occasionally hoovers up data from nearby Wi-Fi networks
> Google+ social network and communications platform
> The Google blacklist of dangerous websites that other search engines refer to before they display the results of individual queries
> Widgets
> YouTube

Epstein's list is impressive but it's not comprehensive. He doesn't include:

> Blogger, which was acquired in 2003 and now hosts an estimated 35 percent of the world's blogs
> DoubleClick, the massive advertising network that is present on one-third of the world's websites. It leads the pack in the controversial practice of inserting cookies on browsers to track users as they roam the Web.
> Google Checkout, the original online payment processing program that has now been replaced by Google Wallet
> Google Docs, the suite of cloud-based productivity tools that enable groups to collaborate and share documents
> Google Drive, which collaborators can use to archive and store documents
> Google Now, the amazing smartphone app that knows where users are going and can make recommendations based on its prediction of what they will do when they arrive
> Google Talk (gTalk), the instant messaging feature in Gmail
> Google Voice, the online voicemail/phone management system
> Google Chrome operating system, which runs on laptop computers and keeps track of every click
> Google+ Hangouts, the instant messaging and video-conferencing service

> Picasa, which allows users to view and edit photos online
> The cloud backup service for Android devices, which stores Wi-Fi passwords and data from third-party apps
> Your last known location, previously recorded in an app called Google Latitude, which was phased out and replaced by Google+ Location in 2013
> Your location history, which is recorded from mobile devices that run the Android operating system

Use of these services provides Google with unmatched insight into the habits of hundreds of millions of individual Web users. Once a user logs into Google, all search queries are recorded in Google Web History. Even when a user is not logged in, the pages visited are recorded by Web cookies and that information is gathered by Google Analytics and AdSense. Today more than 10 million websites, including 55 percent of the top 10,000, use Google Analytics. Moreover, Google records every visit to YouTube: what was watched, what was searched, and what channels were subscribed to. As users roam across the Web from one Google-owned service or device to another, the company's understanding of our behaviors and preferences continues to grow. If knowledge about user behavior and habits is a strategic advantage in digital media, we can conclude that Google has achieved knowledge supremacy.

Google's use of the data is guided by three core principles, as Peter Fleischer, the company's global privacy counsel, explained to *Computer World* in 2009: "We don't sell it. We don't collect it without permission. We don't use it to serve ads without permission." However, most people have only a dim understanding of the trove of data that the Internet giant has amassed. Google classifies everything it knows about us into two distinct categories: user-generated content and server log data. Personal content created by users, such as email messages in Gmail, can be managed by a user who logs into his or her account settings. But the server log data, which is collected from the cookies embedded in a computer's browser, is not accessible or even visible to end users. This information includes the time and date of web page requests, Internet protocol (IP) addresses, the Internet service provider that connects an individual computer to the Web, the unique hypertext transmission protocol (HTTP) cookies inserted in the browser, and more. Google doesn't consider this information to be personally identifiable (although others contend it can be). Google also asserts that server log data is never combined with personal information.

In the two years since Robert Epstein's article was published, Google has amassed several new ways to track us—even in the non-digital world—via a series of strategic acquisitions. On average, it acquires one company a week. We'll learn more about some of these in Chapter 7.

Google has also launched an ambitious series of projects to enable high-speed Internet access in various regions around the world, which further extends its reach and its ability to collect more data. For example:

> Fi is Google's new mobile phone service in the United States. Referred to as a mobile virtual network operator (MVNO), Google won't own the actual cell towers and spectrum but instead will operate virtually by leasing capacity on Sprint and T-Mobile's networks.
> Google Fiber is deploying gigabit-speed Internet access to thirty-four cities in the United States.
> Project Link provides broadband service via fiber-optic networks in Africa.
> Project Loon places high-altitude balloons in the stratosphere to bring Wi-Fi to remote and rural parts of the Southern Hemisphere. Google also acquired Titan Aerospace, a manufacturer of unmanned solar-powered drone aircraft, to deliver Internet connectivity from the skies in conjunction with Project Loon.
> And, in 2014, Google announced a $1 billion program to provide Internet access to unwired areas of the world via a fleet of 180 low-orbit satellites.

As the next two billion consumers in various corners of the globe access the Internet, Google has positioned itself to serve as the world's onramp to broadband Internet as well as the operating system, browser, email, search engine, video and photo site, map provider, and one-stop shopping-and-travel portal. Analysts predict that Google will be in a position to track some or all of the activity of 90 percent of the people online, and now Google is in the process of extending its tracking capabilities into the home and on to the streets.

Epstein points out that we can never erase our digital footprints. Google scans the content of our email, our web searches, our map searches, our social sharing, every click and scroll on its browser and two operating systems.

The company doesn't deny it. On the contrary, Google executives boast about it. As Eric Schmidt, Google's chief executive officer, said to *The Atlantic* magazine in September 2010: "With your permission, you give us more information about you, about your friends, and we can improve the quality of our searches. We don't need you to type at all. We know where you are. We know where you've been. We can more or less know what you're thinking about."

ASK YOURSELF
> What is your proprietary data asset? When you consider your company's approach to generating information, would you describe it as a "data geyser" or a "content sink"?
> Can you describe transactions in your field as a kind of graph? What types of data are generated around each transaction? How might you unlock the value of the information that is generated in your company's graph?
> How does your company track data to improve performance?
> How does your company account for the value of data assets?

7

SMART THINGS AND THE DATA LAYER

EVERYTHING THAT CAN BE
CONNECTED WILL BE

I n 2013, a new buzzword gained currency in the technology world: the Internet of Things (IoT). The term first began to circulate widely in 2007 when companies such as Cisco Systems, SAP, and General Electric started to use it in their marketing materials to describe smart appliances that can talk to each other. Thanks to the plummeting costs of chips and connectivity, microprocessors will be added to every conceivable product in the next five years. And then smart devices of all sorts, ranging from wearable computers to smart cars to smart TVs, will find their way into our lives, improving them and making life richer, easier, and more entertaining. At least, that's what it says in the brochure.

In this chapter we'll take a look at some of the strategies and competitive dynamics that will influence the rollout of the IoT. The leading Internet companies are vying against the makers of consumer electronics and cars for platform hegemony. Once again, it's a winner-take-all game and there are bound to be a few sharp elbows and a jab or two thrown.

From a consumer standpoint, everyday life is about to get strange or amazing, depending upon how comfortable you are with devices that talk back. Our appliances are about to wake up. They will recognize us. We will encounter responsive screens in stores that light up to offer instant real-time rewards and promotions tailored to our shopping habits. Data about our presence will be collected and transmitted from one device to another as we move about on our daily errands. At home our networked devices will communicate silently to each other, optimizing energy consumption and adjusting automatically to our presence, alerting us only when there is an unusual pattern in our physical health or safety.

In businesses as disparate as health care, manufacturing, and transportation, smart machines will monitor the consumption of resources, the disposal of waste, and the overall well-being of the system, whether it is the human body or an industrial plant. At least that's the vision. What could possibly go wrong?

ERASING THE BOUNDARY BETWEEN DIGITAL AND REAL

The Information Age used to be confined to a computer screen connected to a broadband pipeline. Then it leaped to a smartphone connected to a mobile data network. Now it's everywhere. Today information exists in a vaporized state much like atmosphere, surrounding us. And thanks to oddly named wireless protocols like Bluetooth, ZigBee, Z-Wave, near field communication (NFC), and more, the increasing data smog generated by any type of motion or activity will no longer be lost; it will be captured, organized, and analyzed. The by-product of interaction with smart devices is information, and plenty of it.

For the past twenty years, we have shuttled between two separate dimensions: online and offline. That is about to change. Mobile data already infuses the flavor of Internet into every routine of our daily lives. Soon the Internet of Things will siphon data from every fixture in our homes and workplaces and suck it back up to the cloud for storage. No longer a separate destination, the Internet is expanding into an unseen dimension that is everywhere at once, a vaporous overlay on top of the physical world.

Security expert Bruce Schneier observed that surveillance is the business model of the Internet. Quite soon that business model will extend far beyond the confines of the personal computer into the real world around us. Soon the persistent tracking, profiling, and hypertargeting that are fundamental to the business of the Web will become a normal background condition in the gym, the kitchen, the car, and in our city streets, malls, and shopping centers.

Data is a big business, and the Internet of Things opens up a huge new trove of bits to be mined. During the next five years, the biggest trend in durable products and consumer electronics will be the addition of intelligence in the form of a microprocessor and wireless connectivity. Every product, appliance, vehicle, garment, accessory, building, sign, streetlight, pallet, shipping container, storage bin, warehouse, railroad car, vessel, and package that can possibly be connected to a digital network will be. Every interaction will be tracked and recorded and sent to the cloud for storage.

When that occurs, the usual dynamics of the Vaporized Ecosystem will come into play, but this time the conflict will occur in staid old manufacturing industries instead of in the cutthroat computer and mobile phone sectors. Entire product categories will be reinvented, mature businesses will be upended, and new entrants will dominate.

> Closed proprietary systems will be pitted against open systems
> Corporations will struggle to maintain ecosystem hegemony
> New competitors will enter the market, spurring innovation
> Entirely new use cases will emerge
> An entirely new data asset will be defined

THE REINVENTION OF FORMS AND FUNCTIONS

Consider the humble lightbulb. Thomas Edison didn't invent it, but he did perfect it. At least, he improved it sufficiently to sell lightbulbs in huge quantities. He did such a good job that the industry named the lightbulb after him. The whole world settled on the screw-in bulb as a standard, and it hasn't changed much since his time. In fact, the standard Edison lightbulb is so commonplace that it is a punch line. The reason lightbulb jokes are considered even slightly funny is that they depend on a universal constant that everybody is familiar with: the same bulb is screwed into the same socket in every fixture in every building. The incandescent bulb has been around so long in exactly the same form that we take it entirely for granted.

Today the lightbulb is changing fast. As Noah Horowitz, a senior scientist in the Natural Resources Defense Council's energy program, wrote on his blog, "We've seen more innovation in the lighting space in the past three years than in the past 125, when the incandescent was invented." Why? In late 2007 then–US President George W. Bush signed into law a bill that passed with bipartisan support in Congress to establish energy efficiency standards for lightbulbs. By 2012 new lightbulbs were required to use 30 percent less energy than the classic Edison-style lightbulb. The law specified a target, but it did not specify any particular technology. This spurred innovation: a diverse range of competing formats emerged to meet the new standard, including compact fluorescent lights (CFLs), improved incandescents, efficient halogens, and light-emitting diodes (LEDs).

Of these formats, LEDs emerged as the most versatile of the bunch. They come in a range of hues, from warm "soft" color to bluer daylight tones, and in a range of brightness. They consume one-sixth the energy used by the classic incandescent lights to generate comparable lumens. They last a lot longer too, up to 50,000 hours. That's fifty times longer than the old-fashioned bulbs. According to the US Department of Energy, LEDs have the potential to reduce US lighting energy usage by nearly one-half.

Initially, LEDs were designed in the same sizes and shapes as the classic Edison bulbs, the better to fit into the 4 billion screw-type sockets already installed in fixtures across the United States. Other LED bulbs are designed to resemble standard spotlights, reflectors in recessed lighting, candles for chandeliers, globes, sticks, and even spirals like CFLs for specialty fixtures. But shoehorning a cluster of LEDs into an old-fashioned form is not the optimal way to use them. That's a transitional step.

Bulbs are necessary for the older incandescents and fluorescents because they rely upon chemical reactions between gases and heated filaments to generate light. That reaction occurs in a vacuum, which can only happen in an enclosed space, and that enclosure must be translucent to emit light. Hence the glass bulb. Light-emitting diode bulbs are different. They don't rely on chemical reactions to generate light, so they don't need a bulb. They don't even need glass. Moreover, LEDs don't generate very much heat: that's a sharp contrast to the old Edison bulbs that lose 90 percent of their energy as heat waste, not light. No heat means that LEDs are cool to the touch, which makes them not only safer but far more versatile than the delicate glass-encased gas-and-filament bulbs could ever be.

By 2010 LEDs began to evolve away from the traditional bulb forms. Some LEDs are produced in long strips, rolled like baling wire, for use under kitchen cabinets; others are freeform resin sculptures in natural shapes like trees and geometric shapes. They can be found in wickless, cordless, flameless candles; and huge flat LED wall panels provide a kind of luminous wallpaper that absorbs sound and provides an ambient glow. The result is an interior designer's delight. In the past five years it has also become common to illuminate places where Edison-style bulbs could never fit. Light-emitting diodes are embedded inside plastic weatherproof containers for patio plants, woven into illuminated garments for pop music stars like Christina Aguilera and Katy Perry, attached to safety vests for construction workers, and incorporated into a lighting safety system for horses called, naturally, Tail Lights. Designer Ben Kokes has even created two titanium wedding rings with diamonds that are backlit by LEDs when the happy couple clasps hands.

The LED is changing the illumination industry so swiftly that the term "lightbulb" may eventually fade from use. Just as the phrase "broken record" is meaningless to a Millennial raised on streaming music, the corny lightbulb joke won't be funny in the future—if it ever was—because lightbulbs will soon be an artifact of a bygone industrial era.

There are so many different LED shapes emerging that an industry group known as Zhaga Consortium has been formed to bring some uniformity to the components by specifying interchangeable parts from different manufacturers around the world. The specifications, known as "books," describe light engines in a range of shapes, from rings and circles to rectangles and strips, but no bulbs. Electric light is breaking free of its Victorian-era constraints.

THE TRANSFORMATION OF PHYSICAL PRODUCTS TO DIGITAL SERVICES

New shapes and uses are not the only changes brought by LEDs. That's just the first tiny step towards an even broader transformation. Designers are in the process of using LEDs to redefine the entire concept of illumination. It's the boldest move since the rural electrification programs that began in the 1930s.

Light-emitting diodes are semiconductors that use a computing technology known as solid state, which means that the devices are built entirely from solid materials as opposed to earlier vacuum tubes. Think of LEDs as miniature computers. Just like any other computer, LEDs can be programmed and networked. The old output of the Edison bulb, *light,* has been transformed into *digital content.* What this means is that we can do things with light that we never imagined before. Consider these examples:

> The Color Up lamp from PEGA Design & Engineering takes advantage of LEDs' ability to render millions of colors. With Color Up, users can use a scanner built right into the base of the fixture to sample a swatch of color from any surface, including candlelight or flame. Then the light will glow in that hue.

> Fos by Erogear is a wearable LED light patch for cyclists and kids who go clubbing that consists of a flexible Velcro-lined patch. It can be applied to any garment or wrapped around a wrist or leg and paired with a smartphone to display streaming video at sixty frames per second. You'd look good dressed in YouTube!

> Anime bicycle lights from ANIPOV turn bicycle wheels into illuminated motion sculptures that can be programmed to display animation and moving messages. It's graffiti in motion, written with light on air.

> The GalaxyDress by CuteCircuit is a prototype on display at the Museum of Science and Industry Chicago. It combines 24,000 LEDs with 4,000 Swarovski crystals to form a lightweight flowing surface for

full-motion video. Thanks to the fact that LEDs don't generate excess heat, this video ball gown is cool to the touch and only requires a few iPod batteries to light up.

This transformation of light into digital content lets manufacturers shift from making low-margin physical products to offering higher-margin services with recurring revenue. Home users might subscribe to or purchase downloadable software programs for lights. Or, as wags put it, it's an opportunity to turn a $1 lightbulb into a $100 service. Flexible, programmable, and personalized products are proof that lighting has become a part of the Vaporized Ecosystem.

In 2012 Philips introduced one of the most comprehensive IoT lighting systems for home use. It included a set of software tools to create novel applications right on top of its Hue lighting system. Now developers from all over the world are adding value to the entire platform by teaching light some new tricks:

> **Light as listener:** Hue Remote replaces the control software supplied by Philips and enables consumers to control the lights in their house via voice command on the iPhone app.

> **Light as paintbrush:** The Switches for Hue app builds upon Philips' concept of "light recipes" by allowing users to record preferences and settings for individually defined situations.

> **Light as decoration:** Goldee allows customers to calibrate the lights in their home to specific tones in a digital photo.

> **Light as messenger:** The Philips Smart Hue channel makes it easy to create a recipe to change the LED color based on a news event, such as a favorite sports team scoring a goal. Similarly, lights can be set to change color to alert customers when a text message or notification arrives on their smartphone.

> **Light as wake-up call:** f.lux software lets customers program the lights in their home to replicate the color progression of a sunrise, so that they can wake up to simulated dawn.

149

> **Light as mood:** Ambilight connects the lights in a house via smartphone to a Philips TV so users can sync the color of the lights with the lighting on a television show or movie displayed onscreen.
> **Light as DJ:** Ambify analyzes the music in an individual playlist, matching the customer's lights to the rhythm.

Other apps link the Hue lights to home telephones, thermometers, weather reports, alarm clocks, and just about any other gizmo imaginable.

The Philips Hue example shows us that a broad and diverse group of programmers will concoct more ways to make use of the system than the original product designers could possibly envision.

As we've seen in Chapters 4 and 5, the company that manages a software ecosystem must place a high priority on attracting developers and encouraging them to write apps that make novel use of the device. Companies that lavish support and attention on their developers tend to prosper.

Adding software controls to any hardware system is risky because it introduces the possibility of a bug or a hacker attack, a malicious programmer writing malware, or an incompetent programmer inadvertently inflicting damage on the system. This risk is managed by providing developers with application programming interfaces (APIs) that limit their access to certain data and system commands but do not permit them to access or manipulate the rest of the system. The API is like a buffer or a protective barrier that enables innovation without inviting chaos.

One side benefit of providing a rich set of APIs to a large pool of developers is that it introduces competition, which always spurs innovation. By opening up the smart device this way, manufacturers will turn old products into a platform for innovation. In turn, new uses create fresh opportunities to improve the product. The most successful companies in IoT will be those that are able to engage constructively with third-party app developers, maintaining the integrity of their systems without exerting excessive control over the imagination and creativity of the developers.

ILLUMINATING BROADER INTERNET OF THINGS
OPPORTUNITIES AND ISSUES

Machine-to-machine (M2M) communication enables automation based on the interaction of smart devices that talk to each other in the background without human supervision. Once these systems are set up, they shouldn't require any further human interaction. Smart lights will know when a connected car enters or leaves the garage, and turn on or off accordingly. When a user turns on her smart home theater system, it will instruct the lights in the room to dim. When the smoke alarm goes off, it will wake up the lights in the house automatically.

M2M is not limited to home appliances. It will also transform equipment installed in public spaces and industrial sites. For example, Luminous Carpets, a collaboration between Philips and Italian carpet maker Desso, consists of super-thin LED panels installed beneath special industrial-grade carpet tiles that are designed to transmit light. The hidden lights can be programmed via a smartphone or tablet to display signage, guides, personalized messages for visitors, and even animation.

An even bigger transformation is underway across the entire urban landscape. Big cities manage tens of thousands of streetlights, and they find LEDs appealing for their lower maintenance and long-term cost savings. Los Angeles is midway through converting 215,000 streetlights to LEDs, a $57-million project that should save more than $53 million a year on electricity. Similar projects are underway in San Jose, San Diego, Chattanooga, Newark, Detroit, and in Buenos Aires, Madrid, and Copenhagen. But smart lights are not just about saving money. The connected lamppost does double duty in the Vaporized Era. By switching to LED streetlights, the city government can introduce some new services, such as blanketing the city in free wireless technology (Wi-Fi), hiding ugly mobile telecom antennae, offering free electric car chargers, and other amenities. Urban streetlights are likely to emerge as one of the most important components of the Smart City of the future because they connect directly to the city power grid, unlike municipal plumbing, sewage, or other systems.

Each streetlight will become a node on a citywide network, and it will serve as a communication hub for a host of networked devices in the vicinity. Author and artist Douglas Coupland has proposed a concept called the V-Pole, which is designed to include hidden antennae for several mobile carriers, a Wi-Fi hotspot, and a touchscreen for parking payment. The V-Pole can even provide wireless inductive charging for electric vehicles. Philips and Ericsson have also designed a similar multi-function lamppost.

Municipal law enforcement and public safety departments are eyeing the new smart lampposts for their own purposes. They hope to add remote monitoring equipment, such as sensors to track sound, motion, weather, smoke, or fire that will notify emergency crews when an incident occurs. Smart equipment can also report on its own condition, streamlining routine maintenance. Such a system could also monitor nearby parking spaces, providing updates to mobile apps that guide drivers to the nearest open spot.

The smart streetlight will make the city self-aware. In addition to providing better mobile phone and wireless data coverage, the system will improve public safety and traffic management without the average citizen even noticing. Most urbanites will take the improved connectivity and smoother traffic for granted and remain blissfully oblivious to the monitoring.

Where consumers probably *will* notice this new, sentient environment is in retail settings. The store is about to wake up too.

TOWARDS SMARTER RETAIL

Until recently, retail stores were shut out of the digital and mobile revolutions because their owners split the physical businesses away from the digital channels. However, rapid innovation in e-commerce and digital marketing lured shoppers out of the brick-and-mortar store onto the Internet. Now, after ten years of punishment from Amazon and other online retailers, the big national chain stores are finally striking back. Thanks to mobile and smart in-store devices, they are fighting fire with fire, co-opting techniques pioneered by online merchants and applying them in their stores.

By 2011 retailers in the shopping meccas of Singapore and Hong Kong were feeling the impact of the smartphone. They were in a full-blown panic about the phenomenon of "showrooming," the term for using a smartphone while in a shopping center to find better deals online. To the store owners' horror, their best customers were comparing prices on a retail website while they were standing inside the shop. In Singapore the trend reached crisis proportions: more than half the customers were seen showrooming inside the lavish boutiques along Orchard Road.

At the time I met with a number of Asian retail and shopping center executives at the MIPIM (Marché international des professionels de l'immobilier) Asia conference in Hong Kong and in a series of follow-up meetings in Asia and Europe. They were plainly furious about showrooming and wanted to know what they could do to fend off the looming threat of e-commerce. Like every big incumbent, the Asian retailers began by exploring the defensive options: legal counterstrikes against online merchants, new regulations, even the possibility of installing special shielding to prevent mobile signals from penetrating the walls of the store. None of these defensive moves would actually solve the problem, I explained, and most of my audience knew it. At best, they felt they might be able to buy themselves some time by slowing down the advance of the e-commerce merchants.

Defense is never the winning stratagem but it sure beats denial. The truly fatal blunder is to dismiss the threat of online commerce as insignificant or pretend it's not happening. That's the approach that Borders bookstore took in the US in the late 1990s. Borders' management felt that the skill of mer-chandising and selling books online was not necessarily a core expertise for a retailer, so it chose the best partner it could find to manage its presence: Amazon. Oops, wrong move. Today Amazon is the world's largest bookstore. Borders no longer exists.

Denial in the face of an existential threat is a surefire way to destroy a business. Today fewer companies make a blunder of this magnitude, but many still underestimate the potential of feisty startup companies to rearrange the strategic landscape. Sometimes they deal with the challenge by appointing a digital czar or digital SWAT team to contend with the threat, but that rarely works either. Trying to contain an existential threat by dumping the problem on somebody else's desk doesn't work. Dismissing or underestimating the threat is just another form of denial.

The first step in dealing with digital transformation is to recognize that understanding technology is everyone's responsibility, not the job of a small under-resourced digital team. Lots of companies still rely on what is known as multi-channel marketing, which means splitting the digital channels (mobile, online, email) from the brick-and-mortar channel. In the Vaporized Era this strategy backfires because digital information doesn't respect those boundaries. It just flows around them. A better approach is to integrate digital technology in every place that the customer expects it, which is an approach called omni-channel marketing. Easier said than done, it requires every department in the company to develop digital skills and to collaborate to ensure that the customer gets a uniformly satisfying experience at every step. How can you transform your business?

Enhancing the in-store experience

The key question for retailers is: what are you great at? Or, better yet, what are you *unreasonably* great at? If the answer is "low prices" or "product selection," it's easy to predict that digital rivals with superior data collection, dynamic pricing, and unlimited shelf space will vaporize your business. My advice is to expand the playing field. Do not attempt to compete against the e-commerce giants on their own terms. If the plan is to do business in person, then offer more than price and selection. Retailers must excel at service and in-store experience, which means focusing on ambiance and fun, product knowledge, and easy returns. They must also find a way to gain a data advantage that offsets the tracking capability of online merchants.

People won't give up shopping in stores. That's almost considered a basic human right in consumer society! But it's easy to shop online. Households will subscribe to staple items delivered painlessly to the home, which means people will require a more compelling reason to leave their homes to visit brick-and-mortar stores. If retailers can't win on convenience, then they'll need to focus on experience and expertise. Shopping in person must become a pleasure trip, or an opportunity for in-depth investigation about a complex product.

The next question is: how might retailers use digital technology to improve the in-store experience? This question demands a shift in attitude. Store owners must cultivate an understanding of technology as a way to build relationships rather than seeing it purely as a competitive threat. Moreover, they need to make room for digital experiences right inside the store itself instead of trying to block the technology. The same principles apply to restaurants, banks, hair salons, and tourist attractions—any business with physical premises.

Consider the following tactics to reinvent retail for the Vaporized Era:

> **Check-ins:** Instead of tracking consumers without permission inside the store or shopping center, why not provide instant coupons, sweepstakes, concierge service, and other goodies to shoppers who voluntarily check in when they arrive on premises? Most grocery chains already have a loyalty card. Why not turn it into a virtual rewards program?

> **Digital delights:** Digital technology can give shoppers a rare jolt of amazement. Hologram mannequins, in-store robot assistants, and interactive displays are one way to add digital bedazzlement. A further step is to network the experience. In Asia, several fashion retailers are experimenting with "social media mirrors" that consist of a video camera and a wall-sized digital display. The shopper can see how she looks wearing a variety of virtual outfits, and with just one click pair her phone to the display and share the image with friends on Facebook. The shopper gets social validation from her friends and the retailer collects demographic data from her social graph shared by Facebook.

> **Gamelike experiences:** Simple game mechanics such as hunting for hidden treasure, collecting items, and trying to displace current "winners" can be applied to retail shopping. These strategies are familiar to the hundreds of millions of people who play social games and they give retailers a tool to drive shoppers to low-traffic areas and test the effectiveness of different displays and different offers. Plus it can be fun for

customers to win prizes and points. A host of startup companies, like Shopkick, are pioneering this approach.

> **Mobile stores:** The boldest idea is to turn the brick-and-mortar store into information and put it where the customer is. We've seen pop-up stores, where sellers lease a short-term space, offer a limited amount of stock to customers, and close the store once they've sold out of their product. In 2011, UK supermarket giant Tesco vaporized that concept. Seeking to expand the number of retail outlets for its Homeplus subsidiary, which is the second-largest retailer in South Korea, it set up a virtual shop inside subway stations and bus stops. Homeplus pasted life-sized photos of store shelves and full-scale product displays right on the station walls. Commuters used the Homeplus mobile app to scan the photo of the merchandise they needed. When the shoppers arrived at their destination, the goods were delivered to them. Homeplus crushed it: online sales jumped 130 percent and the number of registered app users increased 76 percent in the first year.

Harvesting ambient data inside the retail store

The National Retail Federation is the world's largest retail trade association and its exhibition in New York City is known simply as The Big Show. It's where industry leaders and retailers network and where nearly every vendor of technology, including Microsoft, Intel, IBM, Oracle, Adobe, Google, Honeywell, Hewlett-Packard, Samsung, and Qualcomm, now sells sophisticated systems that could turn a big-box store into something like a 3D version of a website. The same data analytics that webmasters have long enjoyed on the Internet are now available to retail chains to apply to traffic in their physical stores.

As I walked around the show just two years after my meeting with the executives at MIPIM Asia, I couldn't believe how much the retail landscape had changed. The list of exhibitors included smaller firms, such as Applied Predictive Technologies, Computer Generated Solutions, Datalogic, and Network Engineering Technologies, whose names made it very clear that they were on a mission to haul old-school retailers into the high-tech twenty-first century.

Their technologies offer a lot of digital goodies to help retailers track who is in their store, who comes in frequently, and who is leaving disappointed. Among the strategies retailers can choose from are:

> **Superior data collection** about shoppers, including the ability to track the unique media access control (MAC) address and service set identification (SSID) numbers in mobile devices. By cross-referencing this information with cash register data, a mobile phone can be matched to a credit card with 99 percent accuracy after two purchases. The upshot: stores will be able to recognize their best customers the moment they step on the premises.

> **Emotion tracking technology** that can read the facial expressions of shoppers, measuring expressions labeled "delight," "joy," "contempt," and "anger." All of this data hints at what the typical customer service rep copes with in stores. Now it can be captured, analyzed, and used to improve the store. This information will provide feedback to help retailers fine-tune their physical environments to their customers' satisfaction.

> **Facial recognition technology** that identifies known shoplifters when they return to the premises or recognizes preferred customers, VIPs, and also celebrities. The information is provided to security staff who discretely escort the shoplifters out and provide special attention to the celebrities.

> **Beacons,** small wireless transmitters that can send a signal to "wake up" an app on a customer's iPhone while she is browsing inside the store. When the beacons ping the phone, a notification will be displayed, reminding the customer to use the app. Beacons are valuable because they add contextual awareness to a mobile phone and provide retailers with a way to integrate their mobile apps tightly into the retail context in order to initiate a dialog with consumers *inside the store*. Beacons allow retailers to obtain data about their customers and personalize the in-store experience: for example, they can sync with robot sales clerks or in-store displays to offer an incentive or reward, guide shoppers to a particular display, or link to mobile payment systems such as Apple Pay.

Beacon technology is rolling out now in US shops. *BI Intelligence,* a market research service, estimates that beacons will influence up to $44 billion of retail transactions by 2016. There will be 3.5 million beacons installed in US stores by 2018. What consumers won't be told is that every time they use a mobile app to respond to a notification sent by a beacon, they release information about their identity, their location, their behavior, and their shopping habits to the retailer.

Whether customers embrace real-world tracking or push back against it will depend on how gracefully retailers introduce the technology. Early attempts to scoop up data without permission from shoppers failed: in 2012 Nordstrom yanked Euclid tracking technology from its stores in response to frantic customer complaints about spying. I've been told anecdotally by vendors as well as by the chief technology officers at two major retailers that every major retail chain has tested such systems without disclosing this fact to patrons. Intelligence about customer behavior is now considered essential just to remain competitive with online shopping sites that record every visit, page view, click, and purchase. And yet no brick-and-mortar retailer is willing to go on the record about tracking because they are terrified of consumer backlash.

What's necessary is a set of guidelines for best behavior. For this reason, I invested in the Wireless Registry, a startup venture that builds software that lets consumers manage their opt-in and opt-out preferences for smartphone tracking. Working with the Future of Privacy Forum, a think tank in Washington, DC, the Wireless Registry managed to persuade the eleven leading vendors of in-retail tracking systems to adhere to a code of conduct. Being able to opt in is the key to consumer acceptance. According to research conducted by Swirl Networks, a beacon-marketing platform, 75 percent of shoppers surveyed said that beacon-triggered content would increase the likelihood of a purchase while they were in the store, and 61 percent said that a personalized message would encourage them to return to the store. However, retailers must proceed with caution since consumer concerns about surveillance are justified.

SURVEILLANCE SOCIETY AND THE OPT-IN PANOPTICON

In the next decade, several Internet of Things initiatives will converge to provide the technological foundation to enable our identity and movements to be monitored, tracked, recorded, and archived in such a way that they can be easily retrieved for subsequent comparison and analysis. A combination of six converging trends will usher us into a brave new world in which most devices on the street and in the home will constantly record human activity:

> Mobile phones, especially smartphones open to Wi-Fi networks
> Global Positioning System (GPS) and other location-tracking technology in mobile devices
> Ever-smaller high-resolution security cameras and web cameras
> Facial recognition, gait recognition, license plate tracking, and other personally identifiable tracking technology used in public spaces by law-enforcement agencies
> Life logging, face tagging, and photo sharing on social networks
> Surveillance systems deployed at massive scale by national intelligence agencies

Some of this surveillance will occur with our consent, some of it will take place without permission, and most of it will remain unnoticed by those observed.

By 2025, it is likely that most (or perhaps all!) of human activity in urban centers will be recorded with a degree of precision that is very difficult to imagine today. One reason this notion is hard to accept is that it reverses the experience our grandparents had during the previous century of migration from rural areas to cities. Their experience fostered the conviction that cities are zones of anonymity. Ubiquitous surveillance technology in our time will betray those convictions.

Much has been made of the intrusions into and erosion of personal privacy in the digital domain. We know that the intelligence services of many countries conduct mass-scale electronic surveillance on private communication by citizens. We know that major banks aggregate data about consumer purchase habits and sell it to marketers, big retail chains, and manufacturers. We know the Federal Communications Commission fined telecommunications giants Verizon and AT&T for breaking the rules on handling consumer data. And we know that Experian has partnered with Facebook, combining the giant credit reporting agency's information about financial records, property ownership, credit, and vehicle leases, with the social media network's data about sexual preferences, relationship status, travel, and hobbies to provide sophisticated customer targeting. Everyone, it seems, is in a rush to vacuum up our personal data.

Several observers, notably journalist Glenn Greenwald in his TED talk "Why Privacy Matters," have drawn the parallel to the Panopticon, an invention by a peculiar eighteenth-century social reformer named Jeremy Bentham, whose preserved body is on display in a wooden cabinet at University College London. Bentham's invention was proposed as a humane alternative to the brutal punishments of the British penal code in the early 1800s. In Bentham's view, miscreants would modify their own behavior if they were confined in a circular prison with a tower in the center. No prisoner could be certain when a guard might be watching from the central tower and therefore, Bentham surmised, they would all conform to what they presumed the invisible watchers would expect. This model prison was known as the Panopticon.

What observers like Greenwald find so objectionable about this type of prison is the psychological effect of the ubiquitous surveillance. The prisoners grow to internalize the rules and then they self-censor in order to comply. Greenwald draws a parallel to the constant surveillance of the National Security Agency (NSA) and concludes that intelligence agencies and law enforcement organizations have in effect turned the Internet into a digital Panopticon. He argues that people in digital environments have actually changed their behavior since former NSA contractor Edward Snowden released the revelations about wholesale government spying.

Critics decry the corrosive effect of such wholesale surveillance on free speech, political speech, the right to organize and formulate lawful political opposition, and the right to unconditional self-expression, that was an early hallmark of the World Wide Web. Now, most of us make no distinction between spying by intelligence agencies or marketers or social networks or data brokers. We assume this passive surveillance is a baseline condition of digital media. What's missing from this critique is the fact that this outcome is optional. If consumers preferred to place a value on their privacy, they could adjust their privacy settings, encrypt their communications, manage their passwords, or even vote for different elected officials. Few of us do those things. Instead, most of us freely post intimate details of our lives on social networks though few of us would ever tell a marketer or researcher the status of our relationships, our career, our children, nor divulge our sexual preferences, our educational and career history, or our private habits of consumption.

Most people say they would prefer private email and web-browsing sessions, but our actions speak louder. We routinely opt for the free webmail, the free browser, the free mobile app, the free social network, the free online news, the free collaboration software, the free storage, the free communications, the free photo album, the free messaging. We freely trade our privacy for convenience. Even when it comes to government spying, most of us complain but reluctantly concede that it is necessary for national security. We can't be bothered to protest, to complain to our elected representatives, or to organize to roll back the intrusions on our civil liberties. We now live in an opt-in Panopticon that we have created—and freely chosen—for ourselves.

THE INTERNET OF THINGS WILL PROBABLY WIN US OVER IN THE END

Given the degree to which people are already subject to tracking in both the real world and digital media, it's probable that there won't be an armed insurrection when IoT blends real-world devices together with digital media. The success or failure of IoT will depend mostly upon execution. How much value will we get in exchange for revealing the intimate truth about our habits at home, in the bathroom, in the living room, and in the car? If consumers feel they are getting sufficient benefit from the devices, they'll trade away data and accept a measure of constant surveillance. In fact, we may come to expect and even welcome life in an interactive world because of the convenience and optimization it will offer us.

A thorough process of reinvention is underway now across many very different product categories. This transformation is at the core of many currently trendy marketing concepts promoted by the high-tech industry, including smart homes, smart cars, and smart cities.

> Smartwatches, smart jewels, and other wearable gizmos are conditioning us to the perception of computers-as-accessories that record body data such as sweat, pulse, and temperature.
> The Quantified Self movement recontextualizes the human body as an information field to be mined. Already, Fitbit and other fitness wearables give us feedback about how many calories we burn on a run, how many steps we climb, how many miles we walk.
> Networked home appliances, kitchen gadgets, and climate control systems will transform the old deaf-and-dumb house into a smart home that monitors the stability and performance of these systems, conforming to our habits and alerting us when there is a problem.
> Connected cars will transform the automobile from mere transportation to a mobile computing platform that records our street-level activity and builds a prediction model about our local travel habits.
> Medical technology is swiftly moving towards "insideables" and "implantables" that will enable physicians to detect individual illness sooner, and harvest health trends from a large cross-section of the population who consent to share anonymized data.
> Responsive outdoor signage, billboards, and posters will welcome us to a responsive urban environment.

What unifies all of these disparate marketing and infrastructure programs is that they tend to involve the same general tactics, namely embedding a miniature computer inside of a familiar product to enable new functionality and then offering a mobile app to connect, communicate, manage, and personalize it. Whether it is a car or a refrigerator or a drill, every smart device will have an Internet protocol (IP) layer and they will all connect to some form of network, either a local wireless network or the Internet in order to track, record, and respond to ambient conditions. The really smart companies will work with developers to build a set of applications on top of the smart infrastructure.

Consumer expectations are shifting. We are becoming accustomed to interacting with the inanimate objects around us and soon we will depend on their intelligence. We will come to expect a measure of interactivity in our retail shopping centers, malls, arenas, and public spaces.

HOW TO TRANSFORM AN OLD INDUSTRY

If you sell a physical product or operate a physical location, this is the time to make it smart. The field is wide open for the moment. You know what to do. Begin with an old product in need of an update. Add a microprocessor, a microcontroller, memory, plus some sensors to track what is happening in the environment around the product. Then connect the whole ensemble to the network.

By combining sensors, connectivity, and computing power with an old product, something seemingly magical happens. The device wakes up and starts telling the network about itself. Data that was previously frozen in the rigid structure of the physical product can now be extracted and sent up to the cloud, where it can be used as the raw material for entirely new businesses. It's not automatic, nor is it magic. Somebody must do the work of telling the device what to do. That's a software project. And it's a big one.

To succeed in the Internet of Things, your company must have a clear software strategy. That means you'll need to make strategic decisions about operating systems, security procedures, partnership, and third-party developers. We can learn a lot by studying what worked—and what didn't—in the first round of IoT deployments.

The Consumer Electronics Show (CES) in Las Vegas is the largest trade show on Earth, where device makers reveal their latest gadgets and make grand predictions about the year ahead. Bullish analysts predicted that by 2020, 50 billion smart devices would be connected to the Internet. That's half a dozen for every person on the planet. At CES in 2013, manufacturers of devices large and small predicted that 2014 would be the Year of the Internet of Things. It didn't work out that way.

Unexpectedly, 2014 turned out to be the Year of the Data Breach. Malicious hackers and foreign agents managed to break into the databases of major companies and purloin data on consumers in record numbers. According to Experian, 47 percent of US companies experienced a data breach that year. USA Today reported that 500 million financial records were stolen in a twelve-month period, exposing the personal financial details of more than half of the adults in the US. Mass hacking attacks occurred in corporate networks managed by Sony Pictures, Target, Home Depot, J.P. Morgan, and many others. And in the background, Snowden's revelations continuously reminded news agencies that the National Security Agency (NSA) and the intelligence agencies from the UK, Canada, New Zealand, and Australia were hoovering up as much of our private correspondence and personal data as they possibly could.

For consumer electronics companies, the timing could not have been worse. After half a decade of plummeting sales and collapsing margins, they needed a win. Vaporization had struck consumer electronics especially hard: sales of cameras, DVD players, video camcorders, GPS units, and other big-ticket items plummeted when consumers migrated en masse to smartphones with features that used embedded software to replicate the functions of these devices. The Japanese electronics giants Sony, Panasonic, and Sharp that had loomed so large in the 1980s were teetering on the brink of economic collapse by 2013.

The collective hope for the consumer electronics industry was that the Internet of Things and smart devices would put them back in the game by reviving consumer interest in their hardware and restoring their profit margins. Likewise, big technology equipment vendors like Cisco Systems, Hewlett-Packard, General Electric, and Oracle were banking on IoT to spur equipment sales. Instead of rushing to the store to scoop up new gizmos, however, consumers reacted with caution. The first round of smart devices was generally perceived as expensive and underpowered.

Most of them failed to deliver sufficient utility for the price. Installation was too complex, and most devices did not play nicely with each other. After three decades of personal tech, most consumers understood that Generation 1.0 of any new device category was likely to disappoint. Better to wait until version 2.0 or, better, 3.0, which will be faster, smaller, cheaper, and better.

Many shoppers also questioned why they needed more networked devices in the home and why these devices needed to record and upload so much information. There were very few good answers to these questions. The IoT was off to a questionable start.

Sales varied from promising to feeble, but no device stood out as a breakaway "must-have" home-run product. By 2015 not a single wearable, smartwatch, or smart gadget had established anything close to the kind of grip on the public imagination that Apple and Google had achieved with smartphones and tablets. Worse, the series of massive data breaches in 2014 had raised serious questions about whether the consumer electronics industry was approaching the Internet of Things with sufficient attention towards security and consumer privacy.

At the CES in January 2015, Edith Ramirez, the chair of the Federal Trade Commission, voiced a grave concern to device manufacturers about implementing better security in connected devices. "In the not too distant future, many, if not most, aspects of our everyday lives will be digitally observed and stored. That data trove will contain a wealth of revealing information that, when patched together, will present a deeply personal and startlingly complete picture of each of us . . . I question the notion that we must put sensitive consumer data at risk on the off-chance that a company might someday discover a valuable use for the information."

Ramirez also chastised the device makers for failing to disclose their practices on handling consumer privacy and managing troves of personal data. "Will your TV-viewing habits be shared with prospective employers or universities?" she asked. "Will they be shared with data brokers, who will put those nuggets together with information collected by your parking lot security gate, your heart monitor, and your smartphone? And will this information be used to paint a picture of you that you will not see but that others will—people who might make decisions about whether you are shown ads for organic food or junk food, where your call to customer service is routed, and what offers of credit and other products you receive?"

OVERCOMING SECURITY AND PRIVACY CONCERNS

There is no doubt that the first generation of IoT devices left a lot to be desired. *Slate* published an article with the title "Pretty Much Every Smart Home Device You Can Think of Has Been Hacked." Hackers just need to find one vulnerability to compromise the whole network. Increasingly, IoT and smart devices look like the weakest link in the smart home. After all, many devices ship from the manufacturer with the exact same default password and no easy way to change it. Many devices offer no easy way to access security patches and software updates.

Against the background of hacking scandals and NSA intrusions, consumers are correct to be cautious. The complaints and concerns about IoT are useful market signals that tell manufacturers what issues need to be addressed in order to succeed. There are six big issues that the IoT companies must address.

1. Poor implementation of privacy-protection features, including unencrypted transmission of data from the device to the cloud.
2. Vulnerability to malicious hacking and intrusions by bumbling amateurs known as "script kiddies."
3. Incompatibility and non-interoperability of software between devices from different manufacturers and competing alliances.
4. Proprietary systems, which will lead to "orphaned" devices that are no longer supported by software updates, instead of open-source software.
5. Barriers to easily downloading and installing software upgrades or security patches.
6. Lack of clear documentation about where the data gathered from the device is stored or how long it is kept.

Some of these issues are in the process of being fixed, but it's also true that millions of devices being sold right now have serious vulnerabilities. Some of the companies making these early products will be acquired or go out of business or they may simply stop supporting the early models. And when that happens, there will be millions of orphan products left running in people's homes, just waiting for hackers to take advantage of any security flaw that remains unpatched.

The lack of interoperability and open standards mean that there will be a lot of dead-end products. At present, no fewer than three industry consortia are duking it out for supremacy and it will take years for the IoT industry to settle on a common standard. In the meantime, millions of devices will be sold. If the software for these devices were open sourced, at least the developer community could take over writing the patches when those products are no longer supported. For proprietary software, however, there's no way to get support once the manufacturer sunsets the product. The prospect of millions of zombie devices running on home networks is a security time bomb.

One of the problems that consumers are just finally beginning to understand is that we don't really own our smart devices and IoT gadgets. At least, we don't own them the way we own a book or a wrench. When we buy a smart thing, we may own the hardware but we don't own the software. We are granted a license to use it. That's different from ownership. It's more like renting. Amazon can remove a title from the Kindle. Apple can force a download of a U2 song whether we want it or not. Every company pushes out software updates until it decides to turn off support for the product, and then it dies. Attempting to modify the device in some way that the manufacturer doesn't condone can result in it being disabled remotely, or "bricked." Unlike a book or a wrench, we can't do anything with these devices once this happens. They simply cease to function.

In the future smart TVs, smart fridges, smart lightbulbs, smart thermostats will all work this way. Consumers will own them until the company decides to stop supporting them. And then we're out in the cold. Bruce Sterling, in his darkly funny book *The Epic Struggle of the Internet of Things,* described the future this way: "Politically speaking, the relationship of the reader to the Internet of Things is not democratic. It's not even capitalistic. It's a new thing. It's digital-feudalism."

WHO CONTROLS THE DATA LAYER?

The struggle for control in the Internet of Things is not really about the Things. It's not even about controlling operating systems or app stores or developer programs. It's about data. Specifically, it is about control of a new layer of data that lies just above the device.

In the first round of vaporization, entire products like movies and cameras and calculators were turned into software. In the latest round, the physical devices still exist but they've been neutered, rendered subordinate to the layer of data that connects them to the cloud. Once that connection is severed, they no longer function properly.

Don't believe me? Consider this. Right now, many people with sub-prime credit scores below 640 can't buy a car unless it comes with a starter interrupt kit. If they are one day late with a single payment, the car shuts itself off completely. It's like a self-repossessing car. It's also dangerous. Sometimes the car shuts off automatically while driving on the freeway. About 2 million vehicles have this device installed. All Internet of Things devices will work like that because the data layer is the ultimate value control point.

While the big consumer electronics companies thrashed and flailed in a privacy and security stew of their own creation at CES 2015, Apple and Google waited and watched. The two smartphone giants were in a prime position to win the IoT sweepstakes simply by letting the consumer electronics companies self-destruct. In the previous year, Apple and Google had each announced a series of initiatives that were carefully calibrated to extend their software ecosystems into every category of smart things, including connected cars, smart devices, health care technology, and wearables.

Unlike the device manufacturers that compete with each other in narrow product categories, Apple and Google aim to span the entire field of devices with a layer of software that reinforces their grip on consumers as they migrate from device to device. By the end of 2014, both Apple and

Google had divulged plans that shared one simple goal: to make the smart-phone the center of the IoT landscape.

Strategies between the two giants differ because each company makes money in a different way. Apple is most profitable from selling its own devices, especially the iPhone, whereas Google makes its profit from selling precision-advertising campaigns informed by Big Data. Google's free Android operating system is typically installed on devices made and sold by other companies, from which it collects data about location, searches, web-browsing history, and voice commands. However, both companies seek to increase the value of the mobile devices at the center of their ecosystems by connecting them to as many other devices as possible.

Neither company necessarily needs to manufacture the whole range of IoT devices: they can accomplish much of the objective simply by offering software toolkits to help manufacturers produce devices that are compatible with the iOS or Android smartphones. The more devices that are connected, the more user data, metadata, and customer loyalty will be siphoned off that hardware by Google and Apple at the expense of the device manufacturers.

The intense competition between old manufacturers and Internet giants will spur the process of change forward. And it will bring the competitive dynamics and strategies of the Vaporized Ecosystem into every industry.

TOOLKITS FOR THE INTERNET OF THINGS THAT PUT SMARTPHONES IN THE MIDDLE

Both Apple and Google have moved aggressively into IoT by offering soft-ware suites, tools, and application programming interfaces (APIs) in the most lucrative categories:

> **Health care and fitness:** Apple is aiming for the health care field with HealthKit and ResearchKit, while Google Fit is aimed more towards fitness and diet apps, which grew 62 percent in 2014, according to Flurry, a mobile analytics company. In 2011 Google shut down its health initiative after only three years because it failed to gain widespread adoption.

> **Home automation and smart devices:** Midway through 2014, Apple announced the HomeKit API for partner companies to build lighting, heating and cooling, security cameras, and other home systems that interface with Apple devices. Google's approach was to acquire Nest Labs, the maker of smart thermostats and smoke detectors, for $3.2 billion. Nest has subsequently acquired security system maker Dropcam and home-automation hub maker Revolv. In 2014 Nest Labs announced that more than 5,000 developers and device makers expressed interest in adopting the Nest API.

> **Automotive:** Apple and Google entered the auto industry via the dashboard. Apple's CarPlay and Google's Android Auto provided connected entertainment and information systems. In 2015, the data information company IHS expects 1.4 million cars to have CarPlay installed, and 1.1 million will have Android Auto. By 2020, these figures are expected to rise to 37 and 40 million, respectively.

> **Retail and payments:** In the five months after Apple introduced Apple Pay, the number of stores that accept this contactless mobile payment system tripled to 700,000 retailer locations in the US. Apple Pay also connects to more than 2,500 card-issuing banks. Moreover, the publicity around the Apple Pay launch seems to have rekindled interest in other mobile payment systems: Google Wallet reported a 50 percent increase in user activity since the Apple Pay launch. Beacons are compatible with any smartphone, but the triangle formed by Apple's iBeacon, iPhone, and Apple Pay will work seamlessly for a superior consumer experience.

Google's long struggle to gain a foothold in mobile payment may finally be gaining traction now that the company has acquired the assets of a rival venture that launched with the unfortunate name Isis. As part of the acquisition deal, the newly-rechristened Android Pay will ship pre-loaded on all phones sold in the US by AT&T, Verizon, and T-Mobile. Google Wallet will remain as a peer-to-peer payment app while Android Pay will compete with Apple's point of sale contactless payment system.

Across these many diverse industries, we are about to see the same strategy repeated as each individual device maker attempts to solve the same dilemma: will the company attempt to build or buy its own software and foster its own ecosystem, or will it join the existing ecosystems dominated by Apple, Google, and other tech giants? Apple will make hardware that commands the fierce loyalty of fans, and most device makers will be tempted to make their products compatible. And Google will continue to provide free operating systems to get device makers hooked on its ecosystem. Google's insight about mobile phones and other smart devices is that they are not just tiny supercomputers. They are also packed with sensors to harvest ambient data from daily use in many locations. For Google it makes sense to give away the operating system in order to gain control of the data layer.

HOW WILL YOU ENTER THE INTERNET OF THINGS?

Manufacturers of lightbulbs, cars, and smart devices of all sorts face a tough choice. Neither option is very appealing.

Option 1: Build your own operating system for your smart devices, launch your own app store and developer network, and attempt to grow an ecosystem from scratch.

Option 2: Drink the Kool-Aid, bite the bullet, walk the plank. Accept Google Android or Apple iOS, become a part of their feudal society, join their massive developer networks, and commit your fate to the ecosystem.

Many hardware companies have attempted Option 1, but nearly all of them fail. Software is hard for hardware companies. It's very difficult to develop and launch and grow an operating system. When I worked as head of digital media for Sony Pictures Entertainment in the late 1990s, I was surprised to learn that a team in one of Sony's legendary Shinagawa research laboratories under the esteemed Mario Tokoro was developing an operating system called Aperios. It was an incredibly ambitious project: an object-oriented reduced instruction set computing (RISC) architecture that would improve performance in smart devices. But for all its virtues, Aperios failed to catch on: it was only installed on a single TV set-top box and in the artificial intelligence AIBO robot pet. Not one of Sony's hardware divisions used it. Not the TV group nor the PlayStation group, not the mobile phone unit nor the handheld game group. Not even the personal computer group. They chose instead to live under the hegemony of Microsoft Windows instead of taking the risk of launching a new ecosystem from scratch. Worse, distracted by this aspect of software development, Sony missed the rise of MP3 entirely, leaving the portable music field that it created with the Walkman wide open to Apple's iPod.

The disastrous experience in 2014 of IoT companies—releasing buggy, insecure, barely functioning software—illustrates the peril of attempting to "roll your own" operating system, especially if it is proprietary. A closed system is often fouled by a lethal stew of malicious attacks, mischief, incompetence, and greed. Although a company may eventually patch the security holes, seal up the vulnerabilities, and make the software more reliable, it won't solve the interoperability problem singlehandedly. As we already know from the smartphone war that crushed Nokia, devices with small app marketplaces and fledgling developer ecosystems tend to get steamrollered by devices with larger ecosystems.

Option 2 is no picnic, either. Once a company accepts Apple's or Google's operating system, it loses control of the customer experience and tends to become just another generic device maker. Apple and Google offer two different flavors of the same bad choice.

Doing business with Apple is tough because you give up a lot of control over your destiny. Apple's strategy is to commoditize complementary products in the iOS ecosystem. Recall that profit margins on content and apps were crushed in the App Dictatorship in order to drive up the value of Apple hardware, especially the iPhone. Something similar is at work in IoT. For makers of smart devices, partnering with Apple means subjecting their products to the ever-expanding iOS ecosystem. They gain access to the world's richest and biggest ecosystem of developers and legions of fanatical Apple loyalists, but by relying on an iPhone app to serve as the remote control for their products, they give up the ability to define their own branded user experience. Ultimately, such products are destined to become faceless appliances subordinate to an Apple device.

Google commoditized its own operating system (OS) in order to thwart Microsoft and other competing OS providers such as Palm and Research In Motion. By making Android free, open, and ubiquitous, Google destroyed the value in the operating system as a business. That's a boon to manufacturers whose biggest item on the bill of goods was formerly the license fee paid to Microsoft. But it comes with a catch. While Google gives the OS away free to manufacturers, they are obliged to install Google apps and set Google as the default search engine, and place the Google Play Store and search icons prominently on the homepage. Of course, manufacturers can (and some do) choose to use the open-source version of Android to build their own custom operating system, but then they will find themselves right back in Option 1 with a small developer network. Not even Amazon has been entirely successful with that strategy on its Fire tablets and smartphones.

THE SMARTWATCH SCENARIO

In the emerging smartwatch category, Apple may eventually sell 20 to 30 million smartwatches annually. All of the producers of Swiss watches together sold only 29 million watches in 2014.

Swiss watchmakers are now boxed in. For decades, they focused on brand and a luxury image without focusing on new technology. When the first smartwatches (not Apple's) were introduced, they were dismissed as underpowered and ugly. But the Swiss watchmakers failed to take prompt action. What they missed is what most incumbents miss. Apple and the other technology companies are not interested in wristwatches per se. The Internet giants look at the wrist as real estate, and they are stunned that the watchmakers have done so little to develop such desirable parcel.

Apple and the other smartphone makers see the wrist as territory that is ripe for colonization. Initially their smartwatches will be underpowered accessories for the smartphone. Over time, however, given miniaturization and the enduring magic of Moore's law, those smartwatches may someday evolve into a substitute for full-featured phones.

As for the Swiss watchmakers, it's far too late to flip their hardware business into a software business. Most of them will fail to develop an ecosystem for software. As Elmar Mock, one of the inventors of the Swatch in the 1980s, told *Bloomberg Businessweek*, Apple's entry "will put a lot of pressure on the traditional watch industry and jobs in Switzerland." There are only two moves left to the Swiss watchmakers: compete against Apple by fostering their own fledgling software ecosystem, or retreat upscale into ultra-high-price luxury, just as the digital camera makers did when the smartphone vaporized cheap compact cameras. Low-end watches will be vaporized.

Traditional watchmakers TAG Heuer, Montblanc, and Swatch Group have all announced that they will launch their own versions of a smartwatch in 2015. Those who persist in the attempt to develop their own software will find the temptation to adopt Google's software and ecosystem increasingly appealing when they face the onslaught of competition with Apple.

THE CONNECTED CAR SCENARIO

Sales of cars connected to Apple and Google's entertainment systems are growing ten times faster than the overall auto market. Seventy-five percent of the 92 million cars sold in 2020 will be connected, according to market analysis by BI *Intelligence*. This is a mixed blessing for the automakers. Like the watchmakers, they will face a tough choice. They may choose to partner with Apple or Google, or they will attempt to launch their own software system for in-car apps and entertainment. As of this book's publication, fifteen auto manufacturers had adopted Apple's CarPlay system, and more than twenty carmakers, including General Motors, Audi, Honda, and Hyundai have adopted Android Auto.

Some carmakers, including Ford Motor Company and Fiat Chrysler, will choose to offer both systems. Previously, both companies had developed their own in-car entertainment and sync systems for smartphones, but the negative feedback from consumers drove them to adopt both Google and Apple solutions and abandon their own.

Today, most automakers believe that they have firewalled Apple and Google away from the critical systems that manage the performance of the automobile. Forty automakers, including Audi, BMW, Chrysler, Ford, General Motors, Honda, Mercedes, Toyota, and Volkswagen, took the unusual step of licensing an alternative OS called QNX from BlackBerry, the ailing smart-phone pioneer. The QNX operating system plays nicely with Apple and Android software for personal entertainment in the car, but it keeps those systems at arm's length from automotive functions. The automakers' strategy depends greatly upon BlackBerry's continued independence, which is far from certain. In other words, the auto industry is just one strategic acquisition away from becoming dependent upon Google, Apple, or another tech giant that might swoop in and acquire QNX, jettisoning the rest of BlackBerry the way Google did with Motorola. If that seems unlikely, consider that Apple has $194 billion in cash on hand. That's enough to buy 483 of the S&P 500 companies. Apple could buy Tesla ($25 billion) and Amazon ($134 billion) and still have billions left over.

The entertainment systems from Apple and Google may be the thin end of a wedge. Gradually, as drivers grow accustomed to the user interface and personalization offered by Google and Apple in the dashboard, consumers may develop a preference for these richer experiences. At that point, carmakers will be unable to rip either system out. They'll be hooked. Once the Internet companies gain a beachhead in the car, they will naturally seek to expand.

Later, in the mid-2020s, when robot vehicles finally become commercially viable, Google's and Apple's grip on the in-car experience might be strong enough to enable either firm to ram the fat end of the wedge into the vehicle, sliding a layer of proprietary software between the hardware of the car and the apps, content, and passenger experience of an autonomous vehicle, just as Microsoft did with the PC. At that point, cars will become less about driving and more about riding passively and using mobile apps. If this happens, Ford, General Motors, and Volkswagen may begin to resemble the former consumer electronics giants Panasonic, Sharp, and Sony. Or Compaq, Dell, and HP, the bygone leaders from the PC industry. Or like Nokia, Motorola, and Ericsson, to compare the carmakers to the vanquished colossi of the mobile phone industry. The Internet companies will attempt to steal the value right out of the automotive industry by controlling the data layer in the car, leaving Detroit stuck with the low-margin metal, leather, and rubber.

In the meantime, Silicon Valley tech firms are already cranking up the competitive pressure, recruiting talent from Detroit automakers. Apple has hired more than 200 people to work on an electric car project called Titan. And Google has already demonstrated its own version of an autonomous vehicle that will debut in prototype form on the streets of Mountain View, California, in summer 2015. The fact that Silicon Valley is working on vehicles is enough to keep future-minded Detroit executives awake at night.

ASK YOURSELF

> If your company produces products, how might these be transformed by the addition of computer power and network connectivity?

> How might a third-party developer enhance your smart product with an app?

> How might a broad deployment of your smart products be connected into a smart network? How will that change usage? How might that generate new value or new business opportunities? Who else might benefit from participating?

> What is your company's policy regarding consumer data? How big a priority is this for your firm? Does your company conduct routine security audits on your software products? Are they resistant to tampering, hacking, and data interception?

> Who controls the data layer in your industry?

8

THE RISE OF THE PEER-TO-PEER ECONOMY

EVERYTHING THAT CAN BE DECENTRALIZED WILL BE

The vaporized concept is just a metaphor, and every metaphor breaks at some point. It's always instructive to find out where. I recognize that certain things will never be replaced by software—for example, we all need buildings and food, bridges, and vehicles—which is why the motto is not "Everything will be vaporized," but rather "Whatever can be vaporized will be."

REINVENTING OWNERSHIP WITH ON-DEMAND MOBILE SERVICES

Uber is the textbook example of a vaporized enterprise. This car-sharing company, which was founded in 2009, doesn't own any physical assets: no cars, no garages, no drivers on staff. Yet, without owning a single car, Uber manages to provide transportation to millions of customers by leveraging the thousands of cars that have already been purchased by private drivers. In 300 cities around the globe, customers now simply pull out their smartphones and order a car and driver via the Uber app. Within seconds, they are reviewing bids from nearby drivers who have enrolled in the Uber network. One click later and the driver is on her way to pick up a fare. It's so effortless that everyone who uses Uber for the first time has the same reaction: "Why didn't somebody invent this ages ago?"

Uber is not just a ride-sharing service, however: it is vaporizing car ownership. In just five years, according to the company's blog, each Uber driver has removed nine cars from the road. The US reached peak car ownership in 2006, when the ratio of cars to licensed drivers reached 1.156, but the economic crisis of 2008 and the migration away from suburbs and back into cities have changed attitudes towards ownership. Uber makes "access instead of ownership" preferable in many cases because of three factors that have aligned: a) a critical mass of smartphones that are always connected via wireless broadband that can link passengers with drivers anywhere at any time, b) Internet software platforms that extend real-time transactions, mapping, and dynamic pricing to mobile phones to enable transactions in the real world, and c) an available pool of people with cars who are looking for work.

Uber represents the most prominent of a new class of companies sometimes referred to by ungainly acronyms such as ODMS (for "on-demand mobile services") or AEMs (for "app-enabled marketplaces"). These designations are cumbersome because they strive to combine three distinct concepts that are the heart of our vaporized theme: mobile, market, and services.

> **Mobile:** The smartphone in a purse or pocket is the remote control that summons the service instantly, whenever and wherever it's needed. The app in the phone is completely different from a service designed for a static desktop computer. It takes advantage of all the communications and sensors built into the phone: Global Positioning System (GPS) technology, text messaging, dynamic maps, mobile apps, and dynamic updating. No matter where a customer happens to be, as long as he or she is standing in a city where Uber operates, a car will find and come to a pre-arranged spot.

> **Market:** Instead of a limited number of drivers on the payroll, Uber offers access to a much wider pool of providers who work when and where they want to. In cities like San Francisco and New York, Uber offers a larger pool of drivers than the local taxi services combined. And

Uber's app provides the consumer with better information about each driver, so that a more informed choice can be made.

> **Services:** Uber replaces car ownership with access to transportation on demand at a competitive price. It turns transportation into a service instead of a durable product.

Compare the Uber experience to the typical taxi experience in North America, and it's no surprise that Uber is insanely popular. In many nations, the taxis are clean but expensive. But in the US, taxi service is frequently atrocious *and* expensive. To hail a taxi involves standing on a street corner, defying weather, waving a hand in the vain hope that an approaching taxi driver might see it and stop to provide a ride. In comparison, the ease of Uber's mobile app and cloud connection makes the old taxi experience feel positively medieval.

On Uber, nobody hails anything. The driver and passenger *choose each other* from a field of offers in a real-time marketplace that is constantly updated. The Uber app provides the passenger with visibility into the location of the car, the exact license number, contact information, and historical performance data for the driver, including the ability to phone or text him with a single click as he is en route to the pick-up.

Likewise, the driver gets to see the passenger's name and contact information and ratings from previous drivers. Nobody negotiates price. They don't even necessarily need to speak the same language. The customer simply gets into the car and the driver takes her to the destination she tapped into her phone. At the end of the trip, she exits the car and the driver rides off to pick up his next fare. No money is exchanged because the transaction goes from a customer's phone to Uber's central servers, where the customer's credit card is billed and the driver's account is credited.

What Uber provides is the most efficient switchboard marketplace for transportation as a service. The brilliance of this approach is that Uber doesn't really compete with taxi service. Instead, it renders taxis obsolete. Like all vaporized services, Uber simply routes around the existing incumbents to go direct to the consumer with a new proposition. A row of yellow cabs lined up at a taxi stand is a relic from the pre-smartphone era. Why stand in a queue or hail a cab on the street when it's possible to order transport on demand with one touch of the smartphone screen?

The ways Uber can be used are limited only by customer imagination. Need a ride home from an unfamiliar neighborhood? Take Uber. No cash, no wallet? Use a smartphone to pay for Uber. Need a ride from a hotel to a business meeting in an unfamiliar city? Uber. Want to indulge in an extra round of drinks without the risk of being arrested for driving under the influence? Take Uber. Need to collect the kids after a play date? Send an Uber.

A growing segment of Uber customers have come to rely upon the service so heavily that they no longer rent cars when they travel. They book an Uber driver from the airport to the hotel and meetings, then another Uber driver back to the airport. No rental counter, no gas stations, no shuttle bus, no rental contracts.

BENDING THE REAL WORLD TO CONFORM TO THE INTERNET

A lot of customers love the convenience and ease of Uber's service, but many others love to hate the company and everything it represents about the Vaporized Era. It's as if all the fear and loathing that people feel towards disruption, volatility, and tech-driven change have been distilled into a single negative impulse and projected onto an obnoxious, over-exposed company that just happens to offer a killer product.

Uber employs no drivers, yet the firm's chief executive officer boasts about job creation. All of the company's drivers are independent contractors who bring their own vehicle and bear their own expenses, including gasoline bills, and yet Uber rakes in fees on top of their property and hard work. To many people, even though Uber is making existing individual investments in car ownership more efficient, its tactics feel exploitative.

Poor communication skills don't help the company's cause. Uber's management prides itself on passion, drive, and what it refers to as "principled confrontation." To critics, those principles look more like "asshole culture," the term coined on tech blogs to describe the pugnacious and sometimes overbearing style of the new disruptors.

For example, in October 2014 several publications reported that Uber CEO Travis Kalanick demonstrated God View to journalists gathered at a reception in Chicago. God View shows the location and anonymized data of all current passengers as well as those who are waiting to be picked up. But one guest at the event, Julia Allison, claimed that company executives also demonstrated something called Creepy Stalker View, which enables Uber's executives to zero in on the location of any particular passenger—by name—in mid-trip in real time. The following month, US Senator Al Franken, the chairman of the Subcommittee on Privacy, Technology, and the Law, of the Senate Judiciary Committee, sent a formal inquiry about the incident to Kalanick.

The list of incidents and indiscretions is long. Quietly removed from the Uber corporate blog was a post called "Rides of Glory" that revealed how easily the company can track and evaluate the commuting habits of people who enjoy one-night stands. (Who knew the people of Boston were such swingers?) After harsh criticism in several publications, Uber's office in Lyon, France, issued an apology for a gratuitously sexist ad that promised a gorgeous female driver would pick up passengers who used a special code. Subsequently, a female journalist who criticized the ad was singled out by a senior vice president of the company as a possible target for retaliation. Even the CEO demonstrated bad manners, joking with a GQ journalist about a sexy new service called "Boob-er."

Many Uber customers will forgive the management's sexist remarks, they'll overlook the lack of discipline, they'll even ignore the critics, but there is one feature that generates enormous controversy among even the company's most ardent fans: surge pricing.

Here's how it works. At times of peak demand, there are not enough drivers available to satisfy all of the people who need transport. To lure more drivers out of their homes and onto the roads to pick up passengers, Uber cranks up the price: sometimes up to three or four times the normal rate. That's great news for the drivers. Unsurprisingly, customers hate it. It feels like a gouge.

In Sydney, Australia, in December 2014, demand for Uber's services soared during a hostage crisis in a downtown café. Customers wanted transportation to get away from the danger zone, and it seemed to them that Uber was exploiting the crisis for gain by cranking up prices. What these passengers failed to understand is that during times of peak demand, the alternative isn't lower prices. It's no cars at any price. Under the old taxi system, at rush hour when every driver had a passenger, there were no more cars available at all. Uber solves that scarcity problem by applying the same dynamic pricing common on Internet shopping sites to expand the supply of cars on the road. At peak times the service may be expensive, but it sure beats having to walk—or missing an appointment altogether. Uber is literally warping reality to conform to e-commerce: that ability to expand supply dynamically to meet demand is one advantage of a vaporized marketplace.

As entertaining, or dismaying, as all of the controversy around Uber and its pricing strategy may be, it is just a sideshow. In fact, what's behind the undercurrent of resentment are some deeper questions about consumer society and property ownership. Uber challenges the conventional notion of liberty and the romantic visions of the highway as an endless ribbon of freedom that have been baked into the American psyche by the auto manufacturers for three generations. Any time a startup company challenges people's beliefs about their own identities, it is bound to run into some resistance.

Uber has exposed a fault line between the old economy and the new digital economy, and its management team is gleefully dismantling our assumptions about how consumer society is supposed to work.

GROWING THE COLLABORATIVE ECONOMY

The trend towards "access instead of ownership" and the rise of on-demand markets represent two significant shifts in consumer behavior. And as Uber's success shows, it turns out that vaporizing auto ownership is an enormous opportunity. In less than six years, Uber has become one of the most valuable privately held ventures on the planet. The ballooning valuation tells the story. In an eighteen-month period, a share of stock in Uber increased in price tenfold.

On August 22, 2013, Google raised eyebrows by leading a round of investment in Uber, putting $285 million into the then-four-year-old firm, at a heady valuation of $3.8 billion. Less than one year later, on June 7, 2014, Uber announced that it had raised $1.2 billion at a valuation of $17 billion. Less than six months after that, the firm set out to raise an additional $1 billion: by February 2015 the company had expanded this Series E round to $2.8 billion at a staggering $40 billion valuation to accommodate "overwhelming demand" from such investors as China's web services company Baidu, the mutual fund giant Fidelity Investments, and the sovereign wealth fund of Qatar. From $4 billion to $40+ billion in eighteen months. That's not bad for a company with no physical assets. At the time of writing, the company was rumored to be preparing to raise more financing at a $50 billion valuation, which would make it the most valuable startup company in history.

Uber is on a roll. Kalanick sees opportunity to expand into home delivery: "If we can get you a car in five minutes, we can get you *anything* in five minutes." And given the company's skyrocking value and potential for expansion, it's not a surprise that startups are rushing out with copycat business plans. "Uber for Health Care" or "The Uber of Power Tools" or "The Uber of Grocery Shopping."

Not every business can be vaporized and replaced by an on-demand market app for the iPhone. The billion-dollar question is: which one might be next? A growing number of entrepreneurs and investors are determined to find out. They are pushing the "Uber for X" concept well past the breaking point. Here are a few examples:

> Uber clones: Lyft, Sidecar, BlaBlaCar, DriveNow
> Uber for licensed taxis: Hailo, Easy Taxi, Curb, Flywheel, mytaxi
> Uber for car sharing: Getaround, Upshift, Zipcar, Car2Go
> Uber for trucking: Cargomatic, Keychain Logistics, Traansmission
> Uber for bicycles: Spinlister, Spokefly, Bicyclette, Spotcycle, Grid Bike Share
> Uber for boats: Boatbound, Zizoo, We are on a boat, TidalWavez
> Uber for dog walking: Swifto, Trottr, Wag
> Uber for lawn mowing: GreenPal, Mowz
> Uber for house cleaning: Homejoy, Handybook, HouseCall, Tidy
> Uber for car washes: Washly, Wype

> Uber for laundry and dry cleaning: Cleanly, DashLocker, Washio, FlyCleaners, Rinse, MintLocker, Dryv
> Uber for house keys: Keys Duplicated, KeyMe
> Uber for beauty services: Swan, StyleBee, StyleSeat, GLAMSQUAD, Uber Beauty, Vênsette, Beautified, Beauty Booked, Stylisted, beGlammed
> Uber for massages: Zeel, Soothe, Unwind Me
> Uber for artwork: TurningArt, Easely
> Uber for courier services: Postmates, Zoom2u, DeliveryCrowd, Deliv, Daily Delivery, Google Express, Favor Delivery
> Uber for grocery shopping: Instacart, Good Eggs, Relay Foods
> Uber for flowers: Bloompop, BloomThat, UrbanStems
> Uber for food delivery: Fluc, Sprig, OrderUp, Zesty, Caviar, RushOrder, Bite Squad, Lish, Peach, Eat24, LABite, foodjunky, FoodNow, Foxtrot, Seamless, GrubHub, Chewse, Pi, EAT Club, DoorDash, Jolt Delivery
> Uber for marijuana delivery: Canary, Eaze, Meadow
> Uber for alcohol: Canary, Drizly, Nestdrop, Thirstie, Sauce, Minibar
> Uber for veterinarians: VetPronto
> Uber for doctor house calls: Medicast, Doctor on Demand, Pager
> Uber for personal errands: x.ai, Fetch, Fancy Hands, Zirtual, The Startup Admin, GladlyDo, TaskRabbit
> Uber for legal advice: UpCounsel, LawTrades, Legal Made Easy
> Uber for car mechanics: YourMechanic
> Uber for parking: CARMAnation, SpotHero, ZIRX, Monkey Parking
> Uber for roadside assistance: Road Angels, Urgent.ly

In a blog post on her website that cites many of these examples, Yvette Romero, an operations and strategy executive in San Francisco, estimated the market size for such services. She notes that there are two key factors that define the potential opportunity for such startups: the size of the undisrupted industry and the potential for what she calls "the convenience factor" to grow the total market size by increasing how frequently such services are used. Romero explains: "While many [of these] seem to present $100bn+ market opportunities . . . actual opportunity is derived by taking a step further in estimating % market share that can be challenged by better distribution, access, transparency, consistency, increased satisfaction via instant gratification using a platform and ease of payment, all while keeping private data private."

A tall order. As we've seen, Uber has managed to accomplish most of Romero's checklist—although even this market leader fumbled on private data. Despite the challenges, thousands of startup ventures are jockeying for position. A gold rush mentality prevails in the race to vaporize ownership.

According to Jeremiah Owyang, the founder of Crowd Companies, these peer-to-peer technologies enable people to get what they need from each other rather than from centralized institutions. It's an economic model he calls the collaborative economy and although the concept is still evolving and the business model is still a work in progress, it's growing fast. Speaking at the LeWeb conference in Paris for digital innovation, Owyang described how, in the space of a single year, this sharing economy expanded from startup ventures in six categories (Money, Goods, Food, Service, Transportation, and Space) in 2013 to twelve (the original six plus Municipal, Utilities, Corporate, Logistics, Health and Wellness, and Learning) in 2014. Dozens of companies operate in each sector, all of them providing some variant on optimizing the use of people, equipment, space, products, services, and other resources.

What's more, collaborative consumption is reshaping the nature of the corporation itself: firms now rely on peer marketplaces to hire temporary workers, on-demand delivery services, mentors for employees, even short-term executive staff. New kinds of companies require new kinds of workspace, like the co-working spaces provided by Galvanize in Denver that include conference rooms and desks-on-demand for more than 140 fast-growing startups that vary in size.

VAPORIZED FUNDRAISING AND THE DEMOCRATIZATION OF VENTURE INVESTING

At LeWeb, Jeremiah Owyang compared the amount of money invested in social media platforms to the amount invested in the collaborative economy. By his math, investor appetite for the sharing economy is at least 25 percent greater than it was for social networks. A whopping $11 billion has been invested by venture capitalists and other early-stage investors in 226 collaborative economy startups in the past fifteen years, mostly from 2010 to 2015. Even if heavyweights Uber, Airbnb, and Lyft are excluded from the analysis, the average total funding per startup in Owyang's report is an impressive $32 million.

These days, it's not just traditional investors who are financing startups. Like so many other things in the digital economy, fundraising has been vaporized too. Crowdfunding, or crowdsourced financing, is the mirror image of a P2P on-demand marketplace for used goods. Instead of matching buyers and sellers for products that have *already been purchased*, crowdfunding matches buyers and sellers for products that *don't yet exist*.

Beginning in 2008, websites like Indiegogo and then Kickstarter started to make it possible for anyone with a good product idea to raise money from fans who are so excited by the idea that they want to help bring it to reality. All it takes is a compelling product description, a statement from the founders about the makeup of the team and their operational plans, and, most important of all, a kickass concept video. Not long ago, it would have been hard to imagine that anyone would part with their hard-earned cash to buy a nonexistent product from a nonexistent company. But that's exactly what now happens every day on crowdfunding sites. Movies, video games, albums, wearables, robots, 3D printers, and a zillion other products have been funded in advance by enthusiastic supporters.

According to crowdsourcing.org, in 2010 crowdfunding raised $900 million for new product ideas. In 2011 more than $1.5 billion was raised. In 2012 that number nearly doubled to $2.7 billion. And in 2013 it nearly doubled again, to $5.1 billion. In 2014 the Crowdfunding Centre in the UK reported that 442 crowdfunding projects were launched daily around the world, collectively raising more than $60,000 an hour. According to estimates from the World Bank, the total crowdfunding market could exceed $90 billion by 2025. That's bigger than today's entire global venture capital industry, according to *Fortune* magazine.

For years, the Lean Startup gurus like Eric Ries and Steve Blank who take a scientific approach to creating and managing startups have recommended that entrepreneurs start with a customer in mind. Today crowdfunding makes it possible for any inventor with a clever product idea to do this with unprecedented ease. An entrepreneur can gather thousands of paying customers before she launches her company or begins production. This is the opposite of demand destruction described in Chapter 1. This is *demand creation* and it can be done globally or hyperlocally with crowdfunding.

In the past, the fundraising process was slow and cumbersome. An entrepreneur needed a business plan and a legally valid private placement memorandum in order to raise money from investors. Those investors demanded budgets, operating plans, product prototypes, organizational charts, and hiring plans, and sometimes evidence of revenue before they would consider putting money into the company. For an early-stage business with no funding, that's a lot to ask. Today, crowd financing means a feisty entrepreneur can bypass the investor class altogether and connect directly to end users to finance the product itself, instead of the company. It's like an inside-out startup.

Venture capitalists (VCs) have paid close attention to crowdfunding since 2008. At first some dismissed this phenomenon as taking "dumb money" from hapless consumers. Yet as the money raised doubled and doubled again, some investors began to wonder if crowdfunding might render the traditional VC process obsolete. They swiftly determined that it is a great enhancement to their due diligence process, and several VCs have begun to embrace it, insisting that any early-stage consumer proposition must be tested first via a crowdfunding campaign. This approach validates not just the product concept and the market appetite but also the team's ability to execute. However, that test is a sword that cuts two ways.

A successful crowdfunding campaign may catapult an unknown startup company to widespread awareness and momentum, thereby reducing its need to take money from any one group of investors. By holding back from the seed-stage investment, VCs risk getting sidelined altogether since crowdfunding can give entrepreneurs more bargaining power. It *is* still quite rare to see a white-hot crowdfunding campaign raise millions of dollars in thirty days, but when it happens, as it did for the Pebble smartwatch and the Oculus Rift virtual reality headset, it resets the balance of power at the negotiating table. Why accept any VC's term sheet when it's possible to raise the equivalent of an angel round plus Series A and Series B from customers via a single month-long crowdfunding campaign, and preserve all of the equity for the founders?

Crowdfunding campaigns raise on average about $7,000, so a lot of startups still find they need traditional venture financing to fund business operations while the company is growing fast. One novel solution is crowd-sourced equity financing. Instead of appealing exclusively to supportive fans to fund the first product run, startup companies can now use a similar crowdfunding approach to sell equity stakes in the firm to accredited inves-tors. This approach expands the pool of investors and, thereby, the pool of capital available, but it also makes it possible for the traditional venture capital firms to participate on an equal footing. That's the logic behind the Jumpstart Our Business Startups Act, known as the JOBS Act, which was signed into law by President Barack Obama in 2012. It is intended to democ-ratize the venture capital process and thereby direct a torrent of fresh funds for investment into startup ventures.

Faster access to capital via crowdsourced financing means more startup companies generating more new products that garner the interest of an ever-expanding pool of customers. It's a global innovation engine that is poised to reconfigure, dismantle, or bypass dozens of vast, well-established industries as these new startups attempt to emulate the template set by Uber and Airbnb, eBay and Craigslist before them. Brace yourself for a tidal wave of new ventures that follow the classic template to building their switchboard marketplaces:

> **Race to scale.** Be the biggest market of buyers and sellers in your cat-egory. Begin with more offers because more offers attract more buyers.
> **Minimize friction.** Strive for a smooth user experience that introduces the least amount of friction in the transaction while maximizing transparency.

> **Make it sticky for the seller by extracting a time commitment.** Encourage the seller to invest time and effort into building an appealing profile page with detailed descriptions, professional photographs, and other valuable metadata. This metadata is an investment in the platform. Over time, reputation ranking and user reviews will make it impossible for successful vendors to switch out of your marketplace.

> **Make it sticky for the customer by cultivating a habit.** The key to capturing all of your customer's available wallet is to focus on optimal user experience: the ease of use of the app, superior search and discovery tools, and better customer care and flawless complaint resolution. Then layer on top as many perks and bonuses, points and rewards, and special offers as you can think of to retain your best customers.

> **Lock in the market participants.** More means more in the winner-take-all dynamic. The law of increasing returns to market leaders propels one player to a dominant position. Over time, as buyers and sellers converge on the platform, both become captive to platform-switching costs imposed by learning a new user interface, establishing a new profile, and rebuilding a reputation from scratch.

> **Extract the maximum data from both parties.** Study the usage and behavior patterns of every participant carefully to glean insights about trends and to identify areas for improvement and opportunities for new offerings, expansion, and bundling.

> **Go global.** Expand like mad to as many cities as possible, as fast as possible, relying on independent contractors and fans to open new territories. Use free offers, discounts, and free trials to generate traction and word of mouth.

> **Collect credit card payment information.** Amassing the largest collection of credit card numbers on file isn't just a way to lock in users but also to evade the clutches of Apple and Amazon. Without direct access to billing information, you're just another serf living in the App Dictatorship.

We've seen this movie before, so we know how it ends. Thousands of new companies will be launched. By the time the dust settles, most will have disappeared: some will fail, some will merge or be acquired, but a few will continue to thrive. The successful companies will transform their corner of the economy. The attrition rate is high, the competition is fierce, but the rewards for the victors are great.

We're heading into uncharted territory. If P2P markets continue to expand, they will penetrate every corner of the economy of physical goods, establishing a new economic model based on access to shared resources instead of outright ownership. Incumbents will see their share of the market erode; some of them will fail. The marketers playing in this zone will earn their reputation by interacting honestly and reliably with consumers rather than by saturating them with brand-marketing campaigns. Access to slightly used high-quality products may supplant sales of newer and pricier items. This will impact advertising strategies and marketing budgets.

The throughline in all of these ventures is to increase productivity by better using our assets, whether they be shared, borrowed, rented, leased, or purchased. Most suburban homeowners have an electric drill; few of those tools are used more than once a month. That's true for many household tools, gadgets, kitchen appliances, and pieces of specialty equipment. They are underutilized. P2P marketplaces can unlock the value that is frozen in these inert products. In this scenario, we're all buyers and sellers, lenders and borrowers. What brings us together is a marketplace vaporized into a mobile app.

COLLIDING WITH RELICS OF THE INDUSTRIAL ERA

Change makes people uncomfortable. That's an axiom of our self-help era. Business managers are no exception. When confronted with technology-driven change, managers face the unpalatable choice of 1) overhauling an existing, stable, profitable enterprise to conform to unpredictable, evolving conditions, or 2) staying the course by doubling down defensively on the old business model. In either case, they run the risk of a catastrophic failure if they get it wrong. No wonder they feel uncomfortable.

Business managers hate to lose control, and this tremendous change imposed by outside forces is beyond their control. To regain some semblance of control over their destiny, some business managers choose to go on the attack. This urge is primal. It doesn't matter if they will win or lose: they just feel the urge to do something, anything, to strike back. They need someone to blame. That's why leaders of technology companies are so frequently portrayed as ruthless villains by mainstream companies under siege.

"Complaining is not a strategy," Jeff Bezos, Amazon's chief executive officer, remarked when Charlie Rose of 60 Minutes asked about the publishers who vilified him. "Amazon is not happening to bookselling," he continued. "The future is happening to bookselling."

In Uber's case, the future is happening to taxis, and those in the industry don't like it. They are fighting back with every available weapon.

Uber is routinely hassled, sanctioned, or sued in nearly every city where the company does business. Traffic came to a standstill in Chicago, Washington DC, London, Paris, Madrid, Milan, Berlin, Moscow, Bogota, Rio de Janeiro, and many other cities around the world where taxi owners went on strike to protest the launch of the Uber app. In China, fistfights broke out when taxi drivers went on strike to protest Uber and similar apps. In Amsterdam, taxi drivers attacked Uber drivers with hammers and brass knuckles. But Uber's most implacable foe is not the cab drivers: it's the taxi owners.

In every major US city lives a powerful local cartel of fleet owners who have amassed hundreds, sometimes thousands, of taxi medallions. The medallion is a tin badge issued by the city and bolted to the hood of the car. It indicates that the vehicle is legally authorized to pick up passengers who hail it from the street. By law, the supply of medallions is severely limited. North America's biggest taxi market is New York City, with more than 175 million paying trips each year. Six hundred thousand passengers per day are served by only 13,437 yellow cabs. That's 3,000 fewer licensed taxis than in 1937 when the Haas Act was introduced to regulate the taxi industry and set the maximum number of cabs at 16,900.

Artificial scarcity is bad news for consumers because it sends prices soaring and makes it impossible to find a cab at rush hour. But it's a great deal for the fleet owners. In fact, medallions in New York City are worth a cool million dollars apiece. For decades, buying a taxi medallion was the best investment decision anyone could make. Medallions outperformed every asset class in America. According to Professors Stewart Dompe and Adam C. Smith of Johnson & Wales University, the value of a New York taxi medallion doubles every four-and-a-half years. Annualized, that is a 15.5 percent rate of return.

The reason medallions grow in value is that the owner is able to rake in most of the profit each time the regulator permits fares to increase. Little of that increase is shared with the drivers, whose annual earnings of $30,000 have scarcely grown in the past decade. Nor does money get plowed back into better cars and better service. Instead, the taxi owners spend money lavishly on lobbying and litigation to preserve their cartel.

Since 2014, however, the price of taxi medallions has begun soften in New York, Chicago, and Boston. With so much unlicensed competition from Uber and Lyft, demand for medallions has begun to taper because the return on investment is no longer clear cut. That's why the War on Uber really began. With so much value at stake, taxi owners in city after city have pushed their local governments and taxi commissions into legal battles against the insurgents by filing regulatory complaints and, if those didn't goad their city officials into action, by filing lawsuits against the city. After all, the medallion owners paid dearly to buy into the regulated cartel, so they expect the government to step up and provide the enforcement they paid for.

Put bluntly, when the taxi cartels purchase a medallion, they are paying for monopoly pricing backed up by the state's power of enforcement. Ride-sharing services jeopardize the cartels' monopoly rent. To protect it, the owners are calling for a regulatory airstrike on Uber and its ilk.

Uber has been sued so many times it's hard to keep track. In the US alone, Uber has been sued by the cities of Portland, Philadelphia, Chicago, Los Angeles, San Francisco, Columbus, Orlando, and more. Taxi drivers in Boston, Chicago, and other cities have also filed suits. Uber has been banned in Nevada, Thailand, Spain, and New Delhi. In Germany, Uber has been banned twice: both times the company continued to operate in defiance of the law. The South Korean government has found Uber's CEO Travis Kalanick guilty of breach of transport law.

All of this heavy-handed blowback has not stopped Uber so far. On the contrary, it seems to backfire, generating widespread awareness through media coverage and thereby creating new customers. Every time there is a taxi strike against Uber, the company sees a spike in the number of apps downloaded, sometimes doubling or tripling its customer base in a city within a matter of days.

The company actively courts the support of passengers in new target markets with email campaigns exhorting the public to sign petitions to allow Uber to move into their city. Its corporate growth objectives are dressed up as a cause for public good, and then it uses its mobile app and social media tools to rally fans. This app-based populism cranks up the pressure on city government. The popular appeal of the Uber app, plus the fact that Uber provides transport services in distant reaches of the city where taxis are scarce, makes it very difficult for elected city managers to fight legal battles with much conviction. They are stuck between the rigid old top-down regulatory schemes of the industrial era and the fast-moving, bottom-up grassroots demands of a generation raised on smartphones.

HOW MUCH REGULATION IS TOO MUCH?

The conflicts that peer-to-peer markets like Uber and Airbnb have encountered with municipal and state governments raise a timely question about government licensing and regulation in general. Some economists decry government intervention in markets. To these critics, taxi medallions, permits, and other forms of licensing are state-enforced schemes that create barriers to job seekers, fix prices, and reduce economic liberty in labor markets. Uber and other collaborative consumption ventures present governments with a challenge: how much regulation is necessary in our hyperconnected era, and how much is that regulation worth?

Nearly one-third of US workers must obtain a license from the state. The number of jobs that require a license has risen from 5 percent in the 1950s to 29 percent today, according to Morris Kleiner, an occupational licensure expert and University of Minnesota professor. Writing on the website of the Cato Institute, a US libertarian think tank, Kleiner maintains:

"Occupational licensing is an enforced labor market monopoly that uses the police powers of the state." Licensing creates barriers to entry for laborers and drives up cost for consumers. In his research, Kleiner also found that there is often no relationship between licensing and the quality of the work.

Most people would agree that medical and pharmacy jobs and other health care work should probably be subject to a licensing requirement. But for many other professions it remains unclear why a license is even necessary, especially when the license is required in one state but not another. "License To Work," a 2012 report published by the Institute for Justice, a libertarian public interest law firm, cites a variety of such professions, ranging from interior designer, shampooer, and florist to home entertainment installer and funeral attendant, as "occupations with no self-evident rationale for licensure." Even in occupations where there is some degree of public safety risk, the training burden bears no relation to the risk. For example, the Institute for Justice report notes that "66 occupations have greater average licensure burdens than emergency medical technicians. The average cosmetologist spends 372 days in training; the average EMT only 33." The training burden for some professions is hugely inconsistent from state to state: Alaska requires a manicurist to train for three days, but other states require four or more months of training. The irrational and inconsistent nature of the licensing burden raises doubt about the need for licenses. High barriers to entry suggest that public health and safety may be less of a factor than the goal of limiting competition among practitioners.

To cynics, occupational licensing begins to resemble a protection racket run by local government, as in pay us fees, do what we say, and we'll protect you from competition. This is the exact opposite outcome from the consumer protection intended when these laws were introduced in the Progressive Era. Worse, a license is no guarantee of satisfactory service. Just because workers have completed a training program and passed an inspection doesn't automatically mean that customers will be happy with the service.

Perhaps in the 1930s the best way to inspire consumers' confidence in the services provided by strangers was to hire an army of government inspectors. Today, however, those official endorsements carry less weight because the mobile phone provides any customer with the instant ability to write a glowing report or a scathing critique of any service. Mobile review apps provide on-the-go access to ratings, rankings, recommendations, and commentary for every conceivable urban service from doctors to plumbers, from pet grooming to gastropubs. The public is just one click away from a social media rating services like Yelp, Urbanspoon, or Foursquare that provide more transparency, accountability, and details of the quality of service than any government inspection.

Clearly, we aren't going to do away with inspections entirely. Yelp can't tell us whether an aircraft has met safety requirements or that a restaurant kitchen is sanitary and rodent-free. But are there some cases in which reputation markets might replace government licensing? Again, Uber provides a useful illustration. On one level, Uber is a classic two-sided marketplace where buyers and sellers are matched, agree swiftly on price, and the business gets done. No cash changes hands. No haggling, no bargaining, no worry about meters and overcharging. But on another level, Uber is a *reputation market* where information about the behavior of participants is exchanged before entering a transaction. Because the buyer and seller both rank and review each other, all participants in the service are transparent. A surly driver can't hide on Uber. Neither can a reckless driver or a driver with a poorly maintained car. Passengers will report the negative experience using the app on their smartphone. Any driver consistently ranked below four stars is terminated by Uber.

As Mark J. Perry, an economics and finance professor at the University of Michigan, puts it in an article on the American Enterprise Institute's website: "Uber and Lyft are already very heavily regulated ride-sharing services, and in some ways they are regulated even more intensely than traditional taxis by a very ruthless group of regulators—the consumers who use their services. The issue really isn't regulated versus unregulated ride services; the issue really is who is the primary regulator: a) government bureaucrats and legislators who are often captured by the regulated taxi cartels or b) consumers. And there's no question that captured regulators almost always put the special interests of the well-organized, concentrated groups of regulated producers like the taxi cartel over the public interest of the disorganized, dispersed thousands/millions of consumers."

On the flip side, rude passengers can't hide either in a two-way reputation market. If a fare pukes in a car after a raucous night of partying, it will be reflected in the score the driver gives. After each trip, drivers post passenger scores to their version of the Uber app so that other drivers can make an informed decision before they accept a fare. Anyone who gains a reputation as an undesirable passenger might well find themselves stranded.

App-enabled P2P markets provide better information in real time to consumers and providers than industrial-era government regulations and licensing schemes. The reputation market provides a check-and-balance system to ensure quality and customer satisfaction. Every participant, buyer or seller, has a strong interest in maintaining a positive reputation, and this desire for high ratings naturally leads to an overall increase in quality and good behavior on both sides of the market. The system penalizes bad behavior and incentivizes the good.

THE VAPORIZED ECONOMY VS THE ESTABLISHMENT

As the peer economy expands into every conceivable niche, established companies in those niches will seek some form of defense. Taxi companies, hotel chains, broadcast TV networks, and other old-school firms increasingly depend upon twentieth-century laws and regulations to protect their businesses from interlopers who apply tactics honed in the digital domain to services in the real world. The battle has shifted. It's no longer digital insurgents versus old-school companies. Now it's digital insurgents versus government regulations.

Technology firms have begun to redirect their attention towards the institutions of government that thwart their progress. A basic premise of the Internet is that the signals reroute around damage in the network. Something similar is happening when tech startups encounter seemingly arbitrary licensing rules. The old-fashioned tactics of lobbying, legislation, and regulation seem like bugs instead of solutions.

So instead of disrupting companies, technologists seek to disrupt government—or render it irrelevant. They seek to deconstruct or bypass the laws, the regulatory bodies, and the central banks and centralized apparatus that governed the twentieth-century economy. They argue for the wholesale reinvention of government institutions. Cheered by taxpayer groups, techno-libertarians, and advocates for small government, and sped by a general trend of declining support for big federal programs and corporate welfare, startups from Silicon Valley have grown adept at inflaming public opinion against government handouts to big business and cartels. All of this politicking is framed in business-friendly terms: pro–free market, pro-entrepreneur, pro-capital, and pro-employment. It's high-tech populism where the insurgents are capitalists and entrepreneurs rather than revolutionaries, communists, or populists with a thirst for redistribution.

And nobody mentions that these new private marketplaces rake in 20 percent fees on every transaction, even as they supplant government and erode the local tax base.

Such resistance is part of a grand tradition of American progress: confronting laws that are out of sync with the times and calling for the removal of policies that enshrine injustice or favoritism. Supporters of the P2P markets cite philosopher John Locke, the father of classical liberalism, who espoused the principle that government is valid so long as the governed consent to be ruled. Citizens have the right to question government, and, if necessary, replace the government. Locke's writing inspired the founders of the US and every subsequent democratic revolution. His principles were enshrined in the Declaration of Independence and echoed in the US Constitution.

It may be grandiose to cast Uber and the other P2P markets in the same light as the American Revolution, civil rights, equal rights, and the labor movement. Fair enough. But Uber does fit squarely in the tradition of American entrepreneurs proceeding boldly to bring a better mousetrap to market even if the law prohibits it. This streak runs deep in American society, and it includes colorful historical figures like homesteaders, Sooners, bootleggers, moonshiners, and smugglers, all the way back to the veterans who started the Whiskey Rebellion. Laws were broken and lawbreakers were punished, but in some cases the laws were changed. For many entrepreneurs, it's worth a shot.

What's in question is the role of government in a rapidly evolving digital economy. From this viewpoint, the government moves too slowly and treads too heavily on free markets.

Is vaporized government next? Technologists are beginning to ask serious questions about the role and function of governments in the age of instantaneous communication and distributed computer power. Many functions of government could, in theory, be done cheaper, faster, and more accurately by software. This line of questioning inevitably extends beyond regulation and licensing into other government activities, and while some dismiss the concept of software supplanting governments as utopian, or technotopian, it strikes me as a mistake to dismiss the question without considering it.

As we spend more and more time and money in digital environments, we owe it to ourselves to contemplate whether the old rules that govern society in the physical world are appropriate or even relevant in this new domain. If not, we run the risk of sleepwalking into the future, dragging the old rules with us.

THE CURRENCY QUESTION

The most heavily regulated industry of all is finance and banking, and the need to maintain stable and reliable currencies ensures that government plays a large role as intermediary and arbiter. Bitcoin was designed to blow all of that infrastructure and regulation away. Cue the eye-rolling and smirking. If you're familiar with bitcoin, you probably know it as the most controversial technology startup of recent years. Or maybe you got burned as a speculator, trying to ride the rollercoaster of bitcoin's gyrating valuation.

Bitcoin was conceived of in 2008 and implemented as open-source code in 2009 as cryptocurrency, a new form of digital cash that could enable payments to be made privately via the Internet without a middleman. The system is great for people who want to bypass the mainstream banking system. In practice, in the early days, that meant the only people who needed bitcoin were those running offshore casinos or scams, or selling illicit merchandise. And a huge number of Chinese investors who had no other place to put their savings. When Chinese speculators began to accumulate huge holdings of bitcoin, the price skyrocketed from $13 to more than $1,000 per bitcoin in a single year, nearly matching the price of gold on November 29, 2013, as reported by CNN *Money*. At that point the total market capitalization for the experimental digital currency exceeded $10 billion.

And then the bitcoin bubble burst. The bubble was pricked by one disaster after another, piled upon an epic fail. In 2014 dodgy bitcoin exchanges in India, France, and the US were raided by authorities; millions of dollars of bitcoin were stolen by hackers; the owner of the Silk Road trading site for illegal goods was arrested by the Federal Bureau of Investigation (FBI); and the Chinese government prohibited banks and payment companies from dealing with it. The digital currency crashed hard, falling below $180 per coin in January 2014. By 2015 it was trading at $200 to $250, less than one-third of its 2013 high value. Cynics wrote it off as a failure: way too volatile to serve as a proper currency, too cumbersome for the average punter, and too tainted by scandal to be taken seriously.

It's tempting to dismiss bitcoin. But that would be a big mistake. Every frontier town attracts its fair share of flimflam men, con artists, and grifters, and bitcoin, operating at the fringe of the shadow economy, was no exception. A big part of the crush in 2013–14 involved clearing these bad actors from the bitcoin stage. And although 2014 was a brutal year for bitcoin currency, it also happened to be the year that venture capital firms poured record amounts of investment dollars into bitcoin startups. One way to look at the company's *annus horribilis* is as a reset: the first wave of dodgy con men were shut down and replaced by a new generation of legitimate businesses building more secure, scalable digital currency infrastructure.

Investors see a boom coming. Fred Wilson of Union Square Ventures described his rationale on his blog, AVC, by comparing the potential of bitcoin to the spectacular rise of social media in the previous decade: "Our 2004 fund was built during social. Our 2008 fund was built during social and mobile. Our 2014 fund will be built during the blockchain cycle." What do investors see that the skeptics miss?

Bitcoin was designed as a medium of value exchange between total strangers. That's different from every other type of digital transaction, which requires a trusted intermediary of one sort or another to ensure that the money flows from one account and arrives safely in the other. Bitcoin presents the possibility of frictionless transactions between individuals with no banks, no credit card companies or payment processing firms, no fees in the middle. No governments, no exchange rates, no manipulation of interest rates by central banks, and no inflation. That's potentially explosive. It is an opportunity to rethink the way transactions work on the Internet.

If bitcoin works as theorized, it matters to far more people than just the fringe players in the shadow economy. Consider any e-commerce site that deals in electronics, for instance. These companies suffer from brutal downward pressure on profit margins exerted by Amazon and the big-box stores. The 3 to 5 percent transaction fee raked off by the credit card company doesn't sound like much, but when competing against Amazon, that slim percentage might be all of the profit margin a business gets out of a transaction. No wonder 50,000 retailers now accept bitcoin.

Banking (and much more) on the blockchain

What makes bitcoin profoundly significant in the Vaporized Era is the remarkable software protocol known as the blockchain. The simple way to describe it is as a "distributed ledger," but this phrase tells us very little until we consider the function of a ledger and the implications of decentralizing it. Introduced in Italy in the late thirteenth century, the ledger combined two innovations: Arabic numerals and double-entry bookkeeping, to record and keep track of economic transactions. Debits and credits are posted in separate columns with an ending balance posted at the bottom. It's a tool to manage a complex business with accuracy and detect errors, and it's considered a cornerstone of modern finance. Now imagine that instead of a ledger that recorded transactions for a single private enterprise you had a universal ledger that tracked every transaction everywhere in the Vaporized Economy. That's the idea of the blockchain.

The remarkable part of the blockchain is that no single entity controls it; instead every bitcoin transaction is part of a networked public record. Anyone can freely download it and inspect it because the data is dispersed across all of the computers in the bitcoin ecosystem, which register and verify all transactions made. And because the blockchain is distributed across multiple computers, it is more secure than centrally stored databases: every computer around the world mining bitcoin is constantly verifying its integrity. What bitcoin entrepreneurs now realize is that the blockchain can be used to record any number of transactions—even those where no money changes hands.

Bitcoin enthusiasts maintain that the algorithm could—in theory—substitute for certain institutions that regulate the economy and society. It could provide a way to conduct any type of secure transaction, including exchanging or transferring contracts or other legal documents, in the digital environment. Here's a sample of some of the topics that are under consideration.

> **Central banks:** The policies of the US central banking system, known as the Federal Reserve, have been blamed for worsening the Great Depression of the 1930s, creating the Great Inflation of the 1960s, pumping up the housing bubble of the 2000s, and a host of other calamities. After the 2008 financial crash, the Fed was lambasted in a letter signed by twenty-three prominent economists for potentially fueling inflation by buying trillions of dollars of long-term treasury bonds in an intervention known as quantitative easing. And in his book *Deception and Abuse at the Fed*, Robert Auerbach, a former economist at the Fed and investigator for the US House Committee on Financial Service (also known as the House Banking Committee), describes a bureaucratic culture of conformity, secrecy, and strict hierarchy that stifles objectivity and dissent. No wonder Nobel Laureate Milton Friedman groused that he would prefer to abolish the Federal Reserve and replace it with a computer. When he made the remark in 1997, it was gruff comedy. Today, bitcoin offers the prospect of doing just that: replacing central banking policies set by bureaucrats with an inviolable rules-based system of regulation by algorithm.

> **Smart contracts:** The concept of self-executing and self-enforcing agreements has been around since computer scientist Nick Szabo introduced the term in 1993. Now, however, it's possible to conceive of real-world applications such as smart contracts that could transfer ownership of

201

property represented by a token that is recorded in the blockchain. This is a step towards automating the transfer of property. Similarly, as computers and network connectivity are embedded in more and more devices, it might become possible for them to transact among themselves, ordering and restocking their own supplies and recording the transfer of data among machines.

> **Digital voting:** Electronic voting systems have been "coming soon" for two decades but, so far, deployments have been marred by malfunctions and dark allegations of tampering. A Danish political party called the Liberal Alliance has already used the blockchain to manage internal polling, a step that may be a precursor to using it to verify the actual voting process for an election. As a member of the party's executive committee was quoted saying in CryptoCoinsNews, "The blockchain removes the need for trust, because the technology can run autonomously without interference from humans, and it is at the same time open source and transparent, so that everybody can look under the hood and see what's going on."

> **Digitally time-stamped documents:** Today getting a document notarized means having to find a notary public, and then driving to the office and signing the document in person. The fingerprints and signature of the document owner are recorded in the notary's ledger, and the document is stamped with the notary's seal. Proof of Existence, a demonstration app developed by a twenty-three-year-old game developer in Argentina, uses bitcoin to verify the date and integrity of a digital document by inserting a unique digital timestamp that is entered into the blockchain. The entire process can take place on a laptop computer, effectively vaporizing the notary public.

> **Decentralized storage:** Cloud computing and cloud storage services are incredibly handy, but they are also completely centralized—and therefore vulnerable to attack. Customers take a bigger risk than they realize when they place their data on the cloud storage. A bitcoin project called Storj is developing a decentralized cloud storage system that uses the blockchain to enable home users to rent excess space on home drives— just like a P2P marketplace.

> **Transparent economy:** Zoom out. If an entire economy ran on a digital currency like bitcoin, economists would have instant real-time access to accurate data about how money was moving through the economy. Bitcoin could present the possibility of a truly P2P marketplace with no central authority, all data about transactions in the free and clear. We'd have a global ledger of economic activity that would enable the entire economy to optimize and improve. Even if bitcoin ultimately fails entirely, the possibilities it presents for a software-defined society have already succeeded in convincing thousands of smart people all over the world to feverishly build ever-more-sophisticated apps and services running on the blockchain.

IN DECENTRALIZATION WE TRUST

Our grandparents were raised in an era when citizens trusted Big Government, counted on lifelong employment with Big Companies, and entrusted their life savings to Big Banks. Those days are long gone. After the financial meltdown of 2008 and the data breaches of 2014, people no longer trust their banks. Lifelong employment went out the window with the downsizing, outsourcing, and offshoring a generation ago. And yet we don't entirely trust the new Internet giants either.

Yes, we rely on digital services every day, but dependence is not the same as trust. It's more like a provisional grant that we are willing to revoke at a moment's notice when a better option comes along or when we finally get fed up with a company revising the rules in its favor again and again. In exchange for free services and apps, we reluctantly grant companies such as Facebook and Google permission to record everything we do while we go about our day. This is strictly transactional. It's a marriage of convenience that's not built to last. Nor have the new on-demand marketplaces such as Uber entirely gained our trust. The obvious zeal of these companies to supplant regulators by establishing a new kind of hegemony over a centralized information marketplace is jarring.

So, whom do we trust? In the vaporized world, we are on our own. We have more information at our fingertips than any previous generation, and much of it confirms our suspicions about the big institutions that we were supposed to put faith in. We're inclined to place more trust in other people who bought the same defective product or who ate in the same grungy restaurant and wrote about it online than we do with a millionaire senator or a faceless city commissioner who reaches out to us only at election time. Social software and always-on smartphones give us a new way to band together for collective power. The emergence of self-organizing, leaderless, autonomous networks of individuals connected by mobile phones is a new feature on the political landscape. The next phase of evolution in digital media may offer more examples of distributed, self-organizing systems designed to resist centralized control.

The newfound versatility of the blockchain suggests that there may be a big opportunity ahead in creating a new kind of trust that can be independently verified. As Ronald Reagan once said, "Trust, but verify." With the blockchain, we may soon see a new generation of vaporized institutions that are provably reliable and demonstrably fair. And that could present a big challenge to today's fast-growing on-demand marketplaces; after all, bitcoin is about doing away with *any* centralized structure, not just government institutions. That's a threat to the centralizers large and small. A distributed, decentralized, truly peer-to-peer network could annihilate the proprietary marketplaces and data silos of the new giants of the sharing economy.

The term "sharing economy," therefore, is misleading. Companies like Uber, Airbnb, and their ilk are hellbent on amassing information about customers and drivers and, most important of all, data that matches drivers and customers together more efficiently than any other company on Earth. Uber has the credit card information, home address, mobile phone number, and email address of tens of millions of users, whom they can segment into globetrotters or local travelers. None of this information is shared. Every company that competes with Uber, and all of the thousands of "Uber for X" wannabes, are equally determined to accumulate their own data assets. They seek to maintain control over their private marketplaces, and one way they do this is by forcing all communication, transaction, and billing to go through their central systems. But therein lies a problem: all that valuable data is locked up in silos and none of these silos communicate with each other. Moreover, those vast information troves stored in multimillion-dollar data centers make a tempting target for hackers, spies, and other interlopers.

At the 2013 Turing Festival, which brings together thinkers to discuss the ways technology is affecting culture and society, bitcoin developer Mike Hearn shared a visionary alternative in his speech called "The Future of Money." Widely reported in newspapers and blogs at the time, Hearn's talk described his vision of an economy fifty years in the future where nobody owns cars. Instead, people who need transportation turn to a P2P market called TradeNet that might be considered a futuristic version of Uber, except the bidders are autonomous robot vehicles. Not only is there no central dispatcher or fleet manager in Hearn's vision, there is no centralized database of customers, no centralized accounting platform, and no centralized billing system. In sum: no Uber. In Hearn's scenario, robot vehicles are programmed to bargain and strike deals with customers directly, using bitcoin to conduct frictionless transactions without the need for a bank, credit card company, payment platform, or regulator.

Just one year after Hearn's speech, some of the first pieces of his vision are already in the process of being assembled. For example, a project called La'Zooz has launched a beta app that uses a cryptocurrency modeled on bitcoin to reward its ride-share participants. No money changes hands. Instead, drivers who respond to ride requests from passengers via the mobile app will earn tokens for every mile they drive. These tokens can be redeemed for rides or, eventually, other services. The objective is to establish a worldwide "Collaborative Transportation Web" that is completely decentralized and wholly owned by its users. It won't be subject to the 20 percent tax imposed by a switchboard market like Uber. Rather than sitting in a central server, the entire La'Zooz system is distributed across the computers and smartphones of its users. It exists nowhere in particular and everywhere at once. Of course there are no robot taxis on La'Zooz yet, but the organization behind the project is already recruiting Uber drivers.

So is Chaincab.com, a new project in Amsterdam that bills itself as a taxi driver cooperative. Every participating driver gets to vote on major management decisions. Chaincab uses bitcoin's blockchain algorithm to manage driver accounts and to track shareholder votes. Under the motto "the disrupters need to be disrupted," the site actively campaigns against Uber.

The main point of these new ventures is to posit an alternative to the centralized quasi-monopolies erected by the privately owned platforms. It is far too early to call these projects more than a proof of concept, but if history has taught us anything in the twenty-five years since the World Wide Web was invented it's that any idea that can be logically expressed in software will probably, eventually, be built. There's no small irony in the notion that the techno-libertarians who started Uber may find themselves disrupted tomorrow by an open-source app that runs on the blockchain. This tiger is eating its own tail.

▶▶ SEMI-EMPLOYED IN LIMBO

Suppose you run a company. You have a lot of workers. Let's say thousands of them. But they are not full-time employees. What are they? They must be independent contractors, right? Maybe not.

In two separate actions, drivers sued Uber and its rival Lyft for wrongly classifying them as independent contractors instead of employees. US District Judge Vince Chhabria, who presided over the Lyft case, concluded that the current employment categories are "woefully outdated." "At first glance, Lyft drivers don't seem much like employees," he wrote in his ruling on the matter. "But Lyft drivers don't seem much like independent contractors either." Justice Chhabria decided that he was unable to make a summary judgment and therefore the case will go to trial where it will be decided by a jury.

"The jury in this case will be handed a square peg and asked to choose between two round holes," Judge Chhabria wrote. "The test California courts have developed over the 20th Century for classifying workers isn't very helpful in addressing this 21st Century problem." There's a lot riding on the outcome, however. If the plaintiffs win, they will be owed reimbursement for fuel and vehicle maintenance, and compensation for benefits, including health care and social security payments. But that's not all. If Uber and Lyft lose, their entire business model could implode. Instead of running a lean technology-based operation with a small staff, the two firms could find themselves saddled with tens of thousands of employees on the payroll, and a massive bill for payroll taxes, health care premiums, and other expenses. Which would make Uber and Lyft look a lot less like groovy exemplars of the collaborative economy and much more like bloated unlicensed taxi companies. And that, of course, is exactly what their opponents have been arguing all along.

The fallout from the legal cases could impact every company that dispatches independent workers in an on-demand marketplace for services ranging from housekeeping to errands to tutoring. In contrast, if Uber and Lyft are vindicated, then it's likely that a lot more employers will push workers off the payroll into independent contractor roles. Already Google and Amazon are poised to launch marketplaces for errands and odd jobs.

The lawsuits shine a spotlight on the peculiar nature of work in a vaporized company. Increasing numbers of workers are opting into jobs where their assignments are issued by software and instructions show up on their smartphones. Ask any Uber driver who they work for and they'll tell you, "I'm self employed." That's because these drivers don't really have a boss. At least, not a *human* boss. An app on the smartphone tells them what to do next. The company has fully automated the process of dispatching a driver to pick up a passenger. So what's been vaporized? The dispatcher.

Writing on his blog about "Replacing Middle Management with APIs," Peter Reinhardt, the CEO and co-founder of Segment, a customer data collection and management company, asserted: "Drivers are opting into a dichotomous workforce: the worker bees below the software layer have no opportunity for on-the-job training that advances their career, and compassionate social connections don't pierce the software layer either. The skills they develop in driving are not an investment in their future. Once you introduce the software layer between 'management' (Uber's full-time employees building the app and computer systems) and the human workers below the software layer (Uber's drivers, Instacart's delivery people), there's no obvious path upwards. In fact, there's a massive gap and no systems in place to bridge it."

Increasingly in on-demand marketplaces and collaborative economy apps, this kind of automated matchmaking is becoming the norm. When you report to a robot, who manages your career? Who gives you advice? Who mentors you? Who is grooming you for the next step up the ladder? In the case of Uber and Lyft, there is no ladder. The middle rungs have been knocked out. These companies have vaporized middle management.

Without that layer of middle management, there's no path to proceed through the ranks and work your way up to a management role. There's no one in that role to spot the rising talent because those middle management jobs no longer exist. Uber's task application programming interface (API) vaporized the dispatcher. Airbnb's task API vaporizes the travel agent. 99designs' API vaporizes the creative director. oDesk vaporizes the vice president of engineering. If you get your instructions from an algorithm instead of from a human manager, you are working below the API. And if you are reporting to a piece of software, what does that make you? A biological robot?

Reinhardt ends his blog on a chilling note: "As the software layer gets thicker, the gap between below-the-API jobs and above-the-API jobs widens. And economic incentives will push above-the-API engineers to automate the jobs below-the-API: self-driving cars and drone delivery are certainly on the way. The gap in training and social groups above and below could mean that new automation technology causes sudden, large-scale unemployment and a surge in demand for subsidized training. I hope we're ready."

ASK YOURSELF

> What would happen to your company if the consumption model shifts from ownership to access?

> Which companies are leading collaborative consumption and peer marketplaces in your industry? Do you view them as friends or foes, or as a business opportunity?

> How might you apply Internet rules to your industry? What would change? What would become obsolete?

> How have regulations shaped your industry? How would you operate your business if there were no regulations? What would improve? What might get worse?

9

ROBOTICS AND THE
.VAPORIZATION OF LABOR

EVERYTHING THAT CAN
BE AUTOMATED WILL BE

Robots are coming to steal our jobs. We know this because every week for the past several years, one news outlet after another has told us so. *PBS NewsHour* asked, "Will your job exist in the future or will a robot have replaced you?" CNBC warned us to "Get ready, robots are going to steal your job." The *New York Times* reported that "As Robots Grow Smarter, American Workers Struggle to Keep Up." Not to be outdone, the *Daily Mail* wailed, "Middle Class Will Be 'Decimated' By Jobs Being Taken By Robots." Even the *Wall Street Journal* ran an article with the ponderous sub-headline "Experts rethink belief that tech always lifts employment, as machines take on skills once thought uniquely human."

As robots and software-driven automated systems take a larger role in our digital and physical lives, the argument goes, they will displace more and more workers. Robots and artificial intelligence (AI) are vaporizing human labor. This firestorm was ignited by a study published in 2011 by researchers Dr. Carl Benedikt Frey of the Oxford Martin School and Dr. Michael A. Osborne of the University of Oxford's Department of Engineering

Science, in which they found that many jobs in diverse fields such as transportation, logistics, and office administration are at "high risk" of automation. Their report, entitled "The Future of Employment," shocked readers as it concluded that up to 47 percent of all jobs in the US economy could be subject to automation or computerization. Forty-seven percent represents roughly 73 million jobs.

Frey and Osborne's 47 percent figure grabbed headlines because the US has barely, even in the most dire phase of the Great Depression, contended with unemployment at even half that scale. The worst year of unemployment ever in US history was 1932, when 23.6 percent of the workforce was out of a job. Since the Second World War, unemployment rates have generally fluctuated between 4 and 8 percent, with occasional spikes. The highest postwar unemployment rate, which averaged 9.8 percent and peaked briefly at 10.7 percent for two months, occurred in 1982. Even today, after the worst recession since the Truman Administration, unemployment remains at 6.2 percent.

ECONOMIC CYCLES AND THE NEW WORKFORCE

In every recession since the Second World War, companies that laid off workers during the downturn tended to rehire as soon as the economy bounced back. Until 1990 this process never took more than one year. However, it has taken longer and longer for workers to find jobs after the most recent recessions of 1991, 2004, and 2009. In fact, the Bureau of Labor Statistics (BLS) announced that not until April 2014 did the private sector in the US regain the jobs lost from its 2008 pre-crisis peak. The so-called "jobless recovery" had lasted six painful years, or longer than the previous two recoveries combined.

According to economist Michael Evangelist, as quoted in the *New York Times,* the new jobs were quite different from the ones that were lost six years earlier: more than 1 million high-wage jobs were never replaced, and, instead, more than 1.8 million low-wage jobs were created. Most of those new jobs, by far, were in the food service industry, which is the lowest wage category in the BLS report. One reason the US employment index responded so sluggishly after the 2009 crisis was that many of the workers who were laid off were not rehired. And they won't be. Ever. Those workers were replaced by machines.

In a paper entitled "Jobless Recoveries" published by the centrist think tank Third Way, economists Henry Siu and Nir Jaimovich observed that in each of the three most recent recessions employment recovered significantly slower than gross domestic product (GDP). This trend is not an economy-wide phenomenon, however. According to Siu and Jaimovich, "It can be traced to a lack of recovery in a subset of occupations; those that focus on "routine" or repetitive tasks that are increasingly being performed by machines." The researchers point out that occupations focused on these routine tasks tend to be middle-waged, which may explain why the new jobs post-recovery tend to pay less than those that were destroyed. It looks like the robots really are stealing our jobs.

Economists also tell us that destroying jobs is a normal part of a healthy industrial economy. For example, automation has been a part of manufacturing since the inventor James Watt added a governor to his steam engine in 1788, and concerns about machines displacing workers have been with us just as long. As early as 1930, economist John Maynard Keynes coined the term "technological unemployment" to describe this phenomenon. So is it really a problem? On the one hand, alarmists suggest that machines might cause a permanent rise in unemployment levels. On the other hand, economists tell us that, historically, the labor market has always generated enough new and better jobs to more than offset the ones eliminated by technological progress.

They point to the cycle of displaced workers devising new crafts and gaining new skills over several months after their layoff and then trading up to more interesting and rewarding occupations. The long-term result has consistently been the expansion of economy, increased productivity, and much better and more diverse jobs. And everyone benefits because prices for machine-made goods are significantly lower, and generally the new jobs pay higher wages than the old ones. For economic progress to occur, a certain amount of job destruction is simply necessary.

This kind of healthy job destruction has been a reliable—and vitally necessary—feature of the economy since the Industrial Revolution. What's changed is the number of recent improvements in robotics. Suddenly, robots are everywhere, especially if we look beyond the humanoid clichés to recognize a robot for what it is: automation. Many observers fret that we are automating old jobs faster than we can create new ones. For the purposes of this argument, any automated non-biological substitute for human labor is a robot.

Mechanized robots were initially a replacement for muscle power; they perform the physical work that would have been done by human beings or animals. Forty years ago, repetitive tasks on an assembly line or food processing plant were deemed suitable for robots. More recently, so were tasks that require stamina and sustained focus in a predefined area, such as a factory floor or a warehouse. Robots can now handle pattern-detection jobs, like pulling weeds in a field of crops. Sorting, stacking, and moving barcoded items for transport is a robot-ready task.

Thanks to rapid advances in technology, the machines are smarter than ever. Robots are now versatile and capable enough to be used in a much broader range of occupations than the factory robots of the 1990s. Today robots perform their work silently in every corner of the urban landscape: as automated teller machines (ATMs) at the bank, self-service check-in counters at the airport, self-service checkout stations at the grocery store, pay-at-the-pump machines at the gas station, and automated payment machines at parking lots and tollbooths.

As they gain dexterity, limbs, and more intelligence and situational awareness, robots look less like stationary kiosks and more like the humanoids we recall from cheesy 1950s science fiction movies. Lowe's hardware stores are experimenting with robot greeters who guide customers to the correct aisle in the store. And Rethink Robotics is selling Baxter, a $22,000 robot with a friendly face, suitable for small businesses and light manufacturing. Add a dash of personality and these anthropomorphic machines are capable of dealing directly with people.

Humanoid automatons are showing up in customer-service roles. In Berlin, there's a robot bartender; in Tokyo's Shinjuku district, a robot cabaret show; and at Germany's giant CeBIT trade show in 2012 there were robot booth babes, gyrating and pole dancing for bemused attendees. Oh, the horror. More and more, robots are taking on roles in some unusual places:

> **Robot hotel staff:** The Henn-na Hotel in Nagasaki, Japan, is staffed by ten humanoid robots. They speak fluent Japanese, Chinese, Korean, and English, and can check visitors into the hotel, carry bags to the rooms, change the sheets, clean the rooms, and deliver laundry. The president of the company expects robot minions to perform 90 percent of hotel services.

> **Robot warehouse staff:** Kiva robots, part of an automated order-fulfillment system, dance an intricate ballet inside an entirely automated Amazon warehouse. They move entire shelving units gracefully to workers who select, sort, and package individual orders. Think of the smart warehouse as a giant computer that routes packages just like packets on a digital network, moving, sorting, stacking, and tracking items.

> **Robot animals:** Boston Dynamics creates impressive robots inspired by biological designs: BigDog, an autonomous packhorse, can carry 340 pounds over hills and through rough terrain for 20 miles; Cheetah, the fastest legged robot on Earth, runs faster than Usain Bolt, the world's fastest human; Atlas, a humanoid robot, walks upright and uses its hands like a human; Sand Flea, a rolling robot, can leap over buildings; and RiSE, a six-legged robot, can climb vertical walls and trees using micro-claws.

> **Robot freighters:** Eight European companies have joined forces with the Fraunhofer Institute to launch the Maritime Unmanned Navigation through Intelligence in Networks (MUNIN) project to design an automated freight ship. Robot ships will operate slowly, at speeds human crews would not tolerate, but they will also save 50 percent on fuel costs, lower greenhouse gas emissions, and, of course, save the money that would have been paid in the form of crew salaries. Eventually, the 100,000 merchant ships on the seas today could be operated by robot crews.

So, should human workers be concerned? Yes and no. Robots are going places that humans can't or don't want to go, including hot war zones, toxic waste dumps, and the stars above us. The US Navy has developed a robot drone that swims like a shark for underwater reconnaissance and may be phasing out manned aircraft in favor of drones. Speaking at the Sea-Air-Space 2015 conference, US Secretary of the Navy Ray Mabus said that the new F-35 Lightning II "should be, and almost certainly will be, the last manned strike fighter aircraft the Department of the Navy will ever buy or fly."

At the same time, artificial intelligence (AI), a type of robot that doesn't need a body, is allowing computers to do more tasks that were previously the domain of human intelligence. Current-generation AIs are like "cloud robots," consisting of software running across multiple servers. They can recognize speech, translate between languages, and make decisions. So it's not a stretch to contend that the global economy recently entered a transitional phase in which far more occupational tasks can be handled by a machine. Factory labor is just the beginning. Next in the queue: the knowledge-processing and analytic skills of white-collar workers. Some jobs that require mastery of a defined body of knowledge, such as law, accounting, journalism, and medicine, can now be partially handled by software robots.

THE BOOMING SECOND ECONOMY

During the past fifteen years, the automated software-driven control systems that operate constantly in the background of every business, every transaction, and every communication have begun to migrate to the cloud along with everything else in the software-defined economy. Now computer systems, payment systems, communication networks, and business process management tools rely on cloud-based automation to function. Soon our autonomous vehicles and smart cities will communicate with the cloud to do their jobs too. Automated systems have merged with the Internet. This, too, is no coincidence. The Internet consists of a vast network of automated systems exchanging billions of messages every day. From inception, it was designed to operate without human intervention, relying on countless software-defined robots that serve, observe, and anticipate what human users will do. For example:

> Servers and routers direct every packet, web page, email message, music stream, and frame of video automatically to the correct destination.
> Automated filtering algorithms and recommendation engines determine which stories appear on individual newsfeeds, which friends are recommended on social networks, which offers show up on e-commerce sites, which fulfillment center will handle a particular order.
> Automated systems handle the real-time bidding, buying, and placement of advertising targeted to individual preferences and behavior.
> Spambots fill online discussion boards with junk messages, create fake accounts to send email, and crack passwords.
> Robotic journalist tools like Narrative Science's natural-language generation platform, Quill, crank out news stories.

More and more of what we experience and consume consists of digital products and digital services. Most of the work to generate and deliver these experiences is handled by automation. As the vaporized digital domain spills out of the computer screen and blends and merges with the real world via the Internet of Things (IoT), more and more automated software systems will permeate our daily lives. According to economist W. Brian Arthur, an external professor at the Santa Fe Institute, this automation comprises a vast, unseen economy. As he explains in a 2011 article in the *McKinsey Quarterly*, "Another economy—a second economy—of all of these digitized business processes conversing, executing, and triggering further actions is silently forming alongside the physical economy." In fact, these everyday processes in the physical economy are now tightly interwoven with the digital world too: as soon as contact is initiated between them, elaborate communication and data processing occurs in the digital domain, unnoticed by humans.

Routine events, such as checking in for a flight at the airport or shipping freight through Rotterdam, involve conversations between servers, satellites, and distant computers. In the past, Arthur points out, human clerks were obliged to manage a sheaf of paperwork, supervise logistics procedures, and physically handle packages. Today the entire process is digitally scanned and automatically dispatched, to be tracked with barcodes, radio-frequency identification (RFID) chips, and other machine-readable interfaces. Arthur says, "What used to be done by humans is now executed as a series of conversations among remotely located servers." Welcome to vaporized labor, expressed purely as digital information.

Arthur calculates that over the long term the second economy will be responsible for a 2.4 percent annual increase in productivity in the overall economy. By 2025 he estimates that the second economy will be as large as the entire physical economy was in 1995. Even if these back-of-the-envelope figures are subject to quibbling and fine-tuning, "What's important is that the second economy is not a small add-on to the physical economy. In two or three decades, it will surpass the physical economy in size."

What's different about this new, networked kind of automation-based economy is awareness. Unlike the robotic brutes on auto factory floors that can neither see nor hear, the invisible automated world of software has eyes and ears. Just like the smart devices of IoT, the automated systems track and respond to events that transpire in the physical world. And detecting changes in the outside world and reacting to them is a form of primitive intelligence. Arthur argues that the emergent intelligence of automated systems is the biggest change since the Industrial Revolution. "With the coming of the Industrial Revolution," Arthur writes, "the economy developed a muscular system in the form of machine power. Now it is developing a neural system."

Thanks to Moore's law, Metcalfe's law, and the growth of really big data sets, we are about to experience a step function increase in the power of automation and robotics. This combination of factors means that the age of artificial intelligence may finally be at hand.

THE AGE OF ARTIFICIAL INTELLIGENCE

The economic logic of robotics and automation is irresistible. Just like every other type of information technology, the price of robotics has decreased steadily while quality has improved. Now, automated systems like Kiva often pay for themselves within the first year of deployment, sometimes faster.

Once a unit of robot labor grows cheaper than a unit of human labor, additional benefits for employers kick in: for many tasks it is safer, more efficient, and more reliable to use a machine than a human being. Furthermore, companies have a huge financial incentive to find ways to eliminate human employees and thereby reduce such associated costs as payroll taxes, disability payments, insurance costs, fringe benefits, plant costs, training expenses, and worker safety claims. The market rewards companies that minimize the number of employees. Which is exactly why Facebook and Google, information technology companies that don't create many jobs, are so highly valued by investors: they create more with less.

The future of companies is lean and leaner. As more industries get vaporized, more firms will begin to resemble info-tech companies, both in terms of their output and their workforce. They will find ways to operate with lower headcount and higher profit. Information technology ensures this outcome, because manufacturing—like every part of society—is increasingly defined by software. And just like everything else defined by software, innovation in this sector is accelerating. No matter what industry your business is in, automation probably already plays a growing role in your operations. And if not, it will soon—competition demands it.

Until 1990, layoffs generally occurred at one company at a time. When a worker was laid off, he or she could find a similar job at a plant across the street or on the other side of town, or wait six months and then get rehired when the economy recovered. Today, entire job categories are being permanently erased by robotics. There will be no rehiring in these categories. If a job at one company is eliminated, the displaced worker will be unlikely to find a similar job at the rival shop across the street because it will have upgraded to the latest robots too.

In this scenario, displaced workers may have no choice but to compete for another job in an entirely different field, and as robots acquire more capabilities, workers may find themselves competing for a dwindling number of positions. Some people are freaking out about this possibility.

TWO VIEWS: THE TECHNO-OPTIMISTS VS THE TECHNO-PESSIMISTS

A long-simmering debate among the techno-elite burst into full boil in June 2014 when venture capitalist Marc Andreessen posted a volley of comments in his signature style, a Twitter "tweet storm." Andreessen's tweets consisted of one side of an argument about robotics and automation. He dismissed fears about worker displacement as "textbook Luddism, relying on a 'lump-of-labor' fallacy—the idea that there is a fixed amount of work to be done."

Andreessen wasn't tweeting into the void. His Twitter account is followed by 333,000 people, including many of the leaders in the venture capital industry. The argumentative nature of Andreessen's remarks drew several responses, including many who took up the other side of the debate. What ensued was the closest thing to soul-searching that happens in Silicon Valley. Here is a radically oversimplified synopsis of the longstanding feud.

Techno-optimists like Andreessen believe that new technology will do more to improve lives than to harm them, by increasing productivity and expanding the economy. Technology gives all of us more for less, delivering valuable goods at lower prices, which raises the standard of living for all. That's especially true of Silicon Valley's bread-and-butter line of products, networked computing technologies. In a grandiose moment, enthusiasts might also argue that technology expands individual freedom, enhances communication, builds understanding and global empathy. It's a pretty appealing vision.

On the other side are techno-pessimists who believe that, left unchecked, new technology (and especially networked computing technologies) will diminish the quality of human life, erode communities and civic institutions, and wreak havoc on the economy by introducing instability, eroding wages, and killing jobs through automation. The pessimists also argue that flaws in technology leave us vulnerable to massive security breaches from malicious hackers, cyber criminals, and foreign spies. In their most extreme moments, the pessimists argue that technology enslaves us, reduces our attention span, and decreases human interpersonal connection which leave us vulnerable to manipulation and control. The techno-pessimist view is a pretty grim vision, inspired by dystopian science fiction and underscored by a steady tattoo of breaking news stories about data breaches, identity theft, societal dysfunction, filter bubbles, and a growing sense of isolation and alienation in our techno-cottages.

Lately the focus of both groups has turned specifically to the possibility of massive unemployment as the by-product of mass deployments of robots and automation.

To the optimists, robots are the source of liberation and abundance. Robots will displace some workers, but only temporarily. Robot workers will save humanity from the drudgery of repetitive tasks and low-wage jobs so that individuals can fulfill their destiny in creative pursuits, entrepreneurialism, teaching, charity, social work, and other projects. For the optimists, the rise of the robot worker signals the dawn of a brilliant age of prosperity, freedom, and choice. A new Renaissance lies just ahead.

To the pessimists, what the optimists miss is that machines are getting smarter, faster. In the pessimist view, robotics will render half of humanity permanently unemployable, mired in poverty, and trapped in a cycle of ever-diminishing opportunity for personal advancement. It's far worse than just the end of the American Dream; it's the Robot Apocalypse and the rise of superintelligent AI that will exterminate the human race. Yikes!

So who's right? There's no doubt that robots destroy jobs. That's a fact and an economic necessity for growth. The debate is whether robots will steal more jobs than the economy can replace, and thereby render a growing segment of the human population unemployable. That claim is dismissed as the Luddite fallacy by techno-optimists. And the Luddite fallacy is considered an article of faith by economists: if it became true, it would undermine the logic of the consumer economy.

The most extreme pessimists conclude with the observation that machine intelligence is improving much faster than humans can adapt or learn new skills. They envision job destruction that accelerates beyond our capacity for invention. In this formula, the human economy will be stuck creating jobs at an arithmetic rate while technology is destroying them at a geometric rate. That's the scary nightmare scenario. If the economy can't generate enough high-wage jobs—or if the human workers can't upskill fast enough to stay ahead of the machines—then the Luddite fallacy may become an economic fact.

PREDICTIONS FOR THE FUTURE: WHAT IS CERTAIN/PROBABLE/POSSIBLE
The optimists and pessimists locked in debate tend to talk past each other. Both sides make some partial points, even if the pessimists do so with more apocalyptic flair. Both parties do each other a disservice by ignoring the opposing case or setting up a straw man argument. This is not a case of either/or. It's a case of both/and.

What is happening is technologically-driven demand destruction for human labor. Thanks to advances in computing and robotics, this process is happening on a much larger scale than in previous eras. We are at the beginning of this process: as robots improve, it may accelerate. By considering both viewpoints, we can speculate about certainties, probabilities, and possibilities for the near future.

Certainly: Robots and automation will continue to replace human workers in every role possible, first in jobs that consist of routine work within a specifically defined domain, and then gradually expanding to broader roles that require more versatility, dexterity, and intelligence. The trajectory moves from narrow expertise to broader versatility: from the checkout kiosk to the robot manager; from the quick-serve restaurant order-taker to the fully automated restaurant; from a single manual task on the assembly line to robotizing the entire factory; from cruise control to self-driving autonomous vehicles.

Probably: Mass displacement of labor won't happen overnight. It will occur gradually, but it may well remain a persistent feature of the economic landscape for decades as the old industrial economy is redefined by software. Technological unemployment will be a chronic condition in every industrial economy rather than an acute crisis. But that's no cause for complacency if large numbers of jobs are destroyed faster than the economy can generate new ones.

Probably: Large groups of workers will be displaced en masse as soon as cheap machines can substitute for human labor across entire job categories. New job creation will remain slower than the displacement. The interval between job destruction and new job creation will continue to grow. The result could be a growing backlog of displaced workers. If a growing number of unemployed workers compete for new jobs, wages will stagnate or decline. That will increase income inequality.

Probably: Most governments will find themselves ill equipped to cope with the growing ranks of the unemployed. Large-scale training programs will be necessary. Unemployment benefits and income assistance programs will need to be topped up in the event that no new jobs will be immediately available.

Probably: Robots will continue to learn, improve, and further displace more workers. This process won't stop with low-level employees. Any job that can be automated will be, including middle management and even senior management positions.

Probably: Prices for goods and services produced by robots will decline, thanks to competitive pressure. Rivals hungry for market share will undercut any company that seeks to extract excess profit. The cost of robot labor will continue to decline, perhaps in line with Moore's law, driving down the cost of production in every field that can be automated. Companies that ride the cost curve down will pass savings on to customers. As a result, standards of living will rise for everyone.

Probably: Automated workforces will yield windfall profits for employers. Investment in robots will bring great returns to investors, some of which will be channeled towards new businesses, which may help some people find new careers in startup ventures funded by the profit from demolishing old jobs.

Possibly: The benefits of automation will not be evenly distributed in society, leading to unrest, political turmoil, and continuing conflict. Some citizens will call for rollbacks or limits on robot technology, but such measures will likely backfire, causing robot owners to relocate their factories to friendlier jurisdictions. Citizens will pressure their elected officials to pass measures to redistribute wealth via confiscatory taxation of profits on robot labor. Already some groups in the US and Europe are agitating for a guaranteed basic income for all citizens, presumably paid for by taxes on gains from investments in robots and automation. The distribution of wealth will remain a divisive political issue for decades. If gains flowing back to investors are reinvested in even more robotics, income inequality will persist and may worsen. This feedback loop will accelerate job destruction while bringing increasing returns to capital.

Possibly: Human ingenuity will devise new ways to work with and around the robots. Artificial intelligence and robotics will make many products cheaper and more ubiquitous, which will paradoxically drive up the perceived value of handmade objects by humans. Entirely new job categories will be devised by humans to serve entirely new categories of wants and needs. These might include a resurgence of handmade craft goods untouched by robot hands, live performances by human/robot hybrid troupes, new forms of education and personal care, and unique experiences such as human-guided adventures, and thousands of other new services that we can't yet imagine.

LIVING WITH HUMAN 2.0

If we think of mechanical robots as non-biological "brawn," then artificial intelligence can be likened to a non-biological brain. Machine intelligence affects human workers in two ways: sometimes as a substitution for human labor and cognition, and sometimes as an enhancement that augments human capabilities. Artificial intelligence is not evolving entirely on its own; the computers must be trained by human users. In that sense, it's not really *artificial* intelligence; it's more like vaporized human intelligence distilled into a computer. It's a reflection of humanity, refracted through the prism of sensor networks and machine intelligence. And we're making it more knowledgeable than any single human being could ever be.

As Kevin Kelly wrote in *Wired* magazine: "It's human-robot symbiosis. Our human assignment will be to keep making jobs for robots—and that is a task that will never be finished. So we will always have that one 'job.'" Artificial intelligence is already in a lot more things than we realize. For example, virtual assistants like Apple's Siri, Google Now, Microsoft's Cortana; gaming systems like Microsoft Kinect and most console games; and mobile apps that translate speech in real time. Financial institutions use AI to manage properties, trade stocks, and detect fraud. Hospitals use AI to improve diagnosis and to monitor life-support equipment. Air traffic control systems rely upon AI to monitor all aircraft in flight. Customer support centers use AI to process natural language in order to interpret and understand human callers. We don't always recognize AI as such because it is invisible to us, but we deal with it every day. And through our interaction and online behaviors, we are teaching these artificial neural networks to mimic the neural networks in human minds.

The field of artificial intelligence was stuck in a permanent dawn for sixty years, but a series of technological advances is now making it possible to bring AI out of the lab into the real world. "We believe we've finally turned the corner because of new algorithms (e.g., see deep neural nets), new hardware (massive improvements in parallelism, throughput and interconnect, all at continuously plummeting prices), and great seas of data to feed to the hardware and algorithms. The second half of this decade will see many of the early dreams of AI theorists finally coming true," said Tom Austin, a Gartner vice president who was quoted in *TechRepublic* in March 2014.

Mechanical robots don't benefit directly from Moore's law, but software robots do. That's why artificial intelligence is progressing faster. Citing "a perfect storm of parallel computation, bigger data, and deeper algorithms," Kevin Kelly predicted that we will soon see AI everywhere. "Everything we formerly electrified we will now cognitize," he says.

The newest AI systems exist in the cloud, offering "intelligence on demand" just like other cloud-based services such as storage and hosting. That's an opportunity to launch a new platform business. Just as Amazon Web Services eliminated a huge barrier to dot-com startups by providing scalable infrastructure on demand, companies that offer intelligence on demand will enable another round of disruptive startup ventures to reinvent existing industries. As Kelly put it, "The business plans of the next 10,000 startups are easy to forecast: take 'x' and add AI."

The first big entrant in the AI platform wars is IBM. Two years after trouncing the top human trivia champions on *Jeopardy!*, IBM's Watson AI computer system has been retooled to assist doctors to diagnose and treat cancer. The best doctors in the world will teach the AI, and then through intelligence on demand, their collective wisdom will be made available to physicians all over the world. Already the Bumrungrad International Hospital in Thailand is using the IBM Watson For Oncology platform to improve diagnoses. "The power of the technology is that it has the ability to take the information about a specific patient and match it to a huge knowledge base and history of treatment of similar patients," wrote Dr. Mark Kris, the former chief of the Thoracic Oncologic Service at the Memorial Sloan Kettering Cancer Center, in *The Atlantic*. "This process can help medical professionals gain important insights so that they can make more informed decisions, evidence-based decisions, about what treatment to follow... Watson's ability to mine massive quantities of data means that it can also keep up—at record speeds—with the latest medical breakthroughs reported in scientific journals and meetings."

The amount of medical research published in journals has been increasing to the point where it would take more than 100 hours each week to consume it all. No doctor can read everything; few of them, in fact, can peel off enough time to read even for one hour a day. At that rate it's impossible to keep up with the millions of new research documents published each year. But Watson is a prodigious learner and a voracious reader. Watson reads everything and can recall it instantly, which makes the AI a useful adjunct to a clinical diagnostician. And institutions are beginning to take advantage of that prodigious knowledge.

By 2014 the IBM Watson program had expanded to other cancer research institutions, including the Cleveland Clinic and the University of Texas. Watson now helps clinicians develop, observe, and adjust treatments for patients with breast and lung cancer and a dozen other common cancers, including leukemia, colon, prostate, ovarian, cervical, pancreas, kidney, liver, and uterine cancers. According to Samuel Nussbaum, the chief medical officer at health care provider WellPoint, doctors who confer with Watson correctly diagnose disease nearly 90 percent of the time, compared to 50 percent for human doctors unaided by AI.

You don't have to be a brain surgeon to use AI, and Watson is not limited to oncology and other medical research. This first iteration of cloud-based intelligence on demand is designed to be a versatile platform for enhancing human capability across many fields. As a result, IBM is spending $100 million to make Watson available as a platform for app developers who are training the system to find answers in fields ranging from cooking to shopping, travel, security, and financial planning. An app called Sofie, developed by LifeLearn, enables veterinarians to use their mobile phones to ask Watson a question just as they would a colleague.

The possibilities of AI are intriguing other industries too. In March 2015 Bridgewater Associates, the world's largest hedge fund manager, recruited David Ferrucci, the scientist who led the IBM team that created Watson's computer system. Why would a hedge fund with $165 billion in assets need a roboticist on staff to create an AI unit? Simple: to help fund managers make better decisions. Increasingly, in white-collar professions, AI will provide tools to augment and assist human workers as they assess complex data sets, identify patterns, and attempt to make smarter decisions. The robots are here to help. And of course, as they help us, we will also teach them. Eventually AIs will know more about each profession than any one practitioner, even the best human in the field. The cloud never stops learning and never forgets. It never retires or takes its knowledge to the grave. And that makes it very valuable indeed.

A MACHINE-READABLE WORLD

This brings us back to those newly smart physical robots on the ground. They are not just for executing orders. Smart robots are different from other machines. What robots have in common with mobile phones (and automobiles and even smart appliances in the home) is that they are not just mechanical devices but also collections of sensors that interpret signals from and react to the world around them: they collect data, process it, and generate it. Therein lies their real value—it's in the data they gather and send back to the mother ship.

The robot car is not just a transportation device—that's a by-product function. It's an emissary from the vaporized realm, coming into the physical world to map it, index it, digitize it, analyze it, and master it. Think of the Google Self-Driving Car as an elaborate mechanism for siphoning data from the real world.

Google's fleet of more than twenty autonomous vehicles, including driverless Toyota Priuses and Lexus RX 450h sport utility vehicles, has driven 1 million miles on California roads. Robot cars are now legal for testing purposes in four US states: Nevada, Florida, California, and Michigan. To make robot vehicles work, Google has created a new kind of map with an immense amount of detail about traffic signals, signs, crosswalks, lanes, and constant changes due to new construction or temporary detours. Google has a lot of experience mapping streets with Google Maps and Street View, but even those audacious projects pale by comparison to the robot vehicle program. Alexis Madrigal, former tech journalist for *The Atlantic,* explained how robot cars generate maps: "They're probably best thought of as ultra-precise digitizations of the physical world, all the way down to tiny details like the position and height of every single curb. A normal digital map would show a road intersection; these maps would have a precision measured in inches."

Google is colonizing the data layer of the physical world by recording it in such precise detail that an artificial intelligence can orient itself and navigate. Think of the robot vehicle like a physical version of the crawlers that index web pages for a search engine. The robot vehicle, loaded with cameras and sensors, is crawling the real world in the exact same way, sucking up data and sending it back to an ever-growing cloud mind. This is an audacious effort to make the physical world machine-readable. The goal is to help machines develop a human-scale understanding of how the real world looks and works. Google is doing something similar with Project Tango, the sensor-laden smartphone that maps the interior of a house or office 250,000 times a second.

Google researchers are teaching the car to record the real world, compare it to the previously recorded data on the servers, and calculate a path. If the road situation changes unexpectedly due to construction or an accident, Google records both what happened and what the car was prepared to do. Both cases can be compared for optimization, just as every drive is compared to the previous routes driven by other cars.

So it's not quite right to think of a robot car as a self-standing machine. It's a networked machine, a node that happens to move through physical space, much like a smartphone. In fact, this connectivity is integral: the robot car will not function properly without access to the cloud services and reference to the other nodes on the network.

WHO WILL OWN THE AI PLATFORM?

Since 2009, $17 billion have been invested in artificial intelligence, reports the business analytics firm Quid. And in the past four years, investment has been growing at 60 percent a year. The best minds in Silicon Valley are betting on it. It's a footrace to be the biggest, fastest. The law of increasing returns to market leaders suggests that the more data is gathered by the leading company, the more likely that company will maintain its grip. Google is vying for that spot, and at the end of 2013 the company made a stunning announcement. In a six-month span, it had acquired eight of the leading robotics companies:

> **Schaft, Inc.,** which won the Defense Advanced Research Projects Agency's (DARPA) Robotics Challenge Trial with a two-legged machine that can climb ladders.
> **Industrial Perception, Inc.,** which specializes in 3D vision for robots in factories.
> **Redwood Robotics,** which specializes in building robot arms.
> **Meka Robotics,** which builds "human safe, human scale" robots that can co-exist with people in homes and in the workplace.
> **Holomini,** which creates omnidirectional wheels for robots.
> **Bot & Dolly,** which specializes in motion-controlled cameras for film and television production.
> **Boston Dynamics,** which builds biomorphic robots such as the humanoids Atlas and PETMAN, as well as a menagerie of four- and six-legged creatures known as BigDog, Cheetah (and its successor, WildCat), and RHex.
> **DeepMind Technologies,** which builds artificial brains.

This spree was followed by several other acquisitions, including:

> **Titan Aerospace,** which makes unmanned high-altitude aircraft.
> **Jetpac, Dark Blue Labs,** and **Vision Factory,** all of which develop artificial intelligence software.

Just a few weeks later, the longtime AI proponent, scientist, and inventor Ray Kurzweil was named Google's director of engineering. Some industry watchers were puzzled by this move. Why would a software company like Google be interested in tackling the messy hardware problems involved in making robots walk and roll and run? And this was only a short time after Google completed the process of dismantling and selling off the hardware divisions of Motorola, one of the last great American electronics companies. They miss the point. Just like Google's entry into the automobile industry, this is not about hardware. It's all about data.

EXTRACTING VALUE FROM SMART MACHINES

Soon, just like smart devices and smart cars, mobile robots will be connected to the Internet, and Google clearly intends to intercept and organize this data before it filters out onto the Web. Google's robot strategy may be the biggest and boldest Big Data strategy of all.

In a way, Google's strategy is a more audacious strategy than Microsoft's in the mid-1990s. Back in its glory days, Microsoft inserted a wedge of proprietary Windows software between computers and the applications that ran them. Today Google is replicating that strategy across an astonishingly broad range of devices. Like Microsoft, Google seems to be less concerned about the actual hardware (car, computer, phone, dishwasher, or robot). It will build these things if it must, especially to make a reference model like Nexus that showcases the full potential of its software, but Google's real interest lies in controlling the invisible layer of data generated by these machines.

The software operating system for robots will be just another value control point in the Google ecosystem that spans from robot workers to robot cars to robot drones and robot cameras installed on Skybox Imaging's satellites, which record data as they orbit 185 miles above the Earth. If any company wants to access the data captured by these machines, or program that data to get useful work done, it will need to go through a proprietary layer of software controlled by Google. And that's where Google can extract a toll.

Even if Google decides to open-source its robot operating systems or provide open access to its robot platforms via APIs, the company will still be in position to reap the data harvest coming from each machine. Like Nest and Android before it, Google's strategic investment in robotics is about software layers: operating systems, a set of APIs, and a suite of apps on top. How might Google use this new data asset?

> Licensing technology to other manufacturers.
> Licensing real-world maps to developers of augmented reality and virtual reality apps; in other words, providing real-world data as an on-demand service.
> Making the huge data sets available to developers through an API and reaping the windfall as more users begin to use the apps.
> Surveilling and tracking items in the real world, including tracking and recovering stolen goods.
> Facilitating virtual presence through teleconferencing and even armchair tourism via virtual reality headsets.
> Creating education and training programs set in virtualized versions of real-world environments. These might be good for crews that must become familiar with an environment before they arrive on site.
> Allowing architects and their clients to do virtual drive throughs of a precise virtual reality rendition of the build site and its surroundings.

Dominance in AI will be propelled by three things that Google has in spades: algorithms, data, and processing power. Now it's gathered the best minds in the field via an audacious series of acquisitions. Given the winner-take-all dynamic in the Vaporized Economy, Google seems poised to dominate.

If you want to access Google's intelligence-as-a-service, you'll feed it with information of your own, thereby reinforcing Google's winner-take-all position. If you want to use Google's operating systems for robots (or autonomous vehicles or smart devices), you'll need to make a similar compromise, allowing Google to harvest the data that you generate from usage. Both of these strategies will reinforce Google's hegemony in this emerging field.

By scooping up talent in the robotics and AI fields, Google sent a clear signal. The search giant is betting big on a future in which a vast range of human capabilities, not just physical labor but also intelligence, will be vaporized, converted into a software platform, and offered as a service. As the leading information company on the planet, Google is enviably positioned to manage the growth of this new field, and thereby transform human labor into pure information running on its software platforms.

Google's stated mission is to organize the world's information. The more information made available, the more profitable Google will become. It really is that simple. Every human worker possesses unique expertise in his or her particular profession, and yet that knowledge doesn't get shared very efficiently, if at all. From Google's perspective, that's a tragic waste of information. Now imagine if that information could be liberated from the human skull and turned into software: what might happen when the best practices of half the workers in America are turned into software subroutines that can be programmed into robots? Human expertise will be vaporized: our best practices will be recorded, captured, analyzed, and turned into invisible software that can be downloaded into our devices.

THE DEMATERIALIZED COMPANY

The history of innovation in manufacturing is a chronicle of machines gradually taking over for human labor. It's a steady progression from mechanization to electrification to machine mass production to robot factories with no human workers at all. However, the process of digitizing human labor and turning this intelligence into an on-demand service is also an occasion to contemplate the nature of "work" in the Vaporized Era. Labor used to be something that a worker possessed. In the future it may be more like an MP3 track, a freely shareable digital file. If labor gets vaporized, why would a company need management? Maybe it's time to vaporize the C-suite too.

The vaporized company is a new possibility on the horizon. Cloud-based services are eliminating the need for a corporation to own many kinds of infrastructure: computing power, storage, and productivity apps. As more business is conducted in the digital domain, more parts of the company will be turned to vapor. Already, non-material assets (also known as intangible assets) such as patents, ideas, copyrights, and brands, as well as business process and procedures and proprietary data, comprise the vast bulk of the value of the biggest companies.

In March 2015, Ocean Tomo, a merchant bank that specializes in intellectual property, released findings from its Annual Study of Intangible Asset Market Value. The report revealed something surprising about the factors that made up the market value of typical S&P 500 firms. In 1975, 83 percent of the average firm's market value was based on *tangible* assets, or physical assets such as real estate, machinery, production plants, and inventory. By 2015 that ratio had flipped. Today 84 percent of a firm's value consists of *intangible* assets. Furthermore, if these intangible assets were stripped away, many of the firms listed on the S&P 500 would have negative value because their debts outweigh the value of their physical assets. We're not so very far away from completely vaporizing the corporation.

ROBOT COMPANIES

Reconceived as AI-managed software systems, firms may be able to run themselves in the future. Vitalik Buterin, the hyperkinetic young CEO of the decentralized web app platform Ethereum, observes that corporations consist of groups of individual people who work together under specific rules in order to achieve a particular mission. Suppose the company's mission statement could be written as software instructions for an AI, he proposes in an article titled "Bootstrapping a Decentralized Autonomous Corporation." "What if, with the power of modern information technology, we can encode the mission statement into code; that is, create an inviolable contract that generates revenue, pays people to perform some function, and finds hardware for itself to run on, all without any need for top-down human direction?" Buterin asks.

The result might be a completely vaporized corporation referred to as a distributed autonomous corporation (DAC). Cloud-based DACs would consist of software running on servers everywhere but existing in no one place in particular. According to Buterin's vision, corporate business objectives would be written as an output maximization function: the AI would divide the tasks into those best be done by computer and those requiring human effort, such as customer service, marketing, or creative design work. All human employees would report to a task-management program (just as Airbnb hosts and Uber drivers do already). And the output of those human workers would be evaluated by other humans or robots and reported back to the robot corporation. All payments, contracts, and infrastructure deals would be handled by a crytocurrency, such as bitcoin or similar.

Turning this vision into reality would require an immense amount of effort, but it's not impossible. We've seen in previous chapters that what is conceivable today will be feasible tomorrow. Bitcoin developers are already formulating plans for the necessary components: tamper-proof rules that machines would not be able to modify, smart contracts with a system for verifying the transaction, and an alternative dispute resolution process because a robot has no recourse to a court of law.

Mike Hearn, the coder quoted in Chapter 8, expanded Buterin's notion into a detailed wiki post that outlined how a robot corporation might operate a business. According to Hearn, a DAC would own capital, make binding contractual commitments, manage supply chains and outsource workers, hire people or robots to do tasks, pay them in stock or digital cash, develop new products, and provide services to other DACs. These corporations would have no physical workspace and no physical presence. Instead, they would reside on the Internet as hundreds or thousands of distributed nodes hosted on stakeholders' computers. Those stakeholders might be shareholders in the corporation or simply service providers that offer infrastructure-on-demand platforms paid by the DAC with digital currency.

The bitcoin blockchain provides the model for DACs: a cryptographically secure, open ledger of transactions distributed across many computers. And bitcoin itself is a kind of proto-DAC. It's an autonomous system that incentivizes doing things that foster it and advance it: writing software, investing and building improved infrastructure, and encouraging adoption.

It may seem preposterous, but from an investor standpoint a corporation with no overhead, no full-time employees, and no bloated salaries for senior management might just be a thing of beauty. Imagine a streamlined, efficient, rules-based profit-maximization machine. Forget the private jets, executive bonuses, marble lobby at the headquarters: this entire corporate ledger would be public and verified.

WHAT JOBS WILL HUMANS DO?

Don't worry. There will still be jobs for humans in the future. The jobs that remain will be jobs that robots cannot do easily, including jobs that involve manual dexterity, good estimates and snap judgments in unpredictable circumstances, custom solutions to unusual problems, and novel approaches and invention. Robots are not very good at these things. Yet. Besides, there's no limit on human ingenuity; we keep devising new needs and wants, which leads to new professions and new ways to get paid. Here are ninety-eight jobs that are highly likely to grow in the Vaporized Economy.

> COMPUTER SCIENCE
- Computer Programmer
- Machine Learning Engineer
- Machine Vision Engineer

> CREATIVE
- Art Director
- Augmented Reality Designer
- Character/Avatar Designer
- Content Creator and Copywriter
- Game Designer
- Gamification Designer
- Virtual World Designer

> DATA
- Adaptive/Predictive System Engineer
- Archivist
- Data Analyst

233

- Data Scientist
- Database Administrator
- Database Architect
- Library Scientist

> EDUCATION

- Admissions Consultant
- Educational Technologist and Information Technology Support Staff
- Instructional Designer
- Instructor
- Online Tutor/Tele Instructor

> ENTERPRISE RESOURCE PLANNING

- Application Performance Architect
- Business Systems Analyst
- Computer Systems Validation Analyst
- Coordinator of Application Development for Wholesale Systems
- Logistician
- Operations Research Analyst
- Project Manager
- Quality Engineer
- Supply Chain Automation Analyst
- Supply Chain Data Analyst
- Systems Engineer
- Technical Architect/Solutions Architect

> HEALTH CARE

- Biomedical Engineer
- Clinical Research Administrator
- Elder Care Specialist
- Health Care Information Technology Manager
- Health Care Navigator/Advisor
- Home Health Aide
- Laboratory Technician
- Medical and Health Services Manager
- Medical Device Quality Engineer
- Occupational Therapist
- Orthotist and Prosthetist
- Personal Care Aide
- Telesurgeon

> INTERACTION DESIGN

- Graphic Designer
- Human Factors Designer
- Human–Machine Interface Designer
- Infographic Designer
- User Experience Designer

> MANAGEMENT

- Financial Analyst
- General and Operations Managers
- Head of Engineering
- Head of Web Operations
- Management Analyst
- Supervisor of Customer Support
- Supervisor of Sales Workers

> MARKETING/SALES

- Pre-Sales Engineer
- Predictive Modeler
- Social Media Manager
- Strategic Pricing Analyst

> MOBILE APPLICATIONS

- Customer Acquisition/ Marketing Manager
- Customer Support Technician
- Mobile App Designer
- Mobile App Developer/Software Application Developer
- Mobile App Product Manager
- Mobile App Software Architect
- Mobile Game Designer
- Quality Assurance Tester
- Web Designer/Web Developer

> REGULATORY

- Compliance Officer
- Sustainability Expert

> RESEARCH AND SYSTEM OPTIMIZATION

- A/B Testing/Multivariant Tester
- Data Mining and Forecast Analyst
- Human Interaction Tester
- Market Research Analyst
- Quality Assurance Engineer
- User Testing Analyst

> ROBOTICS

- Control Engineer
- Mechanical Engineer
- Process Engineer
- Product Demonstrator/Product Consultant

- Robot Sales Advisor
- Robot Service Engineer
- Robotics Software Engineer
- Structural Engineer
- Test Engineer

> SECURITY

- Information Security Analyst

- Network Security Administrator

> SYSTEMS

- Computer Systems Administrator
- Computer Systems Analyst
- Information Technology Manager
- Network Administrator

- Software Systems Developer
- Support/Help Desk/Computer Support Specialist
- Systems Integration Analyst and Engineer

Almost every one of these jobs will rely on computers and automation in one way or another. Whether you are an employer or an employee, your greatest skill in the future could be how well you get along with robots.

ASK YOURSELF

> What kinds of automation have been deployed in your field? What are the next business functions to be automated in your business?
> How might artificial intelligence be applied to automated tasks and decision-making in your business process?
> What percentage of the value of your company is comprised of physical assets? How much of your company's value consists of intangible assets?
> What type of data might a sensor-laden robot gather just by working in your business premises?

10

WILL EDUCATION
BE VAPORIZED?

EVERYTHING THAT CAN
BE DEMOCRATIZED WILL BE

The antidote to technological unemployment, we're told, is education. Even the pundits and economists who breezily dismiss the concept as the Luddite fallacy concede that education and ongoing training are essential for the workforce. In a job market in which technology causes rapid and ceaseless transformation, it's not enough to front-load education during young adulthood. Knowledge workers need continuous lifelong learning and ongoing skill enhancement just to remain employable. Is our current education system up to the task? Are colleges and universities keeping pace with the turmoil in the labor markets?

According to the United Nations Educational, Scientific, and Cultural Organization (UNESCO), by 2025 the world's colleges and universities will contend with the immense challenge of educating more than 200 million young people for a fast-changing society. On top of this huge task, if accelerating technological unemployment occurs, tens of millions of displaced workers will also need to be retrained.

This is a global problem. As routine tasks are automated, every nation will experience a surge in demand for skills training from people of all ages.

Our current university systems are optimized to serve students who have not yet embarked on careers, although a sizeable portion of the student body is older than the core of eighteen- to twenty-two-year olds. However, to meet growing demand, universities, colleges, and two-year community colleges must find ways to serve people at every stage of their careers. And they must be able to do so at a radically lower cost and on demand.

What may be required is a retooling of the education system on a global scale. Not a band-aid solution or a cosmetic fix, but a complete overhaul of the goals, purpose, structure, and outcomes of mass education for the twenty-first century.

HIGHER EDUCATION IN CRISIS

Is any education system in the world ready for this challenge? Not in the United States. Here, educational institutions seem to be in a chronic state of crisis, or rather a bewildering quagmire of ongoing crises. American universities are trying to cope with challenges ranging from rampant alcohol and drug abuse to the presence of guns on campus, diversity issues to sexual assaults and the way in which they are handled. Critics assail US colleges for being too politically correct to the point of stifling free speech. Even the curriculum is under assault: legislators in Oklahoma and Georgia are seeking to ban state funding for the American history advanced placement course because of an alleged "un-American" bias.

These controversies drain college administrators of time, energy, and focus. And the consequences from a legal conflict or a misstep can devour financial resources. Yet, despite the fervor and intensity, these issues are a distraction from the biggest challenge of all. The fundamental crisis facing higher education today is the profound disconnect between the cost and benefit of obtaining a university degree.

THE TUITION TREADMILL

Today a college diploma is considered the essential prerequisite for any professional career. That wasn't always the case. In 1965 only one in ten Americans graduated from college. Earning a diploma was an accomplishment typically reserved for the elite of society. College tended to be a place for privileged young white men to network with peers and grow up somewhat before they began their careers. In 1963 the US government began a massive program to expand college attendance across more segments of society. It worked. Data from the National Center For Education Statistics shows that college enrollment increased from 6 million students in 1965 to more than 20 million by 2013. Today, according to the United States Census Bureau, one-third of the adult population has a college degree.

"The real story is the collapse in economic opportunity for people who do not continue their education beyond high school," says Paul Taylor, an executive at the Pew Research Center (PRC). Taylor was quoted in a *US News* article that covered the center's 2014 finding that those who graduate from high school will earn a median annual income of $17,500 less than those with an undergraduate degree from a college or university. That gap has more than doubled since 1965 and it is still growing. In 1965 a high school graduate earned more than 80 percent of what a college grad was paid; today that same high school graduate would be lucky to earn 65 percent of what a worker with a college degree will take home. The Pew research is consistent with studies from the College Board, the US Census Bureau, and the US Bureau of Labor Statistics (BLS) that show that a college degree correlates with greater earning power and wealth over the course of a career.

This gap will continue to grow. According to BLS, a four-year degree will be a minimum requirement for nearly a quarter of entry-level jobs by 2022. And for increasing numbers of graduates, even that won't be sufficient because the number of positions requiring a master's degree continues to climb. Thanks to a boom of new community college building in the 1960s and new programs funded by the federal government, degrees are available to far more Americans than ever before. But they have not become cheaper to obtain. Paradoxically, higher education has grown much more expensive in spite of government largesse. Some observers conclude that government-issued student loans have fueled runaway tuition inflation.

The cost of a college diploma has increased two-and-a-half times faster than inflation during the past three decades, according to Gordon Wadsworth in *The College Trap*. Since 1985 the consumer price index has risen 115 percent, but the inflation rate for college tuition has increased 500 percent. Today the median tuition for a private college is $31,000 a year. At elite US colleges, annual tuition fees can exceed $65,000. Even at the bottom end of the price range, students who study in their own state at public four-year colleges still paid an average of $9,139 in tuition and fees in 2014–15. That's a 225 percent increase over the average state college tuition of $2,810 in 1984. Has education become a luxury?

Aside from buying a home, paying for a university diploma is the biggest investment most people will ever make. By the time a student completes a four-year undergraduate college program at an Ivy League institution, she may have invested up to a quarter of a million dollars.

The result, unsurprisingly, is a debt bomb. Today Americans borrow money at an unprecedented rate to pay for tuition. More than $1.3 trillion is owed on outstanding student loans, a figure that has increased 84 percent since the 2008 financial crisis, says CNN. Student loan debt is now greater than total US credit card debt, with the average student loan balance being $29,000. Moreover, the average student debt load increases by $1,000 each year. Forty million Americans now have student loans, up from 29 million in 2008. According to the Urban Institute, which conducts research on social and economic policy, one out of five Americans over the age of twenty owes money on student loans, and half of them are worried about it.

An eighteen-year-old is ill equipped to make a decision about his future burden of loan repayments. No high school senior can predict accurately what salary she might earn after college, and therefore it is impossible to make an informed decision about what amount of debt is manageable. Monthly loan payments of hundreds of dollars—currently the average student loan payment is $279 per month, says a study from the credit rating bureau Experian—can be very difficult to manage on an entry-level salary. After rent and car payments, student loans eat up most of what's left of take-home pay. That's one reason why 13.7 percent of those who borrow federal loans for college end up defaulting within three years of leaving school, reported the *Washington Post*. Even more depressingly, one-third of student loan borrowers fail to finish college; they end up saddled with debt and still remain unqualified for high-salary careers. The US is not the only country facing this problem. Students in the UK, Canada, Chile, and Italy have recently protested fiercely against tuition hikes too. In Germany, protests were so severe that the government decided to roll back a plan to charge tuition fees.

Several professional investors, including Mark Cuban, have issued dire predictions that ballooning student loans are poised to trigger the next major debt crisis in the US, rivaling the home mortgage debt crisis for its potential to upend the economy. In part that's because in the US, a tuition loan has a unique characteristic that makes it especially toxic: unlike any other loan, the borrower can't get rid of it by declaring bankruptcy. That permanent stickiness changes people's behavior in ways that are bad for the whole economy.

Students who graduate with debt tend to be cautious, opting for safe careers with a higher degree of stability. It's a rational economic decision: after all, these young graduates seek to minimize the risk of default by finding a steady, reliable income. Unintentionally, however, that decision, made by millions of graduates, drastically limits the number of graduates who approach their careers with flexibility and adventurousness. A fast-changing economy calls for fearless, adaptable workers, not risk-averse desk jockeys.

The result is a negative effect on labor mobility. Once they settle into safe jobs with a steady income, workers burdened with student loans are less likely to switch to a new career in a promising field, particularly if there is risk involved. That deprives innovative companies of much-needed young talent. Similarly, graduates are willing to settle for a lower paycheck as long as they can predictably manage their loan payments. So it should come as no surprise that entry-level salaries for even college graduates have been stagnant for more than a decade, reports PRC.

These factors raise the question of whether the current education system is the appropriate way to prepare workers for the knowledge economy. Can an education process that was originally conceived as a luxury product for the children of the elite serve as the appropriate means to train knowledge workers of tomorrow? Is that the right mission for universities? Change will come to American education because, sooner or later, the market will demand an alternative. That is, if the college bubble doesn't burst first.

CONVERTING HIGHER EDUCATION INTO A BLOATED LUXURY PRODUCT

Why does college cost so much? In a word: it's too physical. At a time when every information-based industry has managed to migrate to digital distribution and vaporize some or all of the old business process, institutions of higher education have done exactly the opposite. More than any other business, the modern American university has vigorously defied vaporization; in fact, US universities have spent the past twenty years betting heavily on physical infrastructure instead of figuring out how to operate more efficiently. When state governments cut back funding for higher education, the colleges simply raised tuition fees, pushing the problem out to the parents and students.

American universities have invested massive sums into luxury dormitories, state-of-the-art field houses, and professional performing arts centers. US colleges now boast country club amenities that include rock climbing walls, tanning beds, shopping villages, gaming rooms, and suite-style apartments with granite counters and ice makers. And the physical expansion continues overseas. Several American universities have embarked on ambitious global expansion projects, establishing more than eighty-three overseas campuses in countries like the United Arab Emirates, China, Singapore, Qatar, and Malaysia. Many of these prestige projects lose millions, and according to the Cross-Border Education Research Team (C-BERT) at the State University of New York (SUNY) at Albany, 15 percent of all international branch campuses have failed and closed.

Is this willful self-destruction or clueless self-aggrandizement? Neither. College administrators are locked in a battle of attrition with rival colleges to attract students who can pay full fare. The way to attract those students is by adding amenities. It's a zero-sum game. "Students these days want the kind of amenities that wealthier schools can provide," James Garland, the former president of Ohio's Miami University, said in an interview with *ProPublica*. "The problematic thing is that it loads up the universities with debt, and with everyone doing it the competitive advantage is quickly lost. If everyone is trying to recruit from the same pool of students, then there are no winners. Everyone just spends a lot of money and gets the same number of students."

The biggest operational cost is employee salaries. Critics highlight the fact that university administration has grown bloated and top heavy. The Goldwater Institute, a public policy think tank, reports that "between 1993 and 2007, the number of full-time administrators per 100 students at America's leading universities grew by 39 percent, while the number of employees engaged in teaching, research or service only grew by 18 percent." One reason colleges can indulge in such extravagance is that they do not yet feel the pressure to reduce costs.

The excess might be justified if all the additional expense were in the service of stellar academic performance and promising payoff in the form of job placement. However, test results suggest that American student performance is lagging behind other industrialized nations. In their book *Academically Adrift: Limited Learning on College Campuses,* authors Richard Arum and Josipa Roksa conducted an analysis of 2,300 undergraduate students at twenty-four institutions. The authors found that 45 percent of the students demonstrated no significant improvement in a range of skills, such as critical thinking, complex reasoning, and writing, during their first two years of college, and 36 percent showed no improvement at all after four years. Students who spend more time in fraternities and sororities show even smaller gains than other students.

Critics such as Harvard professor David Edwards contend that the US education system is training workers for a manufacturing economy that no longer exists. If the money is not buying better learning outcomes, what, exactly, are people paying for?

SOLVING THE SIGNALING PROBLEM

The soaring cost of a college diploma is not correlated with an increase in educational quality. Why do consumers continue to borrow record amounts of money to pay for this expensive product? The answer may have more to do with the perception of its value in the labor marketplace than it does with the actual quality of the education.

Diplomas solve what some economists call a "signaling problem" in the labor markets. A diploma from a recognized college is one of the few ways that a new entrant into the workforce can signal his or her capabilities and achievements to potential employers. Bryan Caplan, a professor of economics at George Mason University, has argued that 80 percent of the value of a college degree consists of the signal it sends to prospective employers. The diploma says a lot succinctly: the bearer of this document was chosen for a university spot from a competitive field of qualified applicants; this person completed his or her assignments satisfactorily; this person is capable of processing and producing complex information; this person completed the curriculum and was recognized for his or her achievements. A college diploma signals an ability to perform in a competitive setting and get results in an information-intensive environment.

As turmoil strikes the labor markets and some career paths turn risky, demand for a proven signal that employers trust is at an all-time high. That's one big reason why people keep shelling out for expensive degrees. Students are willing to pay a premium for the strong signal that a college diploma sends to prospective employers. This also goes some way towards an explanation for the country-clubbing of colleges. If the most valuable thing that students pay for is the signal to employers, then why bother working hard on, you know, actual studying? Why not indulge in excess for four years, party like a rap star, and spend more time in the tanning booth than the library? Academic work is for nerds.

University of Michigan professors Brian Jacob, Brian McCall, and Kevin M. Stange provide an answer in their paper titled "College as Country Club: Do Colleges Cater to Students' Preferences for Consumption?" The authors laconically conclude: "We find that most students do appear to value college consumption amenities, including spending on student activities, sports, and dormitories. While this taste for amenities is broad-based, the taste for academic quality is confined to high-achieving students." In other words, colleges have turned higher education into a consumer product.

They've bolted a bunch of expensive features onto what used to be a no-frills service because that's what sells.

The signaling premise is controversial. Those who accept it believe that college is a ludicrously inefficient way to jumpstart a career. To them, over-paying for four years of lavish consumption of spa-like amenities is like borrowing $30,000 for a luxury vacation before taking a first job.

This signaling problem also creates an opening for deceptive and fraud-ulent practices designed to bilk the least-informed consumers who are desperate to attach the all-important diploma signal to their names. Some for-profit private universities sell snake oil to those who can least afford it. Here's how the scam works: a for-profit firm acquires a small accredited college that has fallen on hard times, converts it to an online university, and then begins using extremely hard-sell tactics targeted at the most eco-nomically vulnerable individuals, selling them unnecessary courses at prices they cannot afford. The victims are coaxed into online degree pro-grams of dubious value, saddled with toxic student loans, and then neglected until they drop out. This occurs at alarming rates—up to 89 per-cent in some for-profit schools.

The high dropout rate doesn't bother the for-profit schools one bit, because the federal loan guarantee system compensates them for the drop-out students' full tuition. Meanwhile, dropout students end up burdened with debts that they will struggle to pay off in exchange for a benefit they never actually received. These unscrupulous firms taint the public view of online learning. More broadly, they generate cynicism about the value of a college education and they fuel resentment towards the current sys-tem of student loans.

OVERCOMING RESISTANCE TO CHANGE

Critics claim that the American higher education system is overdue for dis-ruption. Professor Clayton Christensen of Harvard Business School expects that half of the US colleges will be in "real trouble" in just five years.

The conventional disruption narrative goes like this: costs are spiraling out of control, quality is not improving, this situation can't last forever, and

VAPORIZED

yet the education system itself is incapable of change. It is too bloated, too bureaucratic, too rigid, and too cumbersome to effect a massive transformation from within. Therefore, according to this narrative, the traditional education system is ripe for disruption by nimbler outside forces that can provide a comparable alternative at a lower price. Hurrah for disruption! The whole edifice will collapse, walls will come down, students will be liberated, efficiency will be gained, and magically, outcomes will somehow improve.

That scenario may appeal to some people, perhaps mainly to the feisty startup ventures focused on the education market. But I believe it's not entirely realistic. In my opinion, it's more likely that change will come to the universities slowly, not abruptly, because the US college system is sheltered from normal market forces. Disruptive startups have not yet assembled the full package of components to offer a truly viable alternative to the signaling provided by a diploma. Even when that package is assembled, it will take time for these new learning products to gain widespread acceptance as an alternative to a standard college degree.

The education system is highly resistant to change.

And as long as the disruptive Huns are kept safely outside the gates, there will be little pressure to change inside the ivory tower. There is no mandate for disruptive innovation from within the university. Feeling no urgency, most colleges and universities have grown complacent. They have adopted an incremental approach to change, setting up small startup business incubators and tech accelerators on campus and piloting free online learning programs that don't offer real degrees. All of this activity is deliberately structured to serve in a subordinate role to the traditional curriculum, reinforcing the established system, not undermining it. These timid efforts at innovation will at best be a supplement, not a substitute, for traditional education.

This approach is similar to the strategy of incremental or "defensive" innovation that was pursued by the booksellers, music labels, and TV networks when they confronted the Internet. It never worked for them, and it isn't likely to work for education either. Ultimately, the government would probably intervene to avert an outright collapse of the university system, as banks aren't the only entities that are too big to fail. Until US colleges find themselves losing customers to the Internet, however, they are unlikely to focus on the digital threats or opportunities.

RECLAIMING THE VOCATIONAL MISSION

The ceaseless upward spiral of tuition fees leads to calls for accountability. Critics demand a cost-benefit analysis of obtaining specific degrees. Consumers want some assurance that students will take from their college experience a useful skill set along with their debt. Yet, university administrators resist these demands. They reject calls to publish job placement rates and salary histories for graduates sorted by department. In an era in which detailed price/performance ranking is available for a broad range of goods and services from cars to carpenters, the refusal of colleges to publish similar data rankles.

Unfortunately for the cause of institutional transformation, university leaders simply refuse to accept the vocational mission. They are strongly opposed to skills training on philosophical grounds. For many professors, higher education is about exploring concepts and exposing students to ideas and the insights of great thinkers, not about transmitting practical information and professional skills. Judge us on our research, not our teaching, the American professors seem to be saying. It's a stance that's consistent with the history of American colleges as a four-year playground for the sons of privilege, and the fact that US colleges are modeled on German research institutions. There never was a time when US colleges were expected to transmit professional skills. Why should they start now?

However schools interpret their mandate, there remains a growing need for some organization to train workers for the future. As we saw in the previous chapter, the software-defined society will require workers with a new set of skills. So what skills should we be teaching tomorrow's workforce? I believe that the Vaporized Economy will reward workers who are equipped with knowledge and experience of the following:

> **Critical thinking:** The ability to apply judgment to evaluate, analyze, and conceptualize information from multiple sources, including the

ability to detect bias or inaccuracy in sources, to discern fact from opinion, and to find commonality between dissonant points of view.

> **Abstract reasoning and analogy:** The ability to synthesize facts and evidence into a general theory, to compress multiple facets of a concept into a single piece of data, to simplify a multiplicity of details and arrange them in a coherent order, to transfer meaning from one source to another subject in order to expose common structure or other relationships, to conceive of conceptual metaphors.

> **Systematic innovation and applied creativity:** The ability to apply formal methods for defining problems and designing possible solutions using analysis and synthesis.

> **Modeling and simulation:** The ability to conceive of and describe a representation of a complex system and implement it in software, including the ability to abstract both system process and organization and replicate them in mathematical formulae or computer simulations.

> **Computational thinking:** The ability to define problems and proposed solutions, including modeling entire systems and user behavior, in a way that conforms to the principles of computer science.

> **Applied data science:** The ability to understand and use advanced mathematics, statistics, information theory, data analysis, graph theory, and related fields. And the ability to use data mining, modeling, and analysis in disciplines such as biological and medical sciences, economics and social sciences, finance, marketing, competitive intelligence, and business management.

> **Data management:** The ability to master software programming, visualization, pattern recognition, predictive analytics, data compression, data warehousing, search and retrieval of text, images, video, and other types of information; machine learning, natural language processing, and other techniques for processing structured and unstructured data.

> **Visualization and visual communication:** The ability to express abstract concepts in visual form, such as images, compositions, diagrams, illustrations, infographics, charts, and storyboards.

> **Digital media literacy:** The ability to assess, analyze, produce, and edit content in digital formats, including novel multimedia formats, in order to make compelling and persuasive arguments. This includes an understanding of how social media and participatory media differ from published or broadcast media.

> **Cognitive load management:** The ability to respond to rapidly expanding bodies of information while maintaining a constant awareness of trends, significant patterns, and objectives.

> **Cross-disciplinary collaboration:** The ability to understand and explain problems, solutions, and concepts from one discipline in terms of another, and to encourage participants from a range of disciplines to work together in a constructive way to achieve shared objectives.

> **Project management:** The ability to plan and manage resources to accomplish optimized results against objectives within the constraints of time, budget, and quality. The skill of getting excellent results on time and under budget.

> **Leadership:** The ability to perceive trends and anticipate changes *before* they occur. Leaders are capable of making a strategic and economic argument that justifies a new strategy, and they have the communication skills to persuade others to adopt the new strategies and implement them.

> **Entrepreneurship:** The ability to take risks and make decisions in uncertain circumstances, according to Richard Cantillon, the economist who coined the term in 1730. Nowadays, entrepreneurship is often synonymous with launching a new venture, which involves the skills of planning, managing, team-building, and turning ideas into inventions.

Several of these skills are currently taught as part of some university curricula, but the way these subjects are taught diminishes their applicability outside of academia. First, university departments are organized in rigid silos with little cross-disciplinary exchange, so these subjects are taught in isolation, not in an integrated manner. For example, data science is rooted in the computer science curriculum whereas critical thinking is often imparted in humanities and literature courses. This approach enables specialization and deep expertise but most graduates end up with blind spots because very few of them will be exposed to all of these concepts as students.

Secondly, these topics are typically taught in the abstract, far removed from the everyday world. These subjects gain more meaning when applied to real-world cases. Isolation in the ivory tower diminishes rather than enhances understanding.

Finally, the professor's time in the college classroom is devoted largely to conveying a body of information, rather than giving students a chance to experience its practical application. Critical thinking skills are communicated in a haphazard manner, as a by-product of course work and laboratory experiments instead of being taught directly.

If the university refuses to provide crucial skills for knowledge work, how will students acquire them? The college's abdication of the vocational mission leaves an enormous skills training market wide open for innovation by outsiders.

VAPORIZED EDUCATION TO THE RESCUE

Based on what we know so far about the Vaporized Economy, we can make some predictions about the changes that will occur to higher education outside of the closed confines of the education system. A vaporized approach to education would treat information exactly like atmosphere: free, abundant, shared, available on demand, pervasive, intangible, fast moving, and flexible. Call it a university without walls—a universal university.

> Tuition fees will be driven down towards free or nearly free pricing.
> Education will become available anywhere, any time, and from any device.
> Curriculum will become more relevant to specific contexts in the twenty-first century.
> Course design will evolve from mass market, one-size-fits-all lessons towards personalized programs suited to individual needs.
> Teaching styles will accommodate new formats, including those optimized for two-way participation via digital networks.

> Classroom and school design will shift away from hierarchy and top-down management towards peer education and sharing.
> A switchboard or exchange-based system of value creation and economic reward will emerge to attract more participants.
> Assessments of achievement and the resulting credentials will be relevant to the twenty-first-century job market.

There are two different pathways we might take to get from where we are now to this possible future.

Incumbents

American universities could aggressively develop online education systems that include some version of their highly desirable diploma. However, this approach will present colleges with a brand problem: the low-price online version might dilute or cheapen the perceived value of the classic, expensive on-campus diploma. No company is eager to cannibalize its main source of revenue, and colleges are no different. For this reason, some skeptical observers have cast doubt upon edX, an open-source, non-profit collaboration between the Massachusetts Institute of Technology (MIT) and Harvard University, with courses from many other prestigious universities, including Cornell, Dartmouth, and Caltech.

At first encounter, edX is an amazing development: online courses from the finest universities, offered free of charge to anyone in the world. What's not to love? But skeptics interpret this program as a symbolic gesture in the general direction of online learning without a substantial commitment. That's because the participating universities have been unwilling to push this program to the fullest extent by conferring the same credentials upon students who take the online course as those who pay as much as $65,000 a year in tuition fees for the on-campus experience.

Currently, edX courses are not credit-bearing. In other words, none of the participating universities and colleges will offer students credit for taking the online courses. Instead, students can earn a kind of consolation prize called an "honor code certificate of achievement" or a "verified certificate of achievement." Guess how many employers care about this kind of credential? As a consequence, the edX programs seem like a marketing stunt or a branding exercise. Some university professors have argued that edX is just a bid for an early mover slot in a potentially large market; it's pre-emptive positioning without the substance.

It's entirely understandable why the participating universities are in no rush to offer credit for online courses. Doing so would devalue their on-campus offering. They simply have too much at stake in preserving the old model, and they are unable to alter their cost structure. This is why I believe we are more likely to see these old institutions take a slow, cautious, minimalist and rigorously sandboxed approach to online education.

For the same reason, we can also expect the incumbents, as a defensive move, to cast considerable doubt on the validity of the alternative degrees, diplomas, and credentials offered by online-only universities and by insurgent startup ed-tech ventures.

But even if the incumbents fail to follow through on edX by allowing students to earn transferable credits, they won't necessary succeed in derailing or delaying online learning. The only thing they will accomplish through this inaction is to leave the market open to newcomers. Which brings us to the second player.

Disruptors

Disruptive ventures will fill in the gap with low-priced alternatives. In the classic disruption scenario, a nimble competitor will develop an alternative product that does not match the quality of the traditional four-year undergraduate curriculum, but is nevertheless good enough to satisfy burgeoning demand from a base of underserved consumers at a significantly lower price. Massive uptake will propel the startup venture to go upscale and eventually challenge the incumbents.

This is the universities' game to lose. If they fail to address the opportunity with a comprehensive product that meets the needs of students and their prospective employers, then the opportunity remains wide open to newcomers. Someone will seize it. As we've seen previously in news, music, magazines, film, and lately in television, defense is never the winning strategy when information industries get vaporized. Once the newcomers gain a foothold, the best outcome that the incumbents can hope for is to keep a slice of the market share.

WELCOME TO THE VAPORIZED UNIVERSITY

We're not necessarily trying to find ways to disrupt traditional higher education. We are seeking ways to *maximize* education by enhancing, expanding, and substituting some parts of the education system with pure digital information that can be provided for low or no fees to serve a billion people. If we were going to start a new school from scratch in the Vaporized Era, we probably would do things very differently from the way they're done now.

For starters, we'd probably seek to minimize the physical. We'd avoid building a campus, dormitories, and classrooms, if possible. We'd probably remove the computer lab and language labs, and instead would encourage our students to use the computing devices they already have: laptops, smartphones, and tablets.

We might reconsider the facilities needed for sports and extracurricular activities. Can these be outsourced? If we were to remove those elements, then we'd also no longer need support staff and maintenance crews and janitors. We'd no longer need school security guards, nurses and health care workers, gym instructors, coaches, art instructors, or van drivers.

We might reconsider the role of the teaching staff. Machines and media excel at the task of transmitting information. Human teachers are better at providing questions, reasoned debate, and nuanced critique. So instead of transmitting information in the form of a lecture, teachers might show students how to navigate vast information flows and discern between useful and unreliable sources. In other words, fewer lectures and more dialog, challenge, and debate.

And finally, we might rethink all of the physical accouterments of education: the textbooks, the notebooks, the white boards, and the written tests. Let's ask ourselves how much of that physical matter could be replaced with pure digital information.

Wait a second! Did you just say I've removed everything that makes a good college great? Before you click *send* on your hate mail, hang on! I agree with you. All of those fine things do indeed make for a great educational experience—for those who can afford it. And I'm not arguing that there's no room at all for that classic college experience in the future. But I am suggesting that we need alternatives and complements, not to replace universities, but to go where they cannot go and to do what they cannot or will not do. The way to get there is by leveraging ubiquitous smartphones, mobile data networks, cheap online video, and highly interactive responsive software.

RETHINKING SCALE: ADDRESSING A GLOBALLY DISPERSED STUDENT BODY

One clear lesson from the Vaporized Era is the need to scale the solution to meet growing global demand. The lessons learned in the first round of massive venture-funded online courses prove that is easier said than done.

In 2011 Sebastian Thrun, the former Stanford professor who invented Google's robot cars, taught a course on artificial intelligence with computer scientist Peter Norvig. They decided to open up the Stanford course to anyone who wanted to participate via the Internet, free of charge. Thrun started small, sending a notice by email to a professional networking group, but word spread quickly through the Internet. Within hours, 5,000 people had signed up and by the next day the number rose above 10,000. Ultimately, 160,000 students in 190 countries enrolled in the course. No one had ever taught a university course that large before. As Thrun told National Public Radio (NPR), "We reached many more students, Peter and I, with this one class than all other AI professors combined reached in the last year."

I paid close attention to this phenomenon at the time because I had recently managed Oprah.com, where we produced a series of online courses for Oprah Winfrey. Prior to Thrun's Stanford course, Oprah's Live Your Best Life courses were the largest live online learning initiatives on the Internet. Oprah.com reached hundreds of thousands of simultaneous participants during the live webcast, and once it was finished, tens of millions watched the lessons on demand. Obviously these classes offered completely different subject matter and were designed for a completely different audience. But subject matter aside, the technical challenges of serving educational content to huge audiences were comparable.

How does one teacher address hundreds of thousands of students? How much live interaction is necessary or even possible? Can students really learn from a video on a digital screen? How much of the material is actually retained by students? How can this retention be measured? What is the role of peer-to-peer dialog and sharing in online learning? At the time, these questions were difficult to answer because the field was so new.

The era of the MOOC, an ungainly acronym for the massive open online course, began in 2008 when Canadian professor Dave Cormier coined the term to describe an Internet course called "Connectivism and Connective Knowledge," which was taught by professors George Siemens and Stephen Downes to demonstrate their approach to online learning for the digital age. The two professors had cobbled together a loose collection of collaborative technologies that were sufficiently reliable to permit students to engage and interact via the Internet: rich site summary (RSS) syndication feeds, blog posts, and participatory conversation tools like threaded discussion forums. Some of their students even convened in Second Life, a virtual reality simulation. Since then, the field of large-scale learning on the Internet has matured quickly. In 2012 the *New York Times* heralded the "Year of the MOOC." Thrun left Stanford to found Udacity, a startup venture focused on publishing MOOCs. Two other Stanford professors, Andrew Ng and Daphne Koller, launched a rival firm called Coursera. And that's also when Harvard and MIT launched edX.

Bang! The race to reinvent higher education was on. Fueled by fresh funding from venture capital firms, the new companies hurried to strike deals for content from major universities. It was a land grab to lock up the rights to the best professors, the best university affiliations, and the best curriculum. Coursera and Udacity were angling for an aggregation strategy, hoping to emerge as the YouTube of online courses. Like all software startups, Coursera and Udacity were focused on maximum efficiency at scale, which meant putting every course into a similar template, namely linear lectures on video. This industrialized approach was very different from the ad hoc teaching methods used by Siemens and Downes, whose early "connectivist" MOOCs were designed to encourage all participants to create and generate the learning activities.

The result was a flop. By mid-2013, just a few months after the hype wave crested, a backlash had begun. Experts both within the universities and outside felt the MOOCs fell short in every way: teaching methodology, teaching effectiveness, retention rates, and course completion rates. They criticized how most courses were presented as a digital video stream shot in the university lecture hall, an approach that failed to embrace the two-way capabilities of digital media. The publishers employed painfully uninteresting videography techniques, relying on a static locked-off camera, mediocre audio, and terrible graphics. With such an unengaging user experience, it's little wonder that the average dropout rate for MOOCs exceeded 90 percent.

Even the people who publish MOOCs admit that initial quality was poor. Sebastian Thrun said on PBS: "We have a lousy product." But those who smirked about Thrun's confession arrived at the wrong conclusion: they assumed that his was an admission of defeat, as if there were some fundamental problem with MOOCs that couldn't be solved. That's not the point that Thrun was making with his confession. Instead, Thrun was articulating a crucial point about software products. They improve through an iterative process. Nobody denies that first-generation software products tend to be crappy. Let's call them MOOC 1.0. No shame in that, especially for a free product. Like most things in software, the next release will be better.

Eventually the MOOC providers will work out a formula that uses the strengths of the Internet and blends them with superb production values and excellent teaching. Future MOOCs will be responsive, personalized, and rich with two-way communication and community features. And they will probably link up with universities and colleges in a collaborative way. Today we are a long way from that point, and perhaps it requires a leap of imagination to envision much better MOOCs. Through a continuous process of iteration, however, they will gradually find their niche.

MOOC 2.0: Cooperation, Not Competition

Already there are signs of improvement. Today MOOCs offer much shorter video clips that are optimized for mobile devices. Linear presentation is punctuated by short pop quizzes to test the students' understanding and reap user feedback that will help fine-tune the product. Graphics and presentation styles have improved. Business models are maturing and diverse strategic approaches are emerging. Even the concept of "massive open" courses is under examination.

edX has begun to experiment with SPOCs (small private online classes) taught by a UC Berkeley professor. It's a hybrid approach that blends the classroom and the online program into a unified experience. In this way, the MOOC is evolving into a twenty-first-century textbook; it's an enhancement instead of a substitute for the classroom or professor. Some observers predict that this will be the fate for all MOOCs.

Addressing some of the critiques from their initial offerings, all three providers—Udacity, Coursera, and edX—have begun to roll out advanced college-level courses.

And all three have introduced some type of certificate of achievement, although this aspect remains underdeveloped.

Plenty of weak spots remain. None of the big MOOC platforms has fully taken advantage of smartphones or tablets to enable a truly "anywhere, any device" mode for students. Their community and social features, forums and message boards, remain underdeveloped. The dominant paradigm is still the lecture, a teaching methodology that dates back to the Middle Ages. These shortcomings present an opportunity for new entrants, and hundreds of companies around the world, including NovoEd, Saylor Academy, and Canvas Networks in North America; FutureLearn in the UK; iversity in Germany; OpenLearning in Australia; and ALISON in Ireland, have begun to offer online learning programs. Each firm develops a novel strategy.

Hannes Klöpper, the CEO of iversity, described the current situation to me as a kind of standoff: "So far, MOOCs don't really solve problems. The early excitement wanes while the questions about the business model become more pressing. However, the traditional mode of education delivery is outdated, creating a variety of problems for academic institutions and knowledge-based companies alike." Klöpper's primary strategy to break the logjam is to build a network of alliances among European universities. His company serves as a platform to extend courses from one university to others. "That way," he told me in an email interview, "member institutions can offer all-encompassing interdisciplinary curricula." But iversity is also reaching out beyond academia to corporate partners. Klöpper said that iversity will offer "education as a service" to enable corporations to train not only employees and existing clients, but also to the general public, including university students.

Udacity is pursuing a similar strategy in the US, developing a series of courses tailored to the requirements of corporate partners through its Open Education Alliance. For decades, corporate leaders have complained that universities don't produce graduates with the skills needed in the business world. Now, by partnering with corporations to develop custom courseware, the MOOC platforms will give them a chance to do the job themselves. However, the cloud over MOOCs won't dissipate until they improve to the point where the results are measurable, and valued, by employers.

In fact, what seems to be emerging is a return to the original vision of MOOCs by Canadian professors Downes and Siemens. They did not use a single centralized platform for online learning in 2008 for the simple reason that there were none available for the kind of course they were teaching. So they cobbled together a combination of widely available free tools. The result was greater student engagement than any MOOC has so far been able to demonstrate. The good news is that new tools to engage a variety of student needs are already emerging. Successive waves of digital technology have begun to reshape the learning experience and reconceive of education for highly interactive two-way engagement.

RETHINKING SPACE: THE SOFTWARE-DEFINED CLASSROOM
The digital classroom of the future will eliminate outdated setups like today's dedicated computer lab or language lab. Instead, intelligence will be embedded in the walls and sensor networks that surround students. The entire classroom will become a computing surface with wall-sized screens

operated by eye tracking and gesture control, and smart tables with touch interfaces. Even now, a range of new educational tools is helping to redefine the traditional classroom for digital media.

For years at the grade school and high school level, Salman Khan, the founder of the Khan Academy, has urged teachers to "flip the classroom." Instead of using precious class time to convey basic concepts and lectures, Khan recommends that video lessons be assigned as homework. That way classroom time can be reserved for intensive experiential learning: hands-on learning, demonstration, explanation, and correction. Now some college professors are beginning to try a similar approach, using MOOCs and other online resources as a hybrid tool to enhance, rather than replace, the classroom experience.

Smartphones, phablets, tablets, laptops, and other wireless devices are also moving into the classroom and mobilizing learning. Borrowing a page from information technology managers who, around 2010, began to allow employees to "bring your own device" (BYOD), teachers now permit students to use their personal electronics devices in class rather than telling them to put them away. As a result, bulky resources like specialized dictionaries, thesauruses, historical documents, and even the *National Audubon Society Field Guide to North American Birds* that once occupied a rarely visited shelf in the library, are now just one click away in the form of an app. Even entire museum libraries, such as those from the Louvre and New York's Museum of Modern Art (MOMA), have been vaporized into a mobile app.

And it's not only books that have been digitized. Students are also finding vaporized versions of flash cards, maps and atlases, and spellcheckers, as well as virtual versions of slide rules, graphing calculators, and protractors. One of my favorites is Star Walk, a star map guided by GPS that makes astronomy accessible to anyone with a phone. More than 88,000 educational apps are now available in the Apple App Store, covering nearly every subject for all grades and skill levels.

Apps are for teachers too. Free apps like Google Docs enable group collaboration on shared assignments. Attendance is an app that tracks, well, naturally, classroom attendance. TeacherKit and Teacher's Aide are virtual assistants. Mendeley allows professors to keep track of research and network with peers. In addition to apps, teachers at every level use cloud services like Dropbox, OneDrive, and Google Drive to post and share with students such information as lesson plans, homework assignments, quizzes, supplemental video instructions, answers to frequently asked questions (FAQs), office hours, lecture or lesson videos, white board annotations, previous student projects, and additional resources.

And what about textbooks? Inspired by shared, open-source software, a new generation of open course materials and free digital textbooks are providing an alternative to the expensive proprietary textbooks from major publishers. Several organizations offer free courseware for online teaching, including the Open Education Consortium, which has member institutions in more than thirty countries. Other open education resources (OERs) include WikiEducator and Connexions.

The vaporized classroom

Not only are the contents of the classroom being digitized, the Minerva Project offers the closest thing to vaporizing *the entire classroom* today. A mash-up of online learning combined with the personal camaraderie formed in college dormitories, Minerva is aiming to provide a four-year education superior to the Ivy League universities at less than half the price. A relatively low annual tuition fee of $10,000 buys a room in a dormitory with students from many countries, and all those pupils participate in highly interactive online seminars with a professor who might be located in another nation. Each year, the entire class moves to a different city—Year 1 takes place in San Francisco, and in subsequent years Minerva students live in Berlin and Buenos Aires, Mumbai and Hong Kong, and London and New York.

At Minerva there is no campus, no classroom building, and no gymnasium or other facilities; the "school" is just a dormitory. There are no lectures and nothing remotely like a MOOC. All classes consist of nineteen or fewer students who interact live with a professor through the computer screen. Using specialized Minerva software, the professor can reconfigure the virtual classroom with a click of the touchpad, calling on a single student or dividing the class into teams or superimposing a quiz that displays real-time results. By all accounts, the experience of participating in a Minerva online class is exhilarating and somewhat exhausting because there is no opportunity to slack off, drift, or lose focus. Like all things vaporized, Minerva courses are data intensive. Because the professor has the data-driven ability to monitor student progress constantly, there is no need for industrial-era artifacts like grades or midterm examinations.

RETHINKING SPACE: BEYOND THE CLASSROOM
Just as peer-to-peer (P2P) marketplaces have allowed many people to share underused assets like cars and tools, online peer mentoring gives people the chance to exchange their expertise. Most of us have valuable knowledge and experience but very few opportunities to share it. The rise of efficient switchboard marketplaces for experts will match this know-how with those who seek it.

For decades, most campuses have had tutors and classroom teaching assistants available to help students with their assignments, but thanks to geography, this network of peers is limited. The digital domain provides access to a much broader group of experts who are available at any time. For instance, eTutoring.org manages online tutoring services for 130 colleges and universities in three consortia across North America.

Several firms already operate online tutoring marketplaces. Educational powerhouse Pearson offers a broadly targeted on-demand service called Smarthinking, Inc. that provides a dashboard for teachers to monitor their students' progress. The content covers every subject and is available on all devices, including tablets and smartphones, and it serves both corporate clients and higher learning institutions. In contrast, a Canadian market-place called Rayku focuses exclusively on math tutoring, offering the services of educators with at least ten years' experience who will develop a custom program for each student.

Some services recruit, screen, and manage their tutors centrally. For instance, since 2002 BrainMass has been building a global network of more than 1,000 tutors with graduate-level expertise. Others, however, prefer a decentralized approach. Etutorhub, for instance, operates an open marketplace where students can post a question along with the price they are willing to pay for an answer. Participating tutors submit bids to win the gig, and Etutorhub, acting as escrow agent, rakes a 20 percent commission off each transaction. Similar to Uber, Airbnb and other on-demand marketplaces, Etutorhub provides a reputation graph that helps students find tutors with the right level of knowledge and skill and credentials.

For those outside of college, services such as Thinkful provide one-on-one access to mentors for those beginning their careers or embarking on a new one, although Thinkful mostly involves people who aspire to jobs in software development and Internet technology.

In the future, however, instructors themselves may use software to improve their capacity to give personal attention to each student. Artificial intelligences will monitor each pupil's participation and progress and provide a summary to the teacher on a digital dashboard. Any students in jeopardy of falling behind will be highlighted, and ultimately, AIs may generate customized lessons, assignments, and assessments for individual learners. Minerva provides professors with tools of this type today.

Increasingly, too, online colleges and digital classrooms have begun to adopt game-based programs, which provide clear, concise goals broken down into incremental steps. Instead of long tutorials and didactic teaching methods, these lessons immerse students in an experiential learning process that responds instantly to their decisions. As well, the ability to win and accumulate badges and other tokens of achievement allows students to share proof of their progress with others and earn congratulations. Their individual results are recorded on the teacher's dashboard and can be used to compare, rank, and score each student against others in her cohort as well as to target remedial aid, if needed.

The virtual classroom

Facebook's acquisition of the Oculus Rift, a virtual reality (VR) headset, heralded a renaissance in this technology, which simulates the sensory experience of being in a three-dimensional space. Soon after, Samsung, Sony, Microsoft, Google, and Valve released VR headsets too, not just for use in video games but potentially also in education. For students who have grown up with powerful game systems in their living rooms, using VR in the classroom can make lessons more accessible, relevant, and interesting. For example, it can bend the rules of physics so that students can experience science, history, and foreign languages by exploring a molecular structure from inside a particle, zooming out to fly over the surface of other planets, or roaming through the streets of ancient Rome.

In the future, VR will also allow new forms of telepresence, giving students the chance to interact with learners and teachers in other nations. They may be able to take field trips through time and space to every conceivable setting. And ultimately, augmented reality systems like Magic Leap will allow students to experience a real-world setting, enhanced with real-time data, making the field trip even more informative by erasing the distinction between the real and virtual worlds.

RETHINKING TIME: LEARNING VELOCITY

The use of software to collapse the interval between learning and the application of knowledge is best illustrated by a crop of educational technology startups that focus specifically on skills for the digital economy such as information technology, software development, and digital media. Many companies that provide IT and digital technology courses differentiate themselves by delivering faster results. After all, time is money.

For instance, a site called One Month asks, "What if you could learn anything in one month?" It offers visitors lightweight, self-paced courses that can be completed in as little as thirty fifteen-minute sessions! Currently, topics include web security, software development, programming languages like Python and Ruby on Rails, and some general business topics such as growth hacking, online payments, and digital business management.

Another company called Grovo focuses on "microlearning" to teach digital technology skills by interspersing sixty-second video clips with interactive assessments and quizzes. Some Grovo courses are tailored to specific software tools and programs like Salesforce, Basecamp, and Prezi; others address general digital skills such as search, security, and email efficiency;

and still others cover general business skills such as attention management, leadership, building consensus, and communication.

Bloc is a hyperintensive immersion program that bills itself as the "World's Largest Online Bootcamp." The site offers three- to nine-month self-paced courses in software skills and design, including web development, app design, and user experience (UX) design. These fast-paced programs are designed to give students the skills to keep up with changing technology and apply it in practical settings as quickly as possible.

RETHINKING TEACHING: THE PEER APPROACH GOES DIGITAL

As we saw earlier, online peer mentoring is proving helpful for students who need help with their assignments or want to acquire skills in specialized areas. Technology makes it easier for instructors to deputize their students. "Teaching peers is one of the best ways to develop mastery," said Jeff Atwood, co-founder of Stack Overflow, the question-and-answer website for computer programmers. It turns out it's also a great way to increase student participation, completion, and learning.

Dr. Eric Mazur of Harvard University, who calls himself a "converted lecturer," pioneered the peer instruction approach in the 1990s when he discovered that his students could teach each other physics concepts faster and more effectively than he could using the traditional lecture methodology. Now, with Julie Schell, a postdoctoral fellow at Harvard, Mazur has set up Peer Instruction Network, which uses social media tools to connect teachers around the world who wish to use the method.

Perhaps the boldest of the P2P educational ventures is Peer 2 Peer University (P2PU), a nonprofit organization that bills itself as an "open learning community." Its non-hierarchical approach to learning means that anyone can teach a course or a study group.

OpenStudy dissolves the hierarchical distinctions between teacher and learners at various levels. It is an online study group comprising 40 percent college students, 40 percent high school students, and 20 percent teachers. It's designed to facilitate conversations among geographically dispersed students who are studying the same subject, independent of grade or title.

RETHINKING EXPERIENCE: LEARNING BY DOING

Skills like entrepreneurship, leadership, and collaboration are in high demand by prospective employers. Can these skills really be taught in a classroom? Some universities, like the University of Southern California and Stanford, are trying to find out. They have set up entrepreneurship programs and on-campus incubators for startup projects. Other US colleges rely upon volunteer efforts by professors who teach the entrepreneurship curriculum for undergraduate engineering and technology students provided by the Kern Entrepreneurial Engineering Network (KEEN) Institute.

Harvard's David Edwards describes efforts to cultivate learning through a personal process of "discovering the undiscovered." Writing in *Wired*, Edwards cites programs at Stanford, Massachusetts Institute of Technology (MIT), Arizona State University, and Harvard that encourage students enrolled in business, engineering, design, and even Romance language programs to engage with the world outside academia. These discovery quests are presented in a variety of formats and locations, such as culture labs for exploring experimental projects in contemporary art and design, maker-spaces for sharing tools and other resources, innovation prizes for encouraging and honoring new products and ideas, and after-school activities for promoting real-world awareness and social engagement.

Tech accelerator programs

Outside of academia, there's another way to learn real-world skills: jump in and start a new company. In the past decade, tech accelerator programs — organizations that foster the rapid development of a portfolio of startup ventures — have sprung up in almost every major city in North America, Europe, and Asia. Some call these accelerators "the new college," but they don't much resemble the traditional educational institutions. There's no courseware, no academic curriculum, and no credits. Nor are there student loans and tuition fees. Instead, the focus during an intense three-month burst is on results. For those who succeed, the outcome can be far more valuable than a diploma: it's typically a first round of funding for a brand new venture. Research conducted by professors Yael Hochberg and Susan

Cohen indicates that more than half of the startup companies cultivated in tech accelerators successfully got funding.

An outgrowth of the incubator programs of the 1990s, tech accelerators emerged in the mid-2000s with a novel twist on the formula of hatching startup companies. Whereas incubators relied upon business ideas supplied by the managing partners of an investment fund, accelerators welcomed visiting entrepreneurs who brought their own ideas. Tech accelerators typically provide entrepreneurs with a workplace, mentorship, coaching, access to a support network, and ultimately a small amount of seed funding.

For entrepreneurs, sacrificing 6 or 7 percentage points of equity in their future company in exchange for immediate access to a committed network of instructors, mentors, and alumni can be a much more attractive proposition than borrowing vast sums of money to pay for four years of university tuition. And the condensed time span (hence the term "accelerator") dramatically reduces the opportunity cost of forgoing the traditional college program.

The concept was pioneered by Y Combinator in 2005. Twice a year this seed fund invests in about seventy fledgling startup companies, providing workspace for three months and devoting energy to help them hone a proposition and define a product concept so they are ready to be financed by venture capital firms. Co-founder Paul Graham and his team at Y Combinator have already graduated more than 700 companies, including two bona fide hits: Dropbox and Airbnb. More than 100 Y Combinator startups have exited through acquisition by other firms.

Y Combinator is not the only accelerator program. Techstars has franchised its formula across many cities. And the concept has been copied by corporations, cities, and regional governments all over the world. Today there are more than 2,000 tech accelerators globally, each affiliated with specific industries, regions, and categories.

RETHINKING COLLEGE: TURNING ON, DROPPING OUT, STARTING UP
Billionaire investor Peter Thiel managed to piss off just about everybody in academia when he introduced the Thiel Fellowships in 2010. Larry Summers, the former president of Harvard and a presidential economic

advisor, remarked: "I think the single most misdirected bit of philanthropy in this decade is Peter Thiel's special program to bribe people to drop out of college."

The Thiel program is explicitly intended to persuade talented young scholars to leave university in order to focus on creating a new business or project. Its premise is simple: the fastest way to master the skills involved in entrepreneurship is to start a business from scratch. To do this, Thiel offers twenty participants $100,000 to jumpstart their own companies. In the first four years, eighty-three fellows have raised $72 million in investment and grant money for their startups. And to date these companies have generated $29 million in net income.

One former Thiel fellow, Dale J. Stephens, dropped out of school at age twelve and became, according to his official biography, a "sought-after education expert." Stephens' project in the Thiel program was UnCollege, which bills itself as a "social movement changing the notion that college is the only path to success." As an alternative to the college curriculum, UnCollege offers a structured gap year rich in immersive experiences. The twelve-month program includes an international homestay, volunteer work, a professional internship, mentorship, and the completion of a portfolio project.

VALIDATING THE VAPORIZED EDUCATION

The significance of all of this startup activity in the educational technology category is not whether any particular venture will succeed or fail but the kaleidoscope of new methodologies that will be discovered, refined, and optimized. Ultimately, the goals of education from the learner's perspective are to gain an understanding of the progression and meaning of humanity's greatest insights and to come away with the knowledge and skills for a fulfilling and meaningful life. The potential of education to transform human beings is so great that some people maintain it is a basic human right.

The classic model of higher education whereby students pay huge sums of money to attend lectures given by experts on a sprawling college or university campus is increasingly out of reach for most people. And for many of those who are lucky enough to afford this experience, the enormous burden of repaying their student loans nullifies some of the positive benefits of their learning. The promise of vaporized education, for all its many short-comings and growing pains, lies in the prospect of more equal, affordable access to theoretical and practical knowledge and the credentials that signal mastery of both.

CREDENTIALS ARE THE FINAL FRONTIER FOR ONLINE LEARNING

Suppose you were to take a series of online courses in order to brush up your skills and learn something new. If a prospective employer finds your degree credits meaningful, you've got a shot at getting a better job. However, if that employer fails to see value in your credentials, then your investment of time, effort, and money may not help your cause. You might be smarter but poorer. Establishing credentials is one of the most difficult issues still facing vaporized education.

As we've seen, the big MOOC platforms offer proprietary "honor code" credentials and "verified certificates." P2PU is developing something called "peer accreditation." So far, however, these online-only credentials don't solve the signaling problem because employers have no idea how to inter-pret them. They are too narrowly tied to a single platform, so unless the hiring executive has taken the course herself, she will have no idea what the credit means.

A variety of startups such as Degreed, MyEdu, Accredible, and Smarterer are attempting to solve this problem by aggregating achieve-ments across a number of online learning programs and offering different ways to organize and display credentials uniformly and consistently.

In another approach, Germany's iversity is offering course-completion certificates for its MOOCs that are integrated with the European Credit Transfer and Accumulation System (ECTS). As Hannes Klöpper of iversity told me, "ECTS credits are the official currency of the European education market." So the fact that students of iversity's online education can earn ECTS credits means they can fully integrate into the traditional system of higher education. In fact, a major advantage of the ECTS is that students can earn credits for course work at *any* participating university and make them count towards their degree at their home university. And by cooperating with accredited colleges and universities, iversity greatly enhances the value of online learning in the eyes of employers. However, this strategy may limit iversity's ability to innovate beyond the standard fare of major European universities if the bureaucratic accreditation councils of their not-so-nimble partners can't keep up.

In the US, none of the universities that publish free courseware on edX or Coursera are willing to grant an online degree equivalent to their on-campus programs. So far, only Udacity and the Georgia Institute of Technology (in partnership with AT&T) have worked out a way to offer a traditional degree to online students. When they announced an online master's degree in computer science in 2013 it made news as the first time that a real-world university was willing to confer a traditional degree to online students who pay only $7,000, or about one-sixth the price of the degree earned on campus.

Why haven't the others followed Georgia Tech's example? Simple. If cheap online diplomas gain currency, demand for the pricier on-campus program could erode. Brick-and-mortar universities and colleges may be forced to match the discounted Internet price at a time when they are struggling to amortize huge investments in new buildings and country-club amenities. By withholding their credentials from online learning, these institutions hope to preserve the premium pricing for their core product.

Zvi Galil, the dean of computing at Georgia Tech, sees the future differently: "I thought we could be leaders in this revolution by taking it to the next level, by doing the revolutionary step," he told the online newsfeed *Inside Higher Ed*. Galil expects to scale enrollment from 300 on-campus students to 10,000 online. Galil understands that the winner-take-all dynamic means the advantage accrues to the first mover.

At best, the concepts for online credentials described above merely match what is available at any college or university. To beat the signaling strength of a college diploma, a further revolutionary step may be necessary. Internet courseware needs a new system that is limber and global, defined as an open technical standard so that certification is consistent across every online academy and college around the world. Meeting this demand will require a standardized approach to credentials and a way to track the accomplishments of every learner, regardless of their nation of origin or their socioeconomic background or their local education system. Think of it as a digital ECTS for all online courses.

Say hello to "micro-credentials"

Open Badges may be just the solution. This is the open-source certification scheme developed especially for online education by the Mozilla Foundation, and it offers several features that distinguish it from previous standards:

> The badges are not just static images or cute graphics. Encoded in them are metadata such as the name of the course, the nature of the lessons, the specific test or assessment that was used to grade the student's progress, a link to a gallery of deliverables and, most importantly, the name of the issuer.

> The badges are designed to plug into the reputation graph—they can be posted easily on LinkedIn, for example—but they are not transferable. The badges belong only to the person who earns them.

> The badges can be used as a pivot point to find other people with similar achievements.

> The badges enable a diverse range of options for flexible course design, such as a long course or short, single lesson or series, solo or group, and so on.

> The credits can be permanent or they can be set to expire after a certain date. They can even be remotely renewed by the publisher.

> The badges can be control points for a game-like achievement system: for example, a student might only be able to open up the next level of the course if she has earned the badge for the previous level.

> Meta-badges can be used to organize a group of classes under a single badge, to signal mastery of a coherent body of information.

> The badges can be used to combine unique groups of courses from a variety of providers to create personalized degree programs.

> The badges can be issued by any organization or individual: a college, a MOOC, a charity, a corporation, a government agency, a military division, a public safety department, or an author, expert, or individual teacher. Even a weekend hackathon for app developers can issue badges to those who complete a software project.

> The badges are not bound to the classroom. They can be used to recognize any achievement: sports records, volunteer activity, charitable works, tutoring hours, community service, performing arts skills, or completed travel.

Any organization—not just a college or university—can issue a "microcredential." For instance, Autodesk, the maker of three-dimensional technology software, could issue micro-credentials to people who are qualified to teach computer-aided design (CAD) courses online. Adobe might issue micro-credentials through online courses that teach Photoshop or Illustrator at various levels of advancement.

About 14,000 badge issuers have joined the Open Badges program so far, including major educational publishers like Pearson, government entities like the National Aeronautics and Space Administration (NASA) and the Smithsonian Institution, and corporations like Intel. And, of course, universities such as Purdue and Carnegie Mellon have also signed up.

The advantages of a standardized, software-defined, machine-readable credential are significant. In the future, students will post open badges on a personal website or LinkedIn profile instead of requesting college transcripts. Recruiters and prospective employers will be able to index these smart resumes automatically, keeping track of updates to the badge collection and contacting those with the appropriate credentials when a job comes up.

One major advantage of the open badges and smart resume is that they help to automate the process of matching workers to jobs. Once the credentials are standardized, this process can happen on a massive scale. Did you master a new sales training program? Check. Did you get promoted to sales account manager? Check. Did you make it into the President's Club for closing $5 million in new contracts? Check. All of these badges, issued by independent parties, will appear on the smart resume where they will be noted by prospective employers. It's easy to imagine that a "recruiter bot" employed by a corporate human resources department will constantly scour the Web for prospective candidates. When the bot discovers a candidate with a suitable collection of badges, the recruiter may reach out directly to the candidate. Instead of searching for a job, the jobs will search for candidates automatically.

Open Badges present the possibility of displacing the university's last line of defense: the diploma. Instead of a single document that signals four years' worth of accomplishments with very little detail or a transcript that offers nothing more than the name of a class and a grade, smart badges will enable prospective employers to drill deeper to review the coursework, the test scores, and the entire portfolio of completed assignments.

"The game in academia is that a governing body validates a university's programs and the business community acknowledges and accepts their judgment because they don't want to be bothered," explained Chris Boardman, a professor in professional practice at the University of Miami. "Over time I believe that Open Badges with bots that search out expertise looks like a viable alternative that can meet demand. The question is: 'Who determines the quality of the skill sets acquired?'"

In the future, employers, not academicians, will make that determination. Today universities are accredited by government bodies whose authority is backed up by public funding. By definition, such accreditation boards are detached from the labor marketplace. That situation is ripe for change. In a 2013 speech at the Presidents' Forum, which comprises leaders from a group of accredited national educational institutions, Harvard business professor Clayton Christensen drew a distinction between government-appointed accreditors and employers as the arbiter of online learning's value. He said, "Where the employer is truly the ultimate consumer of the graduates in training, employers—not accreditors—are the only ones who need to be persuaded."

My expectation is that companies will step up to a more active role in determining the merit of digital credentials. Some companies have already begun to issue their own badges that conform to their criteria. And, of course, they will also accept credentials issued by third parties. However, with Open Badges the employers will be able to specify more precisely the skill sets and level of expertise they seek. I believe this is likely to happen because, ultimately, companies face the hard problem of finding the best talent possible. As maddening and frustrating as job seekers may find the labor market, it's even more difficult for employers to find the best candidates for their jobs. The current job market is almost certainly the least efficient, most chaotic, and inconsistent marketplace of all. The hardest problems always present the biggest opportunities. A software-defined marketplace for human talent could be the biggest opportunity in the Vaporized Economy.

ASK YOURSELF

> How does your company currently find candidates for open positions? How effective is that approach? Do you feel that your company is fully aware of all possible candidates? How might machine-readable credentials like Open Badges improve the recruiting process?

> Consider yourself as a candidate for a job. What method(s) would you use today to inform prospective employers about your skill set, experience, and achievements? How might machine-readable credentials improve your ability to connect with prospective employers?

> How do you keep your skills up to date? What tools are available to help you record and post your extracurricular pursuits, non-degree learning, professional development, and personal accomplishments? How might these tools be improved?

> Does your company or organization embrace and maximize digital alternatives? Or does it neutralize or weaken them by withholding a key component of value the way universities withhold credentials from MOOCs? Which approach is more likely to prepare your organization to contend with a vaporized future?

11

THE VAPORIZED SELF

EVERYTHING THAT CAN BE
TRANSCENDED WILL BE

D ematerialization, the process of replacing physical objects with digital information, is a challenging concept because it forces us to reconsider the things we take for granted, including our relationship with the world around us. The Tower Records example reminds us that this digital conversion now occurs in some form in every modern city, every day. A store disappears and we find ourselves subscribing to grocery delivery from Amazon instead. A forest is felled and we replace it with a cell phone tower disguised as a palm tree. Soon the delivery van will be replaced by a drone, the taxi by a robot, the house key by an app on a smartphone, the doctor by an artificial intelligence, the office by a shared document in the cloud.

It is disorienting to discover that the familiar objects of quotidian life are not quite the solid fixtures they appear to be, that they can be here one day and gone the next. And it's hard to embrace this condition when it is not exactly something that we have chosen ourselves. It feels imposed. This realization causes a certain level of anxiety.

Even among those who embrace innovation and new ideas, vaporization evokes a reaction that I describe as truculent sentimentality: we resist change most vigorously when it touches the things we hold dear. Like it or not, humans are hardwired to orient ourselves by the physical things we know and understand, the tangible and familiar stuff of the past.

Even though the process of turning things into software brings benefits to the entire population, the disappearance of each successive product, business, or institution always provokes an outcry from a passionate group of defenders. For instance:

> "There is no education crisis," intones Janet Napolitano, the president of the largest university system in the US. She's in denial about soaring student loans, outdated teaching methods, and the growing disparity between those who can afford education and those who cannot. Her academic colleagues opine that no new system can possibly replace the traditional one.
> Cold, hard cash, or at least bank balances backed by the Federal Deposit Insurance Corporation (FDIC), are tangible and countable and come with all the assurances of fiat currency and government support. "In software we trust" is a dubious proposition for those who question the security and stability of bitcoin and other cryptocurrencies.
> Swiss wristwatches look good, feel good, and have a long history as heirlooms, a reputation earned over centuries and reinforced by lavish marketing campaigns in fashion magazines. Forget apps and connectivity— how can a mini-computer worn on the wrist possibly garner the same prestige?

Denial is powerful because it shuts down the imagination. When we repeat, over and over, that something is impossible, the brain begins to believe it. We lose the ability to think another way. The process of vaporization illuminates so many defects in our current system that we often struggle to say exactly what we are advocating for or pushing against.

For example, Uber excites debate not only because it raises the prospect of a future without car ownership but also because it clearly portends a future without human drivers. Uber-haters find themselves in the awkward spot of defending the local taxi cartels and the old auto industry with all their faults and shortcomings. If they are against Uber, what exactly do they stand for? Defending the past against the future?

The process is relentless. No sooner have we managed to contend with the disappearance of one set of familiar objects than the next round of vaporization looms into sight. Or, more precisely, out of sight. If we can vaporize the university, why not the courthouse? Or city hall? If we can vaporize money, why not banks? Can churches and temples be far behind? How far can we proceed with the concept of vaporizing physical things?

One conclusion is as obvious as it is preposterous: that we will graduate from vaporizing *things* to vaporizing *people*.

We will turn ourselves into pure information: that's the *ne plus ultra* of dematerialization. If we were to liberate the human mind from the human body, we would have no need for physical possessions and their entire attendant infrastructure. Except, of course, the computer networks where the newly digitized You would reside comfortably as long as there is a power supply. Might we eventually transfer our minds to software? Will we exchange our soft biological bodies for hardware?

The idea seems blasphemous, scientifically as well as spiritually. For starters, the technology to back up a human brain onto any other medium is nowhere in sight. How would this even occur? What process would we use? Many neuroscientists and psychologists would argue that we lack sufficient understanding of the human brain to even attempt such a feat. Even if it were possible, few of us would consider it desirable to separate the physical body from the conscious mind. And if we attempted it, how would we be certain that the transfer to the new medium was complete?

Moreover, we *are* our bodies. We operate under the conviction that the body and the mind are inseparable. Every person's life experience is defined by tangible physicality. The most meaningful moments in our lives are physical experiences in concrete settings: weddings, births, moves to a new city, travels to a foreign land, achievements of endurance or physical fitness, creations of something beautiful or important. The sheer physicality of these memories is what keeps them vital, present, accessible, and relevant.

What's more, we derive intense pleasure from our biological bodies: the flavors of a fine meal, the smells of a meadow in springtime, the feeling of crisp sheets or a warm bath, the exhilaration of skiing or skydiving, the rapture of sex, the comfort of a tender embrace. Most people require no persuading to believe that without a physical body, life would not be worth living.

And our legal identities are mapped to physicality: facial features, height, weight, eye and hair color, fingerprints, retina scans, dental records, and DNA. Our voices, our faces, our gaits and physical appearance identify us. Would it be legal to transfer your personhood to a machine, even if you could transfer your consciousness?

Human society depends upon the durable aspects of physical characteristics. Business relationships are founded on trust, and that in turn is often grounded in physicality: a handshake, eye contact, a signature on a document. Our most intimate relationships are consecrated with physical touch and the joining of two bodies. Without them, how could human relationships continue? The more one thinks about it, the more the idea of vaporizing our biological bodies seems to violate every precept of the human condition. And yet, some people believe it will happen. As a matter of fact, a lot of people believe it. They are certain it will happen. It is surprisingly common in futurist circles to speculate about exactly this scenario.

Call it the future of the body or, more accurately, call it the future of human life unconstrained by the limits of the biological body. Call it *digital immortality*. The concept may strike you as absurd, impossible, or pointless. But since you've read this book so far, you already know two things:

1. Every innovation previously discussed in this book has met with that same reaction, yet it did not stop people from exploring those ideas nor did it even slow their progress slightly, and

2. There are already plenty of people working on *this* idea.

So even if the concept of digital immortality strikes you as utterly implausible or even repugnant, let's take a moment to explore it. At the very least, we'll gain insight into the process of vaporization at the earliest stage, while it is still mostly an idea on the drawing board.

DEFYING DEATH

When futurists reach a certain age, they sometimes look ahead wistfully, perceiving a brilliant era that lies just a decade or two beyond their own mortal lifespans. At this point, their futuristic scenarios tend to gravitate to the theme of digital immortality. No futurist demonstrates this proclivity more vividly than Ray Kurzweil, the computer scientist, author, and prolific inventor who has emerged as the principal proponent for the technological singularity.

The concept of a singularity is borrowed from physics, where it describes the point beyond which scale changes so dramatically that all previous methods of measurement fail. Mathematician John von Neumann coined the term to describe the moment at which "technological progress will become incomprehensively rapid and complicated." In Kurzweil's view, this moment will occur when an artificial general intelligence is able to improve itself, triggering a runaway intelligence explosion and, consequently, software-driven improvements to every aspect of society. These changes would occur much faster than human beings could comprehend or manage. Essentially artificial intelligence would rewrite the operating system for the planet. If this sounds like science fiction, your instincts are spot on: sci-fi writer Vernor Vinge popularized the concept years before Kurzweil began to explain why it might actually occur on our watch. In the geekosphere, Kurzweil has attained rock star status for explaining the how, why, and when of the technological singularity.

Kurzweil is Google's director of engineering, tasked with bringing natural language processing to the search giant. However, his broader project seems to be creating a future where human consciousness can merge with computers. In interviews with *Rolling Stone* magazine and in the film *Transcendent Man,* Kurzweil has confessed a personal motivation behind this endeavor. Troubled by his father's untimely death at age fifty-five, Kurzweil feels compelled to generate a digital replica of his father distilled from memories, mementos, and DNA.

I've talked to research scientists, professors, and technologists about Kurzweil's quest. Each of them tends to react the same way: they confess to being aghast, because Kurzweil's candor reveals a motivation so sentimental and personal that it breaches the decorum of detached scientific inquiry. But none of these people will bet against him. That's because he has a remarkable track record of making predictions that come true. Now in his late sixties, Kurzweil is so committed to this eventuality that he has made radical life changes to keep himself fit, to increase the chances that he'll live long enough to see the day when computer processing power is sufficient to replicate—or exceed—the computational power of a human brain. At that point, which Kurzweil contends will occur by the year 2045, human minds might be transferred to computers, where they can commingle for eternity.

UPGRADING THE BIOLOGICAL COMPUTER

Kurzweil's understanding of the human mind is based on concepts borrowed from computer science. Because he sees the human mind as a kind of biological computer, he believes that human-made computing systems will catch up with and even surpass the biological brain's immense processing power. As we have seen in the field of artificial intelligence (AI), computers already greatly exceed the power of a human brain in narrow disciplines, such as calculating huge numbers, scouring through enormous data sets, and even playing chess or *Jeopardy!* Every day, it seems, artificial intelligence gains another power that trumps the human brain in one narrow context after another. Kurzweil is confident that this process will continue until computers surpass biological brains in every capacity. Many scientists and futurists have speculated about smarter-than-human-AI: what sets Kurzweil apart is his conviction that such an AI will enhance human cognition, not render it obsolete.

In Kurzweil's view, the human mind is a side effect of the evolution of brain anatomy. As he recounts it, each of the six layers of human neocortex provided significantly greater computational power than the previous layer. Each increase in power enabled greater consciousness, and eventually imagination and the ability to conceive of models and metaphors. What distinguishes humans from other primates is a by-product of the abstract reasoning power of the higher levels of the human neocortex: all human invention, culture, civics, art, and language arise from the greater computational power in the outer cortex.

In a 2013 Big Think educational video called *Your Brain in the Cloud*, Kurzweil explained that the larger neocortex of the human brain provided a decisive evolutionary advantage over other primates: "That was the enabling factor that permitted the evolution of language and technology, and art and science." In the video, Kurzweil predicted that he and other scientists will create artificial neocortexes that will exceed even the human brain's capacity. He envisions "gateways to the cloud in our heads" that will link human minds with cloud-based supercomputers, wondering: "If the quantitative improvement from primates to humans with the big forehead was the enabling factor to allow for language, technology, art, and science, what kind of qualitative leap can we make with another quantitative increase?"

Kurzweil's habit of making shocking predictions in an utterly deadpan tone incites responses that range from astonishment to scorn. His speculative writing has been subjected to withering critiques by some readers, including scientists who have challenged his science, accusing him of having a slipshod understanding of human biology, the structure of the brain, or the principles of human psychology. Some of these objections sound awfully familiar to me. The naysayers remind me of the people I've encountered in so many other fields, from television executives to game designers to health care professionals to educators, each of whom rejected a new approach without reflection, simply because it challenged conventional wisdom and raised questions they were unable to answer.

Skepticism is good because it forces us to think harder and marshal better arguments. But denialism is unconstructive because it shuts down the imagination and blinds us to possibilities.

TRANSCENDING DEATH: THE TRANSHUMANISTS

If Kurzweil's philosophy can be summarized in one word, it would probably be "transcendence." He believes that human beings are distinguished from all other forms of life on Earth by our ability to surpass our natural limitations—and our impulse to do so again and again. What animates him and his followers is the conviction that humanity will steadily continue to overcome the limits that constrained previous generations on the path towards ever-greater accomplishments.

The saga of human civilization is a sequence of heroic efforts to defy the inevitable, and I think Kurzweil's quest brings a radical high-tech twist to this grand tradition. Our desire to build lasting civic and cultural institutions, our ambition towards immortal achievement in art and science, and our yearning to belong to a religion that spans more than a single lifetime are all by-products of our fundamental existential insecurity.

We know that all human bodies eventually fail: the cages of bone, blood, and muscle that contain us will cease to function because of disease, lethal injury, or slow deterioration. And the costs of maintaining our biological physiology are immense. All of our globe-spanning transportation networks, massive agricultural and pharmaceutical complexes, enormous sewage and electrical networks, and vast health care systems are devoted to just keeping our bodies running.

Yet the costs of death, too, are incalculable. A lifetime of learning and hard-won experience is voided, a family is dealt a tragic blow, an organization may lose a key member, and a chunk of institutional memory is wiped clean. The data in our brains, known as insight, expertise, and wisdom, is irretrievably lost. What if there were some way to back up this information?

Framed in this light, the prospect of replacing the human body becomes the kind of challenge that is irresistible to scientists and inventors of a certain stripe. They are inspired not by the many virtues of the human biological apparatus, but by the prospect of transcending its many limitations.

In 1957 biologist Julian Huxley wrote an article titled "Transhumanism" in which he argued that "the human species can, if it wishes, transcend itself—not just sporadically, an individual here in one way, an individual there in another way, but in its entirety, as humanity." And it turns out that Ray Kurzweil is not the only scientist on this quest. A surprisingly long list of experts are proponents of this concept of discarding the human body.

At a 2013 press conference, Professor Stephen Hawking said, "I think the brain is like a program in the mind, which is like a computer, so it's theoretically possible to copy the brain on to a computer and so provide a form of life after death. However, this is way beyond our present capabilities." Others who share this vision are taking meaningful steps today to bring it to fruition.

Martine Rothblatt, the CEO of United Therapeutics Corporation and the author of *Virtually Human: The Promise—and the Peril—of Digital Immortality*, addressed an enthusiastic crowd at the South By Southwest (SXSW) festival in March 2015 with a message about cyber consciousness, robotics, organ cloning, and what she calls "mind clones," a kind of digital alter ego. Rothblatt, who bills herself as a transhumanist, has invested significant amounts of money into practical prototypes, including a fully functioning robot clone of her wife, Bina Aspen. The robot, BINA48 (short for Breakthrough Intelligence via Neural Architecture, with 48 exaflops processing speed and 48 exabytes of memory) is billed as "cyber conscious" today. In the future Rothblatt expects it to be fully conscious, comparable to a human being. As she told the audience at SXSW, "We are the species that keeps pushing further and further. There is no line in the sand at which point human consciousness has to end."

Russian Internet mogul Dmitry Itskov has gone even further than Rothblatt to promote the concept of digital immortality. In 2013 he organized a summit meeting in New York City to gather futurists, technologists, and transhumanists to discuss his vision of creating digital avatars for the entire human population. He set forth an ambitious multidisciplinary program with aggressive milestones to achieve his goal of a fully disembodied human being consisting of a hologram-like avatar by 2045. One of the objectives of Itskov's 2045 project is to ensure that "Humanity, for the first time in its history, will make a fully managed evolutionary transition and eventually become a new species." His Global Futures 2045 International Congress succeeded in attracting several prominent scientists, philosophers, and religious leaders, and Martine Rothblatt gave the keynote speech at the event. It was titled "The Goal of Technology is the End of Death."

Although a few scientists later distanced themselves from the goals articulated at the congress, others stood by them. Itskov has garnered support from such diverse proponents as the Dalai Lama and the Russian Ministry of Education and Science. The event generated considerable press coverage, including the predictable frenzy of speculation about uploading human minds to computers and storing the contents of our brains in the cloud. What does it really mean? Are these people delusional—or far ahead of their time?

SETTING EXPECTATIONS

In the previous chapters of this book, we've considered several software concepts that have generated controversy and surmounted a wall of resistance as they progress towards their full expression. This topic is a bit different. It is fiercely debated and often scornfully dismissed in its initial concept, long before there is even any evidence that it will actually occur. That shouldn't deter us from a bit of speculative exploration.

The timeline for mind uploading, if it proves feasible, will be much longer than the timelines in the previous chapters about robots, smart devices, and vaporized universities. By 2025, robots and online learning will be increasingly common, even if all of the kinks in those systems have not been entirely worked out. But mind uploading will take at least several decades, if it ever happens at all.

Because we are at such an early stage, there is less evidence to evaluate. Since we're peering into the distant future, the likelihood of getting it wrong is much higher. What follows is an exploration of five completely separate developments that, together, indicate that the concept of migrating human consciousness to a machine is neither a delusion nor a certainty, but an intriguing possibility that is gathering momentum in certain circles. Join me on five leaps of the imagination.

LEAP ONE: WE ALREADY SPEND A HUGE CHUNK OF
OUR LIVES IN DIGITAL ENVIRONMENTS

If you spend time around teenagers, you've probably noticed that most of them spend an awful lot of time staring at the screens on their smartphones. But teenagers are not that different from adults. They are just the newest model human beings. We all seem to have adopted the chronic habit of viewing life through digital displays. They are better adapted to this new perspective.

We're supposed to get 8 hours of sleep each night, but for most people the average is 7.2 hours. Estimates for daily screen time range from 7.4 hours to 12. From the moment we wake up until the moment we go to sleep, most of us are in front of a screen of some sort, whether it is a desktop computer at work, a smartphone while commuting, or a game console or TV set later in the day.

Add 7 to 12 hours of screen time to the recommended 7 or 8 hours of sleep time and that leaves us with roughly 6 to 9 hours each day to talk, walk, eat, get fit, have sex, and do those other things that people with, you know, *bodies* tend to do.

The top three things that we do in screen time will surprise no one: 1) update and manage our social networks, 2) send and receive email, and 3) watch streaming video. In addition to socializing and watching video, we also work, write, learn, design, shop, plan travel, conduct research, play games, listen to music, balance our checkbooks, pay our bills, create, and compose. With virtual reality (VR) headsets like Oculus Rift about to break into the consumer mainstream, we will soon find ourselves *inside* these digital worlds instead of viewing them through a rectangular display. At that point, our screen time may well increase to the point where we spend almost all of our waking time immersed in digital media. During the next five years, virtual reality will literally add a new dimension to the way we entertain and educate ourselves, and how we socialize, converse, and explore the world.

Today's resurgence of VR is happening because of a happy confluence of miniaturization and ever-increasing graphic processing power. However, it is still early in the process and the illusion is not always convincing. Ten or twenty years from now, though, when computer processors are thousands of times faster, we'll be able to explore virtual worlds in super-high resolution with lifelike detail. We may find that we enjoy this so much, we prefer VR to real life.

One of the reasons we're so fascinated with digital media is that we rely on it to extend our human senses or capabilities. Marshall McLuhan, the Canadian media philosopher, surmised that the telephone is an extension of the voice, the car is an extension of the foot, and the television is an extension of our visual apparatus. What sense is extended by virtual reality? I'd suggest VR works like social media to extend *presence* and *memory* into the digital domain.

> **Virtual presence:** What are Vine, Snapchat, WhatsApp, Twitter, Facebook, and Instagram, other than an extension of our physical presence into the digital domain? Microblogging our status updates on social media websites and messaging apps allows us to connect and converse with more versatility than a telephone call because we can reach huge numbers of people who are geographically dispersed. Virtual reality will greatly enhance the bifurcated sensation of being physically present in one place but engaging in social interaction elsewhere.

> **Virtual memory:** Today it is common to record an experience digitally and post it online. Nothing new there. Apps like Periscope and Meerkat make live broadcasting possible in real time. Yet every time we post a selfie, a status update, or a comment, we outsource a huge portion of the task of remembering our experiences to the cloud. And the percentage of our memory of personal experience that is stored in the cloud is growing, as we rely increasingly on passive systems like lifelogging and security cameras to record everything, not just the special moments. With VR these memories won't be simple video recordings or still images from a single point of view; the entire experience will be repeatable from multiple vantage points.

As a society, we seem to be embarking headlong on a migration to a primarily digital existence that includes much of our conscious thinking and communication, and the preservation of our memories. These activities, which we freely choose as individuals, move the whole of society one or two steps further in the direction that Ray Kurzweil described: linking our minds to the cloud. Billions of humans have grown accustomed to entrusting their memories to the cloud via smartphones. Most of us conduct more conversations via the smartphone than we do in person. Since our identities, relationships, and work environments have shifted almost entirely to a digital platform, it might not seem like such a stretch to imagine migrating there entirely ourselves.

LEAP TWO: THE DEPARTMENT OF SCIENCE FICTION IS ON THE CASE

When it comes to borrowing concepts from science fiction fantasies and weaving them into everyday life, nobody does it better than the Defense Advanced Research Projects Agency, or DARPA. Since 1958, this agency has served as the Pentagon's high-tech research arm, but its biggest impact has occurred when military technology was made available to the general public.

It was initially created in a rush after the Soviet Union spooked the world by launching the *Sputnik 1* satellite into orbit. At that time, US President Dwight Eisenhower vowed never to be caught off guard again and created the National Aeronautics and Space Administration (NASA) and DARPA with the mission to regain the technological lead in the Space Race with the Soviet Union. The agency's portfolio gradually broadened from nuclear weapons and ballistic missile systems to include other space technologies, such as weather satellites and a precursor of the Global Positioning System (GPS).

In the late 1960s, DARPA shifted its focus to information processing and data networks, and the agency's record of achievements in this field is remarkable, particularly in technology related to the Internet and computer networks. DARPA supported the development of the foundational building blocks of the modern Internet, including:

> an early computer operating system called Multics (Multiplexed Information and Computing Service) that established concepts used by every subsequent operating system;
> the Transmission Control Protocol/Internet Protocol (TCP/IP) network communication language that underpins the Internet;
> and the first packet radio networks that served as precursors to the mobile data that feeds modern smartphones.

The precursor to today's Internet was ARPANET. DARPA accomplished this on a small budget with a staff of only a few hundred. The full list of DARPA inventions is mind-bending: it includes the microprocessors in smartphones, stealth jets, 3D maps, robots, autonomous aircraft, and even self-driving vehicles. When you use Siri or Google Street View or a GPS-enabled map on an iPhone, this is technology that was first introduced by DARPA. Today we take these technologies for granted because they work reasonably well. In the early days, however, skeptics and budget hawks considered almost every one of them preposterous, outlandish, pointless, or impossible.

A big part of DARPA's mission is still to explore ideas exhaustively for the remotest possibility of a defense capability, even if the ideas lie far outside of the mainstream or current feasibility. The agency's job, after all, is to prevent surprises and come up with a few surprises of its own, too. By definition, DARPA focuses on non-obvious applications of technology.

One reason DARPA has been so successful is that the agency is not proprietary. It doesn't own any of the ideas it funds. DARPA's approach is to serve as a catalyst for research universities and private corporations. In order to attract research partners, the agency's unique approach is to begin at the idea stage by popularizing novel concepts, socializing them among the research labs at American universities and technology companies, and gathering support. DARPA then uses grants and public challenges to galvanize one or more working groups into action. Finally, when the competition teams successfully complete the challenge by advancing the science from the theoretical stage to the threshold of practicability, DARPA releases the ideas to the commercial marketplace where private companies bring them to fruition. Dr. Geoffrey

Ling, the director of the Biological Technologies Office, told me, "We spark and start but rarely finish." Another DARPA employee put it like this: "When it comes to R&D, we do the R and we let private companies do the D."

DARPA's strategic mission requires the organization to focus on technologies that lie so far in the future that even venture capital firms don't yet have the courage to touch them. It's the right organization to embrace crazy, radical breakthrough visions.

Biology is technology

The Biological Technologies Office (BTO) was added as a new unit in 2014 by Dr. Arati Prabhakar, the director of DARPA. In February 2015 I was invited to attend a two-day event in Silicon Valley at which DARPA introduced its BTO projects and the managers of several other biotech initiatives. The name of the event summed up the agency's new approach: it was called Biology Is Technology.

A team at the agency had spent the previous eight years working to improve prosthetics for wounded soldiers and one of its primary goals was to create a new kind of prosthetic limb that could be controlled by thought alone. DARPA staff demonstrated the results of recent work to improve prosthetic limbs, which drew a gasp from the audience. The scientists showed a short video of Jan Scheuermann, a volunteer test subject who is paralyzed from the neck down. In that clip, Jan is shown learning to control a new robot arm with just her mind, unaided by a joystick. Concentrating fiercely, at first Jan struggled. The robot arm lurched unevenly until she succeeded in guiding it to hold a bar of chocolate right in front of her mouth. As she took a big bite of chocolate, the whole room burst into cheers.

Neat demo. But that was just the beginning of the show. The next demonstration showed a patient using a similar neural interface to control not a prosthetic limb but a *flight simulator* with mind power alone. DARPA staff expressed confidence that, with training, a test subject could probably learn to control a drone aircraft with the mind alone. The agency has earmarked $7 million to the development of neural interfaces that will allow a soldier to guide a humanoid robot by brain waves alone.

The cortical modem

These two demonstrations were the set up for a presentation by Dr. Phillip Alvelda about a new project called the cortical modem. Cortical as in *cerebral cortex*. That's right, a modem that connects directly to the brain.

The objective of Dr. Alvelda's project is to develop a direct link to the visual cortex that bypasses the eyes and the optic nerve. If it works, data delivered via the cortical modem could generate a graphic overlay on top of visual sensations from the eyes. Think of Google Glass, Oculus Rift, or any other augmented reality rig, minus the hardware. This is pure data streaming right into the brain, rendering images that mingle with normal vision.

DARPA staff were quick to point out to me that the cortical modem is purely a concept at this point. They expect that it may take five years before they have even a working prototype.

To be sure, the proposed capability of the current concept is crude. At first the images will consist of blurry flashes of light. But every person in the conference understood that computer graphics improve steadily each year, and there seems to be no reason that this would not also be the case for the cortical modem, if it works as proposed. Although the project has barely begun and real-world results lie many years, or even decades, in the future, what matters is that DARPA has told the world that the game is on for the development of a direct digital link to the brain.

Where will this research into the cortical modem lead us? If the project succeeds, it may enable human minds to connect directly to the digital network, sending signals back and forth. Imagine a direct neural interface to a computer nearby or even on the other side of the planet. If it can be done with a computer, then by extension one might be able to connect with a drone or a robot vehicle.

Although DARPA staff did not disclose any military applications for this technology, it doesn't take much to envision how it might be used in the field. Imagine a soldier using the cortical modem to control a drone aircraft to peer above and beyond enemy positions. Sending signals back and forth from the mind via the digital network, the human operator would be able to share vision from the machine. This visual information would flow into the human cerebral cortex from the drone, while control signals would flow out from the human operator. There would be no more joystick or keyboard commands: the soldier will just think of instructions and they'd be sent to the machine. In a weird high-tech way, the operator will become one with the machine. The soldier will be a cyborg connected to a drone through the cloud.

Eventually DARPA projects find their way into non-military consumer applications. If the cortical modem works, the next step could be to connect human minds to all sorts of computers, which means that we ultimately may not need a smartphone to interface with all of the data sets, sensor networks, and smart devices of the Internet of Things. Instead, the network would speak directly to the cerebral cortex and the human operator would be able to extend his or her senses to any device on the network.

Perhaps instead of watching a movie with surround sound on a flat-screen television, in the future you may be immersed in the full sensorial realm of another environment: hearing, seeing, smelling, tasting, and feeling the actual environment of a remote part of the world rendered purely as electronic signals in the brain. It's early in this process. DARPA's Biological Technologies Office is at the beginning of an audacious project with a lot of unknowns. It *is* a tall order, but compared to the next leap, it seems quite achievable.

LEAP THREE: WHOLE BRAIN EMULATION

The next concept, also popularized by science fiction, is known by many names: the backup brain, mind uploading, the mind clone. They all basically mean the same thing: a program that can run your mind on a computer.

Those terms are colorful but they don't quite get at the essence of the project. They each refer to a particular *technique* of preserving data from the brain, but ultimately a different technique may prove successful. For this reason, some scientists prefer to use a different term that spell out the goal without specifying any particular technique: substrate-independent mind, or SIM.

In plain English, we're talking about replicating a human mind on a machine.

Most people tend to stop thinking about an idea once conventional wisdom has concluded it is impossible or even highly improbable. Transferring your mind to a different substrate is one such idea. Even many scientists scoff at the notion. But what if we were to tiptoe right up to the edge of that precipice and peer over the edge? What we'd find isn't a yawning abyss or a howling vacuum. Quite the opposite: SIM is a field teeming with activity. It turns out that a surprising number of people have already leaped into the void. These pioneers are busy right now pursuing their vision of mind uploading.

When embarking on a project that most people dismiss as impossible, there tends to be very little competition, plenty of cooperation, no precedents, and very few guideposts. It's all virgin snowfield, with no footprints. If you are the sort of person who likes to frolic in the wilderness, this opportunity is for you. One such pioneer is Dr. Randal Koene. On the Internet, he's known as "the neuroscientist who wants to upload humanity to a computer." (Go ahead, Google it.)

"Let's be a bit more clear about what we mean by a SIM," Koene explained to me. "SIM means running mind on a platform other than its original biological platform." Can this possibly work? It seems so far-fetched. Koene makes the usual disclaimer that all scientists love to see their theories disproved. But in this case, early evidence suggests that the hypothesis may be valid. "So far, the evidence is on the side of 'Yes, SIM is possible, scientifically and technically,'" Koene said.

One promising approach to SIM is the technique known as whole brain emulation (WBE), or neural prosthesis. Citing as an example the neuroprosthetic work done by Ted Berger at the University of Southern California, Koene told me: "Ted's work aims to build replacement parts for such regions of the brain as regions in the hippocampus—an area that is absolutely crucial for important cognitive functions related to episodic memory. Their team has successfully built neuroprosthetic devices that restored, sustained and, in some experiments, strengthened hippocampal function in rodents and non-human primates within controlled experiments. They are now taking that work to human subjects."

The challenges of mapping brain structure and function
What makes the project of whole brain emulation so daunting is that, today, very little is known about exactly how the human brain actually works. There are several reasons for that.

The first is that the human brain is an astonishingly complex organ containing roughly 86 billion neurons. In order to model a brain, every one of those neurons, and all of their connections, must be mapped. But brain structure alone doesn't tell the story of how signals are transmitted. To generate a functional state, a single neuron may interact with hundreds or thousands of other neurons using a variety of chemicals to transmit signals. Tens of billions of neurons interact with thousands of neighbors, each using multiple chemicals. That's complicated.

Second, the tools to observe and measure brain structure and function remain crude relative to the task of mapping structure. What's needed is ultra-high resolution, fine-grain measurement at the nanoscale.

And that brings us to the third problem, which is that the most effective techniques for mapping the structure of the brain at the right resolution are not, ahem, "acceptable for use on human beings," because they tend to destroy the brain by slicing it into very tiny bits. "It's fine to apply very large electrode arrays directly to Drosophila (fruit fly) brains, or to kill the fruit fly, plastinate its brain, and image that slice by slice for structural data," said Dr. Koene. "It is not as obviously fine to do that to human patients."

You might expect that there would be some sort of brain-scanning device, like a magnetic resonance imaging (MRI) scanner, that could do the job non-invasively. Sadly there is not, yet. Conventional external scanning equipment lacks the fine-grain detail necessary to be useful for mapping the brain at this minute level. It doesn't help that the brain is enclosed in a thick vault of bone. In order to build a functioning model of a human brain, scientists must solve four sets of incredibly complex problems:

> **Large-scale high-resolution structural data** show how parts of the brain communicate with each other, from neuron-to-neuron connectivity to

receptor sites for neurotransmitters and the tiny branches of nerve cells known as dendrites. Consider this the wiring diagram for the brain.

> **Large-scale high-resolution functional data** show how the parts are meant to work together. Scientists gather data directly, recording the types of responses generated by each neuron as a result of interaction with others; however, with 80+ billion neurons, there's a lot of activity to capture. At this early stage, big gaps remain in our knowledge of brain function. We might call this the operating manual for the brain.

> **Automated reconstruction of functional circuits from data:** Computational neuroscientists use experimental data to construct functional models of the brain. Today gathering the data and building the model are painstaking manual processes that will ultimately be automated. The current approach is to spread the workload across a lot of volunteers. For example, while researching the cell networks that govern vision at the Massachusetts Institute of Technology (MIT), Sebastian Seung designed a game called EyeWire that enlisted volunteers to review and correct the maps made by AI. The ultimate aim is to combine the wiring diagrams and operating manuals together to create a complete and accurate model of the entire brain.

> **Tools acceptable for human use:** The brain functions at the nanoscale, and therefore the tools to measure brain activity must also operate at that same tiny scale. One promising approach may be to inject tiny read-write devices into the brain. At the University of California Berkeley's Swarm Lab, a team of scientists has proposed using "neural dust" consisting of particles, each 100-millionth of a meter in size, scattered throughout the brain and connected wirelessly to a transceiver. Neural dust is like setting up a miniaturized sensor network throughout the brain that is capable of measuring electrical activity in neurons and transmitting it to the transceiver.

According to Koene, although these are each enormous tasks, scientists are making headway in all four areas. "These days it is possible to discuss directly the goals of complete connectomics, acquiring all functional data of a mouse brain, and even brain emulation in the setting of research lab grant proposals," he said. "That was not possible ten or even five years ago."

Some skeptics express doubt about the ability to replicate a human brain onto conventional computers. In response, Koene points to progress in alternative chip designs: "There are already advances in new computing architectures such as neuromorphic chips that demonstrate the likelihood that we will be able to build hardware well suited for WBE, possibly even competitive with the extremely low-power optimized wetware in our biological brains." Translation: new computer chips modeled on biological brains and produced by Qualcomm, IBM, and other firms will be able to process sensory data like images, sounds, and smells the way human brains do, very rapidly and without using a vast amount of energy.

Conventional computer designs, referred to as Von Neumann architectures after the mathematician who invented them, send data back and forth between memory chips and a central processor. That arrangement works fine for number-crunching but is hopelessly inefficient for processing sensory data: for instance, the task of recognizing images, something the human brain does effortlessly all day long, would require tens of thousands of dedicated conventional computer chips and a vast amount of energy, expelling enough waste heat to melt a phone.

Neuromorphic chips promise to deliver an energy-efficient way to put artificial intelligence and, potentially, brain emulation onto small devices without requiring massive power or a connection to supercomputers in the cloud. That way, the smart devices that surround us would be capable of reading and reacting to sensory data in the environment, such as the presence of certain people or objects. Qualcomm expects to debut the first generation of its neuromorphic chips, called Zeroth, in smartphones in 2016.

Koene believes it is realistic to expect researchers to gather all of the necessary functional and structural data from something the size of a fruit fly brain within the next five to ten years. If that project delivers results that allow functional modeling, then a whole brain emulation of a Drosophila fly might be possible within fifteen years. From that point, it would become possible to plot a timeline for emulating a human brain. "Aside from scale, there isn't much that seems to be intrinsically different about neuronal networks in Drosophila or human brains," Koene explains. "Sure, the arrangement is different—we have different brain areas, but the components are pretty much the same. The same sort of tools apply to data collection and circuit reconstruction. In other words, there would be very little standing in the way from those results to a human WBE project.

"Timeframes, at that point, become a matter of policy more than a matter of science or technology. How fast do you want to get there? What resources are put into the project?"

LEAP FOUR: THE BRAIN RACE IS THE NEW SPACE RACE

The race is already on to map and model the human brain. Three separate projects are now underway in Europe, the US, and Japan. The scale and ambition of these projects is immense. It's true that these projects have nothing specifically to do with the radical notion of backing up an individual person's mind to the cloud. But they do address the major challenges in developing a functional model of the human brain. And if they succeed, it will accelerate the whole brain emulation project.

Israeli scientist Henry Markram was the first to garner significant government funding for his Human Brain Project. Having successfully modeled the neocortical column of rat brain in 2006, Markram unveiled his plan to build a working model of a human brain at a TEDx event in Oxford in 2009. By 2012 he had raised a whopping €1 billion and scored an IBM Blue Gene supercomputer to begin the ambitious brain-mapping project in Switzerland.

Meanwhile in the US, President Obama parceled out $110 million to the National Institutes of Health, the National Science Foundation, and DARPA to fund the development of tools to record electrical activity at the level of the neuron. Obama's grant was matched by four private institutions: the Kavli Foundation, the Allen Institute for Brain Science, the Salk Institute for Biological Studies, and the Howard Hughes Medical Institute. The US project is known as the BRAIN Initiative, an acronym for Brain Research through Advancing Innovative Neurotechnologies.

Inevitably the scope of the project and the competing teams draw comparisons to previous space race–sized initiatives like the Human Genome Project in 1991 and the competition to build large-scale particle colliders. But Markram suggests that cooperation, not competition, is the preferred approach because the size of the challenge is simply too great. A total of 135 institutions in twenty-six countries are involved in Markram's project. An estimated 7,148 person-years of effort will be required from hundreds of researchers.

The computer processing power required for the Human Brain Project is immense. The current goal for the European project is to move 10 billion packets a second around the model. But this would simulate the signaling of only one billion neurons, about 1 percent of the human brain. The full simulation would require a supercomputer 1,000 times as powerful as those in use today. Hence the demand for neuromorphic chips that mimic the wiring of neurons.

The plan is similar to the approach used twenty years ago to sequence the human genome: start the project by working with today's equipment and assume that better gear will arrive later to speed up the progress. "Well-known manufacturers of supercomputers like IBM, Cray, Intel, and Bull, are committed to building the first exascale machines by approximately 2020," Markram told Fox News. "So we are confident we will have the machines we need."

Within three years, Markram expects that the brain model itself will be able to contribute to the design of next-generation computer chips. The sheer amount of data generated by these models will be immense. The US BRAIN Initiative will generate an estimated 300 exabytes of data each year. That's equivalent to the amount of data that was generated by the *entire Internet* in 2007, according to market research firm IDC.

The project of mapping and modeling the human brain is set to be one of the defining scientific projects of the twenty-first century. It will demand the coordination of contributions from thousands of scientists in many fields, including computational neurobiology, bioinformatics, computer and data science, psychology, and artificial intelligence.

As Gary Marcus, a professor of psychology at New York University, wrote in the *New Yorker:* "To truly reverse-engineer the human mind, we may need a real consilience, to borrow a word from the Harvard biologist E.O. Wilson, a coming together of workers in AI with researchers who study the human mind from a wide range of perspectives—neuroscientists and cognitive psychologists, and maybe even artists, musicians, and writers, too. The challenge of figuring out how the mind works is too complicated for even the smartest of entrepreneurs to solve on their own."

Biology is now an information science
These bold initiatives to model the human brain illustrate a much broader trend: biology has become an information science. The use of computers has not only transformed the study of biology; it has changed the role of the biologist. Instead of observing natural processes, scientists now use computers to reshape and reprogram life at the cellular level. Whereas biology used to be a "wet" science, with bubbling beakers and test tubes, today's biologist is more likely to be working on a computer model based on large data sets than in a wet lab.

In the field of synthetic biology, scientists design new living organisms. Biologists now use computer programs to compose and manufacture novel combinations of DNA. A click of the touchpad sends the code to a lab in China where the new DNA can be sequenced and inserted into a single-cell organism like a bacterium. From that point, the new organism can be observed and tested. If the life-form malfunctions, it is destroyed. If it works as planned, the new organism is packed up and shipped to the biologist for further study.

It seems reasonable to predict that the field of biology will see more change in the next ten years than in the previous century. Rapid advances in synthetic biology, bioinformatics, medical imaging, 3D printing of body organs, and robotics are beginning to yield real-world applications that were previously unimaginable. Information technology has transformed a scientific discipline that was once derided by physicist Ernest Rutherford as "stamp collecting" into the most potent area for applied imagination. We're advancing from "read only" biology to "read/write" biology. That is a major step towards our fifth leap of imagination.

LEAP FIVE: HUMAN-DIRECTED EVOLUTION

The four leaps we've made so far do not make the notion of uploading a human mind any less radical. They are giant steps in a progression, which is part of a much larger trend known as "human-directed evolution." In 2003 Steven J. Dick, then NASA's chief historian, argued that advanced civilizations become "post-biological," and that artificial intelligence is the product of cultural evolution rather than biological evolution. Whole brain emulation is one aspect of post-biological civilization, wherein brains and entire organisms may be redefined by software and exist entirely in environments that consist of digital information.

We are approaching the point at which cultural evolution may surpass and influence biological evolution. As Juan Enriquez and Steve Gullans explain in their book *Evolving Ourselves: How Unnatural Selection and Nonrandom Mutation Are Changing Life on Earth,* human beings now actively manage and guide the process of evolution. We routinely exercise the ability to determine the fate and future trajectory of all living things on the planet, not only ourselves but also the environment and the creatures around us.

Not too long ago it was common to assume that evolution had ceased because human civilization put an end to natural selection. Enriquez and Gullans challenge that assumption. They describe how advances in genomic science enable us to move beyond natural selection and random mutation to human-directed selection and non-random mutation by selecting traits and engineering evolutionary "winners." In the process, we've changed the world incredibly quickly in the past fifty years. We've assumed the awesome responsibility of managing the biological and ecological systems on the planet.

Viewed through the lens of human-directed cultural evolution, the substrate-independent mind is just another evolutionary option for humanity. It's one choice among many. "The substrate-independent mind is desirable and possibly even necessary for the future of our species," Randal Koene told me. "SIM allows our species that was evolved for short lifespans within a very narrow environmental and temporal niche on planet Earth to exist and have an effect on much larger spans of space and time with their very different challenges. Evolution does not move us there, because evolution works through natural selection—merely weeding out losers, not elevating them to become winners. Self-evolution, by gaining full access to that which makes us who we are (which is to a large part within our brains) is the path forward."

OUR DESTINY IN THE STARS

My meeting with DARPA staff and my discussion with Randall Koene brought to mind a conversation I'd had in 2011 while attending Singularity University, a program co-founded by Ray Kurzweil and XPrize CEO Peter Diamandis that is sited on the NASA Ames base in Mountain View, California. I spoke to the NASA base commander, curious to learn why he agreed to host the program on his campus. His reply was awe inspiring: "We believe that a future President of the United States will issue the command for NASA to make a mission to Mars. We intend to be ready for that mission when the command comes." In the admiral's view, every one of the accelerating technologies covered in the Singularity University program will be a necessary ingredient for a successful mission to Mars.

Today it's not hard to find enthusiasts for a Mars mission. They can be found in every nation. Many of them auditioned for *Mars One,* a Dutch reality TV show in 2015 that proposed to send "winners" to the Red Planet. How badly do people want to go to Mars? The contestants are willing to accept a one-way ticket. There is no guarantee they will come back. In fact, no sooner had the competition for the TV show been announced than a group of students at MIT published their conclusions, based on calculations that modeled the mission's life-support systems. They determined that the contestants would begin dying of suffocation within sixty-eight days of landing on Mars. You might think those consequences would deter people from submitting their name as candidates. Think again. Two hundred thousand people applied for a spot on the crew—and a chance to die on Mars.

Like this one, most visions of interplanetary voyages involve human crews. Personally, while I find that notion romantic, I remain skeptical of its feasibility. Human beings cannot survive in space, which is why human astronauts must haul everything they need with them, including all of the supplies needed for the return trip home. That life support for human beings is the biggest cost component of a manned space mission. After all, lifting air, water, food, and medicine into space requires an enormous expenditure of energy. And the longer the mission, the more stuff needs to get hauled along. The trip to Mars would take about nine months, with a price tag in the billions of dollars. The cost of transporting live humans through space is, well, astronomical. A Mars mission manned by human astronauts would be the most expensive meat delivery service ever conceived.

Even with the life support, there's no guarantee that human astronauts would survive. The toll on the human body in space is tremendous. Astronauts suffer physical deterioration the longer they remain in space: not just bone loss and muscle atrophy, but also blindness and other side effects from exposure to high levels of radiation. And besides, even if we manage the feat of sending humans to the Red Planet, we won't get much further. Venus, the next nearest planet, has an atmosphere ninety times more dense than Earth's and a temperature of 872 degrees Fahrenheit. And the clouds are made of sulfuric acid. Mercury is even hotter. In the opposite direction the planets are colder and much bigger, with gravity that would crush a human into a puddle.

That's why the vast majority of the scientific exploration done in space today is conducted by robots.

ESCAPING THE BOUNDS OF PHYSICALITY, TIME, AND SPACE

I envision that if Dr. Koene's work on substrate-independent mind is successful, it might enable human astronauts to explore more distant reaches of space without shipping their deteriorating biological bodies along for the ride. Transferring human consciousness to the robotic systems of the spacecraft would eliminate the need for complex and heavy life-support systems. The human pilot would not be a passenger on the spacecraft. The pilot would be the spacecraft.

Because a substrate-independent mind would not be limited to a human lifespan, it would also be possible to expand the range of exploration greatly: such a robot-human system could conceivably be sent to another star even if it required hundreds of years to make the voyage. Project Longshot, a NASA project from the 1980s, called for a voyage of 100 years to reach Alpha Centauri, the nearest star to our solar system. This journey would be inconceivable for a human being, but not for a robot-piloted spacecraft powered by nuclear fission. Tellingly, the Singularity University program at the NASA base begins with a series of sessions on artificial intelligence, robotics, automation, and robot vehicles, not manned space flights.

Deep space is not for biological humans. The stars may be our destiny, but if we want to reach them we'll have to evolve beyond our biological shells.

BEYOND THE INTERNET OF THINGS TO THE INTERNET OF US

As amusing or inspiring as the thought experiment about interstellar travel for SIMs might be, there's another evolutionary path for human beings right here on planet Earth that is no less radical, and arguably more profound: the meeting of human minds.

In the early 2000s Dr. Phillip Alvelda and I worked at two different companies on the earliest attempts to put video on mobile phones. Today our radical notion has become reality: more than 70 percent of the 2 billion people who own smartphones use them to record and share photos and video. Why is this important? It's been my lifelong passion to use technology to connect people and thereby melt down the barriers of indifference, ignorance, and prejudice. Mobile video is a small step in that direction. Sure, we get a lot of silly pet tricks and StyleHaul videos posted to YouTube, but we also get to experience a great deal more, such as:

> **The faraway has become near.** Today anybody with an Android phone has the ability to share, instantly, what she is seeing with another person in another part of the world. As recently as the 1990s this was impossible without a satellite truck. Now we all carry the capability in our pocket.

> **The extraordinary has become ordinary.** It has become commonplace to see video clips of amazing feats of human performance and physical prowess.

> **Expert knowledge has become accessible to all.** Today there's a video tutorial on YouTube for nearly any skill a person might wish to acquire.

Mobile video gives us all the ability to see through the eyes of others who are nowhere near us and whose lives are nothing like ours. We access radically different perspectives every day just by glancing at the devices in our palms.

THE NETWORKED MIND

DARPA legend has it that Bob Metcalfe, an electrical engineer, was watching two scientists working on a computer that kept crashing and wondered, "What happens when we connect two of these things together?" That spark of curiosity led to Ethernet, computer networking, and Metcalfe's law. Now fifty years later, DARPA is doing it again without the computer. Imagine for a moment what might happen if researchers succeed in networking our minds. As one scientist at the DARPA event described it, "You might choose to let someone else in another part of the world see through your eyes." The concept is mind-bending. Literally.

Randal Koene commented: "It is cool that SIM can allow millennia of space travel and living in non-Earthlike places, but there is a third very important aspect that makes SIM hugely important, namely the connections between us.

"Much of what we think of as progress, civilization, and human development has been achieved through ever-greater and better communication," he explained. "From expressions to language to writing to recordings to the Internet, we keep connecting more people more intimately at greater speed. I think that builds not just collaboration, but empathy, and thereby higher forms of culture. With SIM, we can take that even further."

Whole brain emulation promises to free humanity of more than the constraints of time and space. It will also relieve us of skull-bound isolation.

As much as we love our bodies, they limit us in ways that we can barely recognize because we cannot conceive of an alternative. Every sensation that a human being experiences, from emotion and understanding to memories and philosophical musings, is bound up inside the skull. It remains incredibly difficult for us to convey what we experience inside this three-pound lump of gray matter. The networked mind would free us to share the inexpressible.

CONCLUSIONS

I began writing this book to find the answer to a simple question. Yet, each step of my investigation revealed that the process was expanding quite rapidly to another place, another industry, another field. This change is atmospheric in nature, elemental and all-pervasive.

The shift from the solid industrialized economy of the past to the weightless software-defined economy of the near future means that we are taking leave of many familiar artifacts of the past. Some of them may linger in the landscape longer than others, but a great many of them will erode, whittled to a fragment by the elemental force of information in ceaseless motion.

On the surface, solid strategies for businesses to survive digital transformation might seem to have little to do with human transcendence and mind uploading. But once my inquiry was underway, curiosity led me to pursue it further. It didn't seem right to halt midway out of apprehension of what strange thing might come next—inquiry demands a conclusion. What I've found, and attempted to show here, is that all of these changes exist on a continuum. And that vast continuum itself is contained within the broad scope of the human imagination.

In this book we considered a range of certainties, probabilities, and possibilities—or, some might say, wild speculation about *impossibilities*.

My thesis is simple: whatever solid thing can be turned into information will be.

In some cases, that's already an irrefutable fact. Many tangible goods have already been turned into downloadable apps. Most of the money supply exists only in electronic form. Intangibles comprise 85 percent of the value of the S&P 500. This process will continue because vaporization is unstoppable. Probably, it will transform education, labor, and corporations. Possibly, our government institutions and even our biological bodies will follow.

Plenty of people are overwhelmed, caught in a gridlock of denial about this rapid change. Some deny even the possibility of what has *already occurred*. Resist the impulse to pretend that vaporization isn't happening. It is. It will continue. It doesn't matter whether one person likes the outcome or another doesn't, nor whether society accepts or resists these developments. It only matters that you pay attention. Don't ignore the trend.

Once conceived, ideas have a habit of finding expression in human affairs. My hope is that you might be inspired by the ideas and ambitions described here to pursue big visions of your own. After all, this book is not just a rallying cry to rethink your business model or even to reinvent your industry, although vision and courage are needed for both. More broadly, this is a call to open the aperture of your imagination a bit wider by asking big questions.

When we ask ourselves questions, the mind begins to generate images in response. That's how we envision the future. Will autonomous cars really prowl the roads in 2020? How might that change things that we take for granted today about our cities, architecture, commuting, parking, safety, travel, and the independence of the disabled, the elderly, and young people?

Will there really be robot corporations in the cloud? Will robot corporations be considered "persons" under the law? How might that change human employment? The people with the imaginative capacity to envision such possibilities are the ones who will find out first if there is a business opportunity. And then they are going to seize it.

Will bitcoin work? Will it even last another year? Nobody can say for sure except the people who are working on making it happen. If you ask them, they will tell you that they are 100 percent certain that it's going to be the basis for the next round of software-defined transformation. If it turns out they are wrong, they'll just get busy on the next idea until they make that one work. Or the next.

Don't waste time or energy arguing in the face of it, or even trying to decide whether it's wrong nor right. It's neither. It's both. It's different. What is certain is that no positive outcome can be achieved in any situation unless someone first imagines it.

Will the vaporized university be effective? If so, how might that change our world? Imagine it and find out. Imagine a smart, ambitious individual in the poorest corner of the globe gaining access to training and even employment opportunities through a mobile device. How might that change things?

Will the cortical modem really connect our minds? It's certainly a radical idea, but if so, what new experiences could it enable? Imagine an increase in human understanding, insight, compassion, sympathy in the truest sense of the word, not as a condolence but "feeling with" another person on the opposite side of the globe.

The capacity for speculative vision, a level of comfort while embracing radical possibility whether it's accurate or wildly off base, is the kind of athletic mindset that will shape the world of the future. Get in the habit of cultivating your "what if?" intuition. That's going to be the thing that guides you through the bewildering times ahead. And trust me, there will be some really strange times indeed.

Instead of saying "That will never happen" or "That can't happen," ask yourself instead "How might that happen?" or "What would happen if?" The answer to this question illuminates what we already know and frames what we need to discover. All of a sudden you'll begin to imagine a universe of crazy, reckless, madly disruptive, possibly impossible, perhaps certifiably insane ideas about what may come in the future. Some of them will come true.

I know this because I've been launching new business ventures for twenty-five years. I've done it for major corporations and for very small startup companies, and I've done it all over the world. The one thing that each of those very different projects had in common was this: in the beginning, all we had was an idea and a launch date. Often we did not even have a clear plan to get the job done. We just got busy. We worked our butts off to bring the product into existence with sheer willpower, persistence, and enthusiasm. Most often, we succeeded in inventing or designing something entirely new: a new technology, a new genre, a new device, a new mobile app, a new company, a new standard, a new habit. These breakthroughs were built on the innovations of others, and they in turn became a layer of infrastructure to support the next round of innovation. Our reality is constructed from ideas conceived and executed by others, and it can be reconceived and reconfigured at any time by someone with a new, better idea.

These successes only happened because the people on the launch team asked themselves the right questions. How might it happen? What would that be like? How would it work? How would that change things? And then they went ahead and built it, just like they imagined it.

So, what kind of future do you want to be a part of? How will you make it happen? How will you lead your organization, your family, or yourself through it? These questions confront us as we encounter the most breathtaking economic, societal, and perhaps even evolutionary leap that any single generation of human beings has ever experienced.

Now it's your turn. There's a whole world out there ready for you to reinvent. Pick a topic, any thing or institution or company or product or service or tradition, and ask yourself: how might I replace that with software? You can do it if you want to. All you have to do is jump in.

WITH GRATITUDE

M ost of the events in this book occurred during the past seven years, but in some respects I've been gathering material for this project since my career began. Along the way I have had the good fortune to learn from truly excellent business executives who taught me, sometimes by example and sometimes through firsthand experience, how the convergence between traditional mass media and digital technology would really work in practice. At MTV I was inspired by Judy McGrath, Sara Levinson, Vinnie Longobardo, and Abby Terkuhle; and at Sony Pictures Entertainment by Andy Kaplan, Yair Landau, and Jon Feltheimer; by David Zaslav at Discovery Communications; and by Ira Rubenstein at PBS. Of all my business mentors, I learned the most from Lauren Cole, who has an unerring instinct for spotting the strongest and weakest parts of a new business model.

During the past five years, several organizations have invited me to conduct workshops with their technology, marketing, and strategy teams to develop plans for the evolving digital media landscape. I consider such work a privilege. I wish to thank David Levy, Donna Speciale, and Joe Hogan at Turner Broadcasting; Katrina Cukaj at CNN; Paula Kerger, Rich Homberg, and Juan Sepúlveda at PBS; Kevin MacLellan at NBCUniversal International TV; Paul Zilk at Reed MIDEM; David Gale and Tom Tulloch at NASPL; Stacey Philpot at Pivot Leadership; Adam Carroll and Saira Khan at Interpublic Group; and Leslie Billingsley at FCBX. You've given me ample opportunity to refine my concepts and apply them to real business challenges.

Several brilliant technologists have been mentors and professional colleagues. They include Dr. Jim Brailean, Ed Knapp, Dr. Eric Bilange, Stillman Bradish, and Andrew Hessel, who have encouraged me to follow my intuition about technology trends and keep asking questions.

Nicholas Negroponte graciously agreed to write the foreword to my book, and he welcomed me warmly at the MIT Media Lab, where I have met several research scientists who have inspired me since I first learned about this laboratory in 1985. Nick has been wonderfully encouraging to me in this book project, my public speaking, and my other pursuits.

Every Saturday morning, my friend Ken Rutkowski hosts a three-hour breakfast seminar for Los Angeles entrepreneurs to discuss and debate trends in technology and the broader economy. At one such breakfast, the original question about Tower Records was posed to me. That question sent me on this quest, and since that time I've returned to speak with the group each year to report on what I've discovered. Thank you, Ken, for giving me a forum to test my ideas-in-progress.

Every book is a collaborative undertaking. I've had the pleasure of working with Canada's finest editorial team under the leadership of Maggie Langrick, the most persistent, patient, professional, and positive editor I've ever known. I also wish to express my gratitude to Lucy Kenward, a superb copy editor, fact checker, and my touchstone for jargon-free vernacular; and to Paris Spence-Lang for his cheerful assistance. My publicist, Jane Wesman, has made it possible for the public to discuss this book and find it in those retail shops that have not yet been vaporized.

I could not have completed this project without the contributions of experts in several fields who graciously answered my questions and who provided me with insight, information, and in some cases very lengthy interviews. They include Dr. Randal Koene, Brad Burnham, David Orban, Hannes Klöpper, Martin Schmucker, Kim Zetter, Reese Jones, Chris

Boardman, Steve Hershberger, Rob Mesirow, Patrick Parodi, Philippe van Nedervelde, Volker Hirsch, John Szeder, Jeffrey Borneman, Phil Braden, Arturo Pelayo, and Peter Rothman, as well as some contributors who wish to remain anonymous. Your commentary was instructive and your corrections astute. Any errors that remain in the text are my responsibility.

Several authors generously gave me permission to quote their work, including Kevin Kelly, W. Brian Arthur, Mark J. Perry, Yvette Romero, and Peter Reinhardt. My brief citation cannot adequately summarize the valuable insights in their books and articles. May my reference serve as the merest introduction in the hope that readers will delve more deeply into these works.

Many friends and professional colleagues have been steadfast supporters, encouraging me to write this book. They include Kathy Eldon, Ron Deutsch, Alex Lightman, Sally DeSipio, Brett King, Mark Pesce, Brendan Harkin, Mark Cuban, David Saintloth, and Gabe Zichermann.

Appropriately, perhaps, for an author devoted to dematerialization, I was delighted to discover that social networks enabled me to establish connections to virtual acquaintances who provided much-needed international perspective. I was encouraged by a group of friends whom I've never met in person, including John Eden, Chien Yu Lin, Fredrik Bränström, Markus Sandelin, and Jason Benlevi. One of the great pleasures of the past five years has been the opportunity to meet these friends, one by one, on my global travels.

Early readers provided suggestions to streamline the text and refine the arguments. I am especially grateful to Jay Samit, Gerd Leonhard, and Jarl Mohn for their close reading and recommendation to add practical business takeaway.

Dr. Geoffrey Ling and Dr. Phillip Alvelda of the Biological Technologies Office at DARPA invited me to join them at a lively two-day seminar in San Francisco, where I was frankly astounded by the audacity and scope of their vision.

The most enlightening week of my life was spent at Singularity University at the NASA Ames base with Ray Kurzweil, Peter Diamandis,

Salim Ismail, and an eclectic cast of technologists and research scientists. The lectures, seminars, and other activities that constitute Singularity University confirmed many of my hunches about the future and provided a fact-based orientation to the accelerating technologies that will shape the pace and scope of change in every imaginable field for decades to come.

Oprah Winfrey and her tireless book club team, especially Jill Davis, restored my faith in the enduring power of books at a time when digital media seems to be absorbing everything in its path. It was a professional honor to work alongside them, managing Oprah's presence in the digital domain, and together we developed some powerful new ways to connect with readers via the Internet. I remain deeply grateful because Oprah's Book Club cultivates the most important resource for every author: a vast number of avid readers with an abiding respect for the power of the printed word.

INDEX

ABOUT THE AUTHOR

F or twenty-five years, Robert Tercek has been a pioneer in the field of
digital media. He has supervised the design and launch of new services
for every digital platform, including satellite television, game consoles,
set-top boxes, broadband Internet, and mobile networks. His credits include
milestones such as the launch of the world's first streaming video to mobile
phones, the first multichannel television service in Asia, the first interactive
game show broadcast in the United States, some of the earliest multiplayer
games on the Web, and live online learning events for massive audiences.

He has served in executive management roles at MTV, Sony Pictures
Entertainment, and most recently at OWN, the Oprah Winfrey Network,
where he was president of digital media. He has also been an entrepreneur
in five startup ventures. He has lived and worked in Asia, Europe, and North
and South America.

An enthusiastic advocate of the digital future, Robert is a frequent
speaker at industry events and consortia, and for several years was a lecturer
and adjunct professor in interactive media at the School of Cinema-
Television, now known as the School of Cinematic Arts, at the University
of Southern California. Today he provides strategic insight to major media
companies and technology firms. Since 2010 he has served as the chairman
of the board at the Creative Visions Foundation in Malibu, California.